Praise for

FORTY CHANCES

"Howard Buffett's new book redefines risk taking in philanthropy."

—*Forbes*

"Howard Buffett's account of his long battle against food insecurity conveys his deep respect for poor farmers and his conviction that they can be empowered to feed the world. His work is amazing and will inspire you to join his crusade."

—President Bill Clinton

"Howard has three passions: his devotion to the fight against hunger and misery; his love for farming; and his ability as a photographer and writer to share his amazing journey. Through the stories in *40 Chances*, Howard invites all of us to join his efforts to fight poverty."

—Carlos Slim

"*40 Chances* is easy-reading earnestness from a dedicated do-gooder."

—*Mother Jones*

"The Jewish Talmud teaches that if you save one life you save the entire world. Howard Buffett has lived this prescription, and in the process has saved the world many times over. *40 Chances* illustrates that his commitment and passion to help folks out of poverty, at home and especially in the developing world, has had a remarkable and measurable impact on the lives of farmers and rural citizens worldwide. *40 Chances* should be a primer for all our citizens on how one man has the passion to save the world, and how we can all follow his lead in our own way."

—Secretary of Agriculture Dan Glickman

"[An] inspiring manifesto . . . Buffett's work is both an informative guidebook and a catalyst for igniting real changes in the world."

—*Booklist*

"An impressive example of how an individual's diligent work can truly affect the world."

—*Kirkus Reviews*

"Whether we are driving his combine in Illinois, meeting with farmers in Guatemala, walking across the border from Mexico to the US, or indulging in our shared love of Dairy Queen, a day spent with Howard Buffett is one spent learning and laughing. Howard's intellect is only surpassed by the size of his heart. This book will give readers a chance to learn from him in the way that I have, and form their own plan for making the most of the 40 chances we all have."

—Eva Longoria

"*40 Chances* is an immensely readable, important and inspiring book with essential lessons about doing business in difficult circumstances."

—*Success*

"The book successfully blends personal stories with a tough look at the struggle to fight domestic food scarcity and world hunger. Those interested in these issues or global philanthropy are sure to find this a satisfying read."

—*Publishers Weekly*

"Howard Buffett has figured out a way to tell 40 stories about hunger, farming, poverty, and war, while delivering a readable account of a formidable challenge."

—*Bloomberg Businessweek*

FORTY CHANCES

Finding Hope in a Hungry World

Howard G. Buffett

WITH HOWARD W. BUFFETT

FOREWORD BY WARREN E. BUFFETT

SIMON & SCHUSTER PAPERBACKS
New York   London   Toronto   Sydney   New Delhi

Simon & Schuster Paperbacks
A Division of Simon & Schuster, Inc.
1230 Avenue of the Americas
New York, NY 10020

First Simon & Schuster trade paperback edition October 2014

SIMON & SCHUSTER PAPERBACKS and colophon are registered trademarks of Simon & Schuster, Inc.

For information about special discounts for bulk purchases, please contact Simon & Schuster Special Sales at 1-866-506-1949 or business@simonandschuster.com.

The Simon & Schuster Speakers Bureau can bring authors to your live event. For more information or to book an event, contact the Simon & Schuster Speakers Bureau at 1-866-248-3049 or visit our website at www.simonspeakers.com.

Some images have been enhanced for appearance, for black and white, or in accordance with nondisclosure agreements.

Designed by Jill Putorti

Manufactured in the United States of America

10 9 8 7 6 5 4 3 2 1

The Library of Congress has cataloged the hardcover edition as follows:

Buffett, Howard G.
    40 chances : finding hope in a hungry world / by Howard G. Buffett ; with Howard W. Buffett ; foreword by Warren E. Buffett.
        pages cm
    1. Food relief—Developing countries. 2. Agricultural development projects—Developing countries. 3. Humanitarianism—Developing countries. 4. Hunger—Developing countries. I. Title. II. Title: Forty chances.
    HV696.F6B84 2013
    363.809172'4—dc23
    2013031452

ISBN 978-1-4516-8786-6
ISBN 978-1-4516-8787-3 (pbk)
ISBN 978-1-4516-8788-0 (ebook)

This book is dedicated to the two most important women in my life: my wife, Devon, and my mother, Susie

Contents

Foreword

My late wife, Susie, and I had our first child soon after we were married—though not, she would want me to add, so soon as to raise questions in that more judgmental era. We named her Susie as well, and she proved to be such an easy baby to handle that we quickly planned for another child. The difficulties of parenthood, my wife and I concluded, had been vastly overhyped.

And then Howard Graham Buffett arrived seventeen months later in December 1954. After a few months of coping with him, Susie Sr. and I decided an extended pause was essential before our having a third (and last) child, Peter. For Howie was a force of nature, a tiny perpetual-motion machine. Susie had plenty of days when she felt life would have been easier if she had instead given birth to some boring triplets.

Howie was named after two of my heroes, men who remain heroes to me as I write this almost six decades later. First, and forever foremost, was my dad, Howard, who in his every word and act shaped my life. Ben Graham was an obvious choice as well, a wonderful teacher whose ideas enabled me to accumulate a large fortune. Howie began life in big shoes.

Through Howie's early years, I had no idea as to what direction his life would take. My own dad had given me a terrific gift: he told me, both verbally and by his behavior, that he cared only about the values I had, not the particular path I chose. He simply said that he had unlimited confidence in me and that I should follow my dreams.

I was thereby freed of all expectations except to do my best. This was such a blessing for me that it was natural for me to behave similarly with my own children. In this aspect of child raising—as well as virtually all others—Susie Sr. and I were totally in sync.

Our "It's *your* life" message produced one particularly interesting outcome: none of our three children completed college, though each certainly had the intellect to do so. Neither Susie Sr. nor I were at all bothered by this. Besides, as I often joke, if the three combine their college credits, they would be entitled to one degree that they could rotate among themselves.

I don't believe that leaving college early has hindered the three in any way. They, like every Omaha Buffett from my grandfather to my great-grandchildren, attended public grammar and high schools. In fact, almost all of these family members, including our three children, went to the same inner-city, long-integrated high school, where they mixed daily with classmates from every economic and social background. In those years, they may have learned more about the world they live in than have many individuals with postgrad educations.

Howie started by zigzagging through life, looking for what would productively harness his boundless energy. In this book, he tells of how he found his path and the incredible journeys that resulted from his discovery. It's a remarkable tale, told exactly as it happened. As Howie describes his activities—some successful, others not—they supply a guidebook for intelligent philanthropy.

Howie's love of farming makes his work particularly helpful to the millions of abject poor whose only hope is the soil. His fearlessness has meanwhile exposed him to an array of experiences more common to adventurers than philanthropists. Call him the Indiana Jones of his field.

It's Howie's story to tell. I want, however, to add my own tribute to the two women who made him what he is today: a man working with passion, energy, and intelligence to better the lives of those less fortunate. It began with his remarkable mother. Fortunately, the genes from her side were dominant in shaping Howie.

Anyone who knew Susie Sr. would understand why I say this. Simply put, she had more genuine concern for others than anyone I've ever known. Every person she met—rich or poor, black or white, old or young—immediately sensed that she saw him or her simply as a human being, equal in value to any other on the planet.

Without in any way being a Pollyanna, or giving up enjoyment in her own life, Susie connected with a multitude of diverse people in ways that changed their lives. No one can match the touch she had, but Howie comes close. And he is on a par with her in terms of heart.

Howie nevertheless needed Devon, his wife of thirty-one years, to center him. And that need continues. Much as Susie provided the love that enabled me to find myself, Devon nurtures Howie. Both he and I were not the easiest humans to deal with daily and up close; each of us can pursue our interests with an intensity that leaves us oblivious to what is going on around us. But both of us were also incredibly lucky in finding extraordinary women who loved us enough to eventually soften our rough edges.

His mother's genes and teachings—usually nonverbal but delivered powerfully by her actions—gave Howie his ever-present desire to help others. In that pursuit, his only speed is fast-forward. My money has helped him carry out his plans in recent years on a larger scale than is available to most teachers and philanthropists. I couldn't be happier about the result.

Most of the world's seven billion people found their destinies largely determined at the moment of birth. There are, of course, plenty of Horatio Alger stories in this world. Indeed, America abounds with them. But for literally billions of people, where they are born and who gives them birth, along with their gender and native intellect, largely determine the life they will experience.

In this ovarian lottery, my children received some lucky tickets. Many people who experience such good fortune react by simply enjoying their position in life and trying to ensure that their children enjoy similar benefits. This approach is understandable, though it can become distasteful when it is accompanied by a smug "If I can do it, why can't everyone else?" attitude.

Still, I would hope that many of the world's fortunate—particularly Americans who have benefited so dramatically from the deeds of our forefathers—would aspire to more. We *do* sit in the shade of trees planted by others. While enjoying the benefits dealt us, we should do a little planting ourselves.

I feel very good about the fact that my children realize how lucky they have been. I feel even better because they have decided to spend their lives sharing much of the product of that luck with others. They do not feel at all guilty because of their good fortune—but they do feel grateful. And this they express through the expenditure of their time and my money, with their part of this equation without question the more important.

In this book, you will read about some of Howie's extraordinary projects. Forgive a parent when I say I couldn't be more proud of him, as would his mother be if she were alive to watch him. As you read his words, you will understand why.

Warren E. Buffett

Introduction:
One Shot at a Warlord

The camp commander had just told me that two of the soldiers on our side were eaten by crocodiles the previous week. That got my attention. But as I stood in a clearing of scrub trees in the hot, dry desert of South Sudan, I realized that the thin man walking toward me, leaning on a cane, was much more dangerous than any croc. Crocodiles attack when they are hungry or their turf or young are threatened. I was about to meet General Caesar Acellam, an African warlord who had helped lead a campaign of murder, rape, torture, and enslavement across at least four countries. He was a top lieutenant in the psychopath Joseph Kony's Lord's Resistance Army. As such, Acellam had hunted the most vulnerable people on the planet—poor, starving children—to turn thousands of boys into sadistic soldiers and girls into sex slaves.

It was May 2012, and the temperature was over one hundred degrees. I had flown into this remote camp in a Cessna Caravan turboprop just minutes before, and the sweat was pouring out of me. There were tents and Mi-8 transport helicopters and Mi-24 attack helicopters parked under camouflage tarps. The dirt landing strip and the camp clearing were barely visible when we began our descent. There was an unmistakable, almost electrical, charge of pride among the Ugandan army leaders who hosted us. For months their men had camped in the jungle and tracked and finally ambushed Acellam just a few days before along the banks of the River Mbou in the nearby Central African Republic (CAR)—the same river where crocs had claimed their comrades.

The LRA's evil campaign is more than a quarter century old. Its soldiers are vicious fighters with a twisted loyalty to the messianic Kony. He and the LRA are blamed for displacing around two million people and forcing upwards of sixty thousand children to fight for him during his more than two decades of spreading mayhem through what's called the Great Lakes region of Africa.[1] At the time of my visit, Ugandan soldiers had been leading an effort to hunt the LRA down in CAR. Kony and his followers have been on the run and have lost many supporters in the last several years, but they are skilled jungle fighters and difficult to find.

Kony has left a trail of death, mutilation, and misery. A young woman who looked to be about twenty also walked toward me with the forty-nine-year-old Acellam. The Ugandan commander explained that she was one of the thousands of girls Acellam and his followers had abducted and raped, and had been living as Acellam's "wife." She was holding the hand of a little girl with an angelic face who looked to be about two years old: Acellam's daughter. The young woman's body language was striking. She clearly felt she had to stand near Acellam, yet she leaned away as if she were a magnet being repelled by a colliding charge. I fished in my pocket and produced a Tootsie Pop and handed it to the child. Her mother smiled at me and helped the little girl unwrap it.

Acellam was being held under armed guards, but the Tootsie Pop was a weapon for my own personal mission that day. Others included my cameras, jars of peanut butter and jelly, and a few slices of bread. I am an experienced photographer of life in the developing world, both its fragile beauty and its dark, difficult sides. A friend of mine who is an advocate for impoverished and exploited people all over the world, and who supports the hunt for Kony, had asked me to take photographs of Acellam and his family. I was told that Acellam needed to look relaxed and smile in the photographs. Not for the sake of journalism or art: the photos were for laminated flyers urging the remaining members of the LRA to surrender. These would be dropped over the jungle by C-130 transport aircraft. It was important for the photograph to convey Acellam being treated well and with respect.

Stiff and wary at first, his eyes bloodshot but still sharp, Acellam surveyed his surroundings as one experienced in dangerous situations would do. But there was a resignation to him. He was tired; he knew he was done. He was no longer in control of his fate. I reminded myself that I was in the presence of an evil predator. The good I hoped to accomplish with photographs required me to bury my disgust for a man who, at this moment, I needed to like me.

Acellam, I could tell, was accustomed to underlings attending to his needs. I jumped up to get him water, and I prepared what for him was exotic fare: a peanut butter and jelly sandwich. He liked it. He told me he and his family had been eating "roots" in the jungle. His English was very good. He began to relax. He smiled when I asked if he liked the peanut butter. I got the pictures, and over the next few months, 565,000 laminated flyers with my photographs of a smiling, apparently happy Acellam—with quotes from him urging LRA fighters to surrender—rained down over the jungles of the Central African Republic. In the year that followed, dozens of fighters and hundreds of victims emerged, including a barefoot, one-eyed combatant in a tattered suit who surrendered in Obo, CAR, by holding the flyer with the photographs of Acellam and his family over his head. He later explained that he had fought with Kony for sixteen years.

This member of the Ugandan army was part
of the brigade that captured General Caesar
Acellam in May 2012. *Photo: Howard G. Buffett*

The photographs used in this flyer represent a disarmed Acellam. They disproved
rumors of his torture and death and encouraged many victims to seek out safety and
escape Kony. *Courtesy of: CLRA Partners*

This was one of my more unusual high-adrenaline encounters in a decade of trying to attack the causes of hunger and create more sustainable, lasting solutions. It's been a wide-ranging journey, peppered with dangerous, even bizarre experiences. Why was a meeting with a vicious warlord part of the hunger equation? Because one of the most challenging elements in battling hunger, especially in Africa and Central America, is conflict. Individual stories of the bloodthirsty barbarism of Kony and his followers are horrifying, but two million people displaced and sixty thousand children kidnapped over the last twenty-plus years continue to live a fragile, hungry existence.

Conflict is ugly and takes a long-lasting toll on children and families. It ruins agricultural production, disrupts the shipping of food, and destroys land. It creates mass dislocation as people flee for their lives. And that is a dislocation from which there is no easy or ready recovery. It can mean months, even years, spent in a filthy, crowded camp for displaced persons. It can mean returning home only to find that one's land and home have been taken over by others who feel entitled to remain there. And as those former child soldiers escape or are released from the only life they know—uneducated, traumatized, disconnected from their families—how are they to feed themselves? They have spent their childhoods murdering on command, often high on drugs. They typically have limited skills and are often hated by their own people.

In 2005 the Food and Agriculture Organization of the United Nations (FAO) said that conflict was the world's leading cause of hunger.[2] In 2007 Oxford University economist Paul Collier, writing in *The Bottom Billion: Why the Poorest Countries Are Failing and What Can Be Done About It*, analyzed the states that are home to the world's poorest people, most of them in Africa. He found that 73 percent have recently been in, or continue to be in, a civil war. But poverty and hunger exacerbated by conflict exist all around the world. I've seen firsthand the human toll the drug wars are taking in Central America. In some regions of Mexico, for example, families living in remote villages have been forced to convert their corn and bean crops to marijuana and are starving at the point of the drug lords' guns.

I confess: I am personally drawn to intense, high-stakes situations such as that South Sudan jungle. I am drawn to conflict-related challenges, as they are among the hardest problems we face. I am comfortable going where other philanthropists and aid groups may not or cannot go. But this kind of adventure is not my day job.

As you're about to learn, I'm a farmer. Mostly, I approach food insecurity—when a person is routinely unsure of when, how, or where they will access their next meal—and poverty from the perspective of a farmer who operates planters and combines and who understands soil, seeds, and fertilizer. The bulk of my battles are with weather, insects, and weeds. However, I'm committed to addressing the full picture and complexity of hunger—even the most difficult realities. And I can promise you that even in far less dramatic situations in agricultural agencies or food-security conferences or the back rooms of Washington, DC, there is a waste of resources, corruption, or unintended consequences from failed policies. These impediments and the slow pace of politics and bureaucracy are almost as maddening to me as a warlord's sneer. We know that millions of people die of nutrition- and hunger-related causes every year, more than three million of them children.[3]

This mission did not come to me quickly or easily. To understand how I ended up making a warlord a sandwich, however, we have to leave the jungle and travel back in time to a much quieter spot in America's breadbasket.

PART 1

The Roots of "40 Chances"

Story 1
The Day I Heard the Clock Tick

I farm 1,500 acres in central Illinois, and I buy a lot of farm equipment from Sloan Implement Company in Assumption, a town of about 1,200 people that is south of Decatur, where I live. Outside Sloan's, John Deere tractors, combines, planters, wagons, and trailers line up like a big green machine army, begging to be walked around, climbed on, and imagined at work in your fields to make some chore go faster or better. Inside, there is every kind of part, oil, and tool, and then a cavernous building in the back where they repair equipment. During spring planting and harvests in summer and fall, the place jumps with activity. But it takes on a little different character in the winter. As snowdrifts pile up on fallow fields, a lot of farmers come trooping in to ask questions, complain about the price of corn or soybeans, and talk about new ideas and equipment. Good farmers love to learn and swap experiences. Some time ago, Sloan's started hosting an event called "Planter's School."

My first Planter's School was in the winter of 2001. In addition to farming, I was still a partner at nearby GSI, a global manufacturer of grain bins, and I also served on the board of Lindsay Corporation, which makes center pivots: the irrigation machines responsible for those big, circular planted areas that air travelers can see when flying over the Midwest. Deere & Company had some interesting new equipment, and Sloan's advertised that it was bringing in some outside speakers. One Saturday I made my way to the back shed, where they'd set up twenty or thirty folding chairs. The first speaker started his talk by saying something that changed my outlook on life. I didn't write it down at the time, but as I remember, it went like this:

> Most of you think of farming as this continual process of buying seed, planting, fertilizing, harvesting, then starting all over again. But think about the period between the first time your dad had you climb up with him on the tractor to plant and the day you will turn your acreage over to your son or daughter. If you're pretty healthy, and you're like most farmers, you're probably only going to do this about forty times. You'll get forty chances to plant your crop, adjust to what nature throws at you, and hope for the best. It's enough time to learn to do it well. But it's not forever.
>
> Some of you are well into your forty chances already. You've learned from your mistakes, but I'd guess that none of you feel you can afford to take a single year left on your string for granted. What we're trying to do here is make sure we're giving you the best possible tools and the best possible advice on how to use them. That way you can make the most of those forty chances.

This idea hit me. I had never thought of farming like that before. In some ways, farming is predictable: cycles of planting and harvesting, rewarding but consuming work day after day, year after year. As a farmer, you're always in catch-up mode, trying to get the next task done but looking around the farm and seeing another twenty projects you wish you had time to do. It sometimes feels as if the work will never end. He was reminding us that it does. When

I thought about it, forty didn't seem like all that many chances, and I had used up a bunch already. I thought, "There is no time to waste!"

I spend about half the year working as a farmer; here, I'm loading a bag of seed corn into a planter at our Illinois farm. *Photo: Howard W. Buffett*

I started thinking a little differently about farming, but I also realized that this idea applied to a lot more than farming. It's easy to slip into a rhythm in life and just plod forward. Whether you love or hate what you're doing, whether you're good at it or struggling, life is not a treadmill—it's a moving walkway. There are no do-overs. We get a limited number of chances to do what we do, whatever we do, right.

I started asking myself, "Am I making the most of my chances? Am I trying to improve and perfect my methods every single year?

Am I listening to people with new ideas? Am I learning the right lessons from my mistakes?"

Beyond farming, I was trying to align some other important developments in my life. I had been blessed and honored by my parents, Warren and Susan Buffett, with the gift of significant funds that established the Howard G. Buffett Foundation. Through the foundation, I had been able to support causes that were important to me and to my wife and children, primarily in the area of wildlife conservation. I had traveled extensively in Africa, Asia, and Latin America on business, and also to pursue my other passion, wildlife photography—particularly of endangered animals such as mountain gorillas and cheetahs.

But during these travels, the more I viewed threatened habitats, the more I could see the truth of what Dennis Avery, an expert in global food issues, had once put to me succinctly: "No one will starve to save a tree." As I saw the larger context of these situations, I realized why so many animals were endangered and why rain forests were disappearing. From a distance, it was easy to blame greedy poachers and corrupt government officers for the decimation of important ecosystems. But I also saw that the people who shared these ecosystems with the endangered species were endangered themselves. Many were starving. If I thought I had no other way to feed my hungry child than poaching an endangered animal, what would I do? If the land on which I was trying to grow the food that was all my children had to eat stopped producing because it was worn out, would I worry about preserving the adjacent rain forest, or would I slash and burn it down to use the soil beneath it? The answers seemed obvious.

If I cared about endangered species, if I cared about habitat preservation and biodiversity, I realized I had to shift my efforts to a more fundamental issue. I had to work on the hunger side of the equation. Pretty soon the size of those numbers began to haunt me.

The United Nations estimates that roughly 870 million people suffer persistent, chronic hunger today.[1] Everywhere in the world, malnutrition and hunger create lifelong physical and developmental burdens for children; they interfere with learning, and they are linked to other threats such as terrorism and human trafficking. Hunger is a factor in every war. Occupying military or rebels take the locals' food, and starving people fight for the side that feeds them; isolating villages and withholding food is a slow but effective way to render enemies impotent, or even kill them. Food is power.

One-sixth of the people in my own country, or almost 50 million Americans—16 million of them children—qualify as food insecure.[2] And for all these current challenges, realize that there are just over 7 billion of us on Earth today, and the world's population is projected to top 9 billion people by 2050. That's less than forty years away. During most of our lifetimes, the challenges of hunger are going to intensify.

Within just a few years of having my eyes opened by that speaker at Sloan's, and in the middle of this transition in my thinking about conservation, fate delivered another jolt. In 2004 the death of my mother, Susan, triggered some new directions in my father's views about philanthropy. My mother was an inspiration not only to my family but also to everyone who knew her. She had a warm and generous heart and a deep commitment to making the world better. My father had planned to turn over the bulk of his assets to my mother to distribute through her foundation. Instead, her death resulted in my brother, sister, and me each receiving a significant commitment from him to fund our foundations on a much larger scale. I now had before me an exciting challenge that most people can only imagine being posed hypothetically at a cocktail party, or maybe as the plot of a movie: If you had a billion dollars to do something important, what would you choose?

I knew what I wanted to work on: feeding hungry people. I was already heading down the path that many other philanthropists had taken. I gave grants to the people already working in areas plagued by hunger and poverty. I supported nongovernmental organizations (NGOs) with a list of interesting projects that needed funding, from drilling wells to trying to improve the livelihoods of former child soldiers by teaching them how to farm. I traveled to countries experiencing severe food insecurity, determined to understand their agricultural capabilities. I asked a lot of questions. Often it seemed that no one had tried certain techniques specifically designed for Africa or experiments at scale. So, our foundation bought a large farm in South Africa in order to conduct our own research. We've subsequently invested in many more acres of research fields in both Illinois and Arizona. I do not have what business-people sometimes call "paralysis by analysis." I jump in and try things.

Over the last decade, our foundation has made more than $200 million in grants to agriculture-based projects that we hoped would help farmers on the ground in the developing world. I've visited over 120 countries, and I'd estimate that I've spoken with thousands of farmers, in addition to just about everybody else working in this arena—from presidents to rock stars to priests to professors.

A NEW INTENSITY

I'm out of antiblunt pills, so I'll give it to you straight: we have to hit the reset button. Chronic hunger has declined in Asia and Latin America over the last twenty years, but it is rising in sub-Saharan Africa, where the population is exploding.[3] To feed the world on a daily basis by 2050, the FAO forecasts that farmers all over the globe will have to increase food production by 70 percent.[4]

Achieving that will demand a new intensity and more productivity from farmers at every level: from the farmers with sophisticated, highly mechanized operations who gather at Sloan's, to the poor, rural farmers of the developing world armed with only a hoe. What's more, we will have to reorganize and redeploy the efforts of all the other participants involved in setting the world's table: governments, NGOs, researchers, philanthropists, and agribusinesses, to name just the main ones. We'll need to come up with solutions to conflicts that embrace the true challenges people face in trying to grow and harvest their own food under these conditions. And we need to rethink our own farming techniques in the developed world as our traditional methods are destroying the topsoil that will be crucial to ensuring agricultural productivity in the future.

I believe we can do it. The global community has stepped in effectively to halt hunger before. In the early 1960s, the so-called Green Revolution saved an estimated billion people from starvation in India and Southeast Asia. Led by some heroic efforts by the late Nobel laureate Norman Borlaug, it was based on large-scale production of a limited number of grains such as wheat and rice. Scientists, governments, farmers, and NGOs all pulled together—and pulled off something of a miracle.

However, that model is not going to work in Africa, which is currently home to pervasive and widespread food insecurity. The continent's diverse geography, its inadequate infrastructure, and the reality that Africa is fifty-four countries and not a single, centrally governed state are not going to allow a Green Revolution recipe to work on the scale of what succeeded in India. Fortunately, there are models and new ideas out there that give me hope, and there are committed individuals who are thinking in new ways and already making a difference. The experience of Brazil, which we'll go into in some detail, is remarkable evidence that a country with the will to change can develop both an improved form of sustainable, environmentally responsible agriculture and a system to ensure that smallholder farmers are included in addressing the nation's larger food-security needs.

Can we convince the global community and governments of nations with huge numbers of food-insecure people to adopt the mindset of the speaker in the back room at Sloan's?

Billions in aid delivered in recent decades have sometimes made food insecurity worse, not better. I've stopped funding the most common type of NGO projects, and I've stopped putting any money into certain countries that do not seem willing to make the structural changes and land reforms needed to lift their populations out of hunger and poverty. We can't use Western thinking to solve African challenges. We need to harvest the right lessons from our past efforts and mistakes, and we have to deploy both new models and cutting-edge technology to make the most of the chances that remain. We can't just fund activities and good intentions; we have to fund self-sustaining solutions.

This book is about how I came to this conclusion and what I think we need to do going forward. It is a collection of stories—forty in all—about how I got involved in trying to attack global hunger, and what my team at the Howard G. Buffett Foundation and I discovered, attempted, unleashed, fouled up, achieved, and learned on our journey so far. In some cases, it's about good intentions but bad execution—our own as well as other people's. It's about ignorance and culture clashes and bankrupt ideas. It's about people we admire, people working in the fields and among those suffering every day, people with innovative ideas, and people determined to stop repeating the mistakes of the past.

It's also about celebrating what it means to be human. I have been to some of the poorest, most difficult places in the world, and, invariably, there will be children smiling and playing, delighting themselves with a little game they've invented or turning a bag stuffed with straw into a soccer ball. In the poorest village, I have seen the pride and kindness in the eyes of women who welcome me with a bit of food or a cup of tea, even though they have so little themselves.

For every sad story I will relate, there are twice as many that I hope will make you grateful to be alive and sharing a world with fine people trying to make a difference, whether in a refugee camp in Africa or a soup kitchen in Decatur. In the pages ahead, you'll meet a twenty-year-old former child soldier named "Little Cromite" who was ripped from his family at age six and who now finds himself without skills, education, or resources to feed himself. You'll see the passion and commitment of one of the world's best-known recording artists, and you'll see how former British prime minister Tony Blair is helping a new generation of African leaders learn management and governance principles. And I will introduce you to a kindred spirit of mine: a Ghanaian scientist and devoted University of Nebraska Cornhuskers football fan who teaches subsistence farmers how to improve their yields, feed their families, and protect their greatest asset—the soil beneath their feet.

My son, Howard W. Buffett (going forward, I'll call him HWB, to avoid confusion), has come along with me on many of my explorations around the developing world, and that has been a rewarding aspect of this journey. I've seen him grow from a shy, typical twelve-year-old when he first started traveling with me. He was a curious boy but sometimes overwhelmed by witnessing shocking hardships and poverty that few of his peers ever saw. He became a man with a unique understanding of the challenges that millions of people face. HWB has had some of his own novel adventures in Asia, Afghanistan, and other areas. He also served a two-year term as the foundation's executive director. Today he is a trustee of our foundation, and he developed some insights and new ideas that he will share as well. He is particularly excited about finding new ways for organizations to work together, utilizing better management techniques and technologies to improve their programs and measure their impact.

One theme that resonates throughout the stories you will read in this book is our conviction that we need to act with urgency. People are dying and suffering *today*. I did not start this endeavor with the idea of building an endowed legacy. I decided not to just go through the motions, pick small, solvable problems to work on, and be content with making a big difference for very few while millions of children starved. I credit my dad with a piece of advice that has carried me through some challenging times: "Concentrate your resources on needs that would not be met without your efforts. . . . Expect to make some mistakes; nothing important will be accomplished if you make only 'safe' decisions."

In the spirit of forty chances, our foundation will disperse all of our funds by 2045. It will effectively go "out of business." HWB has embraced that idea, and when he writes and speaks about the challenges of development today, he urges NGOs to think about reinventing their approaches, even asking, "Do you have a strategy that can put yourself out of business?" As I write, we have about thirty more chances to get this right.

Story 2
Prague, 1968:
The Soviet Army Eats First—
"We Just Get What Is Left"

I have never personally known hunger as more than an inconvenience, even in some pretty extreme situations. I've gone many hours without food bouncing on dirt roads through the African savanna and then been offered goat eyes and fried rats when I arrived at my destination. I've had to fake swigging high-octane alcoholic home brews so as not to offend my tribal hosts as I waited for food. But I can only imagine the pain that I once saw in the eyes of a woman in an Angolan village decimated by famine. Her three-year-old child had starved to death the week before I arrived. Spindly, eyes yellowed from likely liver failure, teeth crumbling against her swollen gums, and probably not long for the world herself, she thrust her infant at my chest. "Please, please, you must take my child," she begged. "My body is broken."

I cannot imagine the depth of that woman's pain, but I have seen similar examples when I travel to areas of the world suffering extreme poverty and food insecurity. However, the first time I realized how vulnerable people feel when there is not enough to eat—and also how quickly conflict can undermine food security—it blindsided me. I was a naïve teenager from Omaha, Nebraska, and I thought I was just going on a sightseeing trip overseas to visit a friend of the family.

I was born in White Plains, New York, but I grew up in Omaha, my parents' hometown. Nebraska is the heart of America's breadbasket, although none of us were farmers. Rather, my father, who was the son of a US congressman, was busy building a financial investment empire piece by piece while I was busy playing with Tonka trucks and collecting Cub Scout merit badges.

One of the most often repeated "factoids" that intrigue people about my father is that he still lives in the Dundee neighborhood house in Omaha where he and my late mother, Susan, raised my sister, Susie, and my younger brother, Peter, and me. It's a nice, two-story, five-bedroom brick house in a neighborhood of similar homes. It's not what most folks would probably consider a billionaire's house. When I was growing up, there were five of us—my parents and us three kids—which left one extra bedroom. And as I've thought about some of the experiences that helped shape what I'm doing today, that extra bedroom played a surprisingly important role.

A lot has been written about my father—some of it even true. My dad is a financial genius but also a no-frills, commonsense kind of guy. It's his belief that people should make their own way in the world, and my sister, my brother, and I have always known that we were not destined to live a life fueled by unlimited spending allowances and luxury. When asked, he would say he was figuring out how to give us enough to do anything but not enough to do nothing.

I respect that. And I would add that my dad is a lot of fun and has the greatest sense of humor of anyone I know. He does almost nothing that is considered extravagant, so some people say he is cheap. One of his standing jokes is, "I don't buy cheap suits; they just look cheap on me."

I had a normal childhood. I was never hungry, and I never lacked any basics as a child or teen. But we never did much of what you might consider fancy. Vacations were often long trips in the family station wagon, where we fought and whined and drove our parents nuts. One memorable adventure was a trip to Massachusetts so that my dad could take a look at the textile company called Berkshire Hathaway, which he was considering as an investment. My vivid memory of the trip was that each of us was allowed to take one toy or book in the car. I chose a big coloring book but discovered at one point that it was fun to hold it out the window and listen to the pages flap. My dad kept saying, "Howie, you're going to lose it, and I'm not buying you another one." I did—and he didn't.

My dad supported my education and my desire to travel. He encouraged all three of us to pursue our interests, and he gave us help and support, but few handouts. We made a deal that I would get no birthday or Christmas gifts for three years, and when I graduated from high school, he would give me $5,000 toward my first car. I earned the other $2,500 myself. When I realized in my twenties that I wanted to farm, he purchased some land near Omaha—and I paid him a competitive rent that he insisted return 5 percent annually on his investment.

For all of my dad's success as an investor, he didn't talk about it much at home except in the sense of life lessons that were aligned with his investing philosophy. The idea of investing for the long term was a frequent theme, as was paying attention to basic underlying value, not some quick hit. I think he was always more intrigued with value as opposed to money itself. He'd say, "You know, Howie, it can take thirty years to build a reputation and five minutes to ruin it." He did not subject us to nightly investing seminars or lectures about cash flow. In fact, my sister tells the story of how she once filled out a form at Dundee Elementary School when we were kids, and under my father's occupation, my mom told her to write "securities analyst." According to Susie, "The other kids saw that and thought it meant he went around inspecting burglar alarms." Somehow I got the idea that it meant my dad was a security guard, and I think I told Peter, and the two of us thought that was pretty cool—although I'm not sure why we didn't ask where his gun was, why he didn't wear a uniform, and how he could protect the security of anything but us, since he spent so much time reading and on the phone.

My mother was a loving, caring person who looked out for us and made sure we stayed on track. In my case, this was sometimes a challenge. I was a high-energy kid with a healthy dose of rebel in me. I once did something obnoxious when I was a teenager, and she sent me to my bedroom and locked the door with a key from the outside. She said she wanted me to think about my behavior for a few hours. I climbed out the window, went to a local hardware store where we had an account, bought a bolt lock on credit, climbed back up into my room, and installed it on the inside of the door, thus preventing her from entering when my sentence was up. I look back and wonder where she found the patience to put up with me.

My mother helped us develop an appreciation for the world beyond our own yard and beyond Omaha as well. And that's where the extra bedroom comes in. She had a curious spirit and a generous soul, and when I was a young child, she started hosting exchange students studying at what was referred to locally as Omaha University (now the University of Nebraska Omaha campus). Over the years, a half dozen or so exchange students stayed with us for several months at a time. The first I remember was an elegant young African woman named Sarah El Mahdi, who was from Sudan.* It was 1960, and I was only five, so I can't recall many details. I can picture her in her colorful

---

* Sudan gained its independence from Egypt only four years before Sarah stayed with us. I have since visited Sudan four times. There has been chronic food insecurity in this conflict-plagued region for decades. I once spent three nights sleeping near Nyala in the Darfur region, and every night I could hear the sound of helicopters that were headed out to attack villages filled with starving people. The government in Khartoum categorically denied it, but I saw the camouflage-painted Mi-24 attack helicopters myself and even managed to take some low-resolution photographs of them by hiding a disposable camera in a potato chip bag. In the morning, local people could tell you which villages were bombed the night before.

print scarves and dresses, although my sharpest memory overwhelms any other: while Sarah was there, I was stung by a bee for the first time. I remember being terrified and in pain. She took care of me.

BILLY CLUBS AND LONG LINES

Another exchange student who stayed with us would make a more lasting impact on my life. Vera Vitvarová was from Prague, Czechoslovakia, now the Czech Republic. She stayed with my family during a dramatic and tumultuous period in her country's history. The brief "Prague Spring" flowering of intellectuals and writers and a more liberal government in Czechoslovakia began in early 1968. There was great optimism that reforms might take hold in this Iron Curtain country, but USSR leader Leonid Brezhnev was having none of that. By August, he had sent hundreds of thousands of Soviet troops to invade and occupy the country, many concentrated in Prague.

Vera joined us shortly before the invasion. Her family wrote letters about the developments, and wire service and television reports described the turmoil in Prague. I recall that the Beatles' song "Back in the U.S.S.R." was popular during the time she stayed with us. I liked it, but Vera would become upset and ask me to turn it off whenever it came on the radio.

I turned fourteen in December while Vera lived with us. Susie was a year and a half older, and she was more involved with her own friends and high school life, and Peter was too young to pay much attention to Vera. But when she left in the late spring of 1969, she invited us to visit her family in Prague. I wanted to go.

My mother was against it. I can't remember exactly how much detail we had seen on television or in the newspapers, but she knew it was a volatile situation. We forget how much time it used to take news to travel and how cursory news from abroad could be. It wasn't anything like the speed of information we have today. I kept asking and arguing with my mom. I remember one day my dad was sitting in the living room listening to us while reading the newspaper, and he finally put it down and said, "Susan-O [his nickname for my mom], let him go. I think it will be a good experience."

Off I went by myself to Prague for a month. From almost the moment I arrived, I realized that our family had not understood the magnitude of what was going on there. As we taxied down the runway on arrival, I saw tanks and other military vehicles and army personnel all around the airport. I've always been fascinated with big iron anything, and I thought that was cool. But after I got off the plane and walked toward Immigration, there was a big soldier with a gun and a grim look on his face checking passports. For the first time in my life, I felt very alone. "Will they let me in? What if he does not let me through? What if Vera is not there to meet me?" I did not speak Czech; cell phones weren't around then. My adventure took on a new edge. Vera and her family appeared, and I could relax a little, but the mood on the ground among passengers and airport and military personnel was stressed and intense. I would soon learn some of the reasons why.

Vera's family lived in a fourth-floor flat in a building about a half hour from the Old Town area of Prague. Her father, Milos, had what was then considered a good government job as general manager of an import-export company and made the equivalent of about $120 a month. Her mother, also named Vera, and sister, Helena, lived in the apartment. Her cousin Jarslov lived with them as well. By moving Jarslov to the living room floor, I ended up with my own bed, on a couch in Milos' den. The family also had a sign of affluence at the time: the only television in the building.

There were so many "foreign" impressions that are vivid in my mind to this day, such as no hot water. We could bathe only once a week, and had to boil water on a stove and pour it into a bathtub. But my most vivid memory was about the food. There wasn't much of it. I'd had no idea just how difficult life had become in Prague since the Soviet invasion.[1] I'm not sure that even Vera had either, since she had spent most of the previous year with us. I went to the grocery store with her several times and can remember standing in line for two or three hours just to get in, and then being able to buy only a small amount of potatoes and bread. We had money, but the shelves were practically bare. I was used to having unlimited amounts of food anytime I wanted it. During my month there, I don't think we ate more than twice a day, and often just those same starchy, bland items. I remember asking, "Why can't we get hamburger or some kind of meat?"

"Because the Soviet army eats first," Vera replied. "They take all the meat and most of the vegetables. We just get what is left."

Prague had a surreal quality. There were tanks in the street, bullet holes in the walls of buildings, and soldiers everywhere. I once watched as a group of young people in a square protested the occupation of their country. Several black vehicles pulled up, and men got out and attacked the protesters with billy clubs. This was the first time I remember feeling as though I could not believe what I was seeing. I felt that I should do something, but I knew I was helpless. Another day, we got word that a monk had set himself on fire to protest the occupation. I wanted to go see what had happened, but the family's mood told me not to even ask.

After I'd been there a week or so, I asked Vera, "Why are the soldiers on the street corners *Czech* soldiers? Why wouldn't they be Soviet soldiers, since they were the ones who invaded?" She explained that when the streets were crowded, Czech citizens were sneaking up behind the Russian soldiers and knifing them in the back. So the Soviets forced Czech soldiers to man these dangerous posts and then positioned their soldiers in safer locations to watch and to make sure the Czechs did their jobs.

Another surreal moment was watching Vera's black-and-white television set as American astronauts walked on the moon for the first time on July 20, 1969. The moment that Neil Armstrong set foot on the moon, I felt a surge of pride. I wanted to cheer. In the United States, we had been hearing about the moon launch for months. Every boy in America dreamed of being an astronaut. But the mood in Vera's apartment, which was crammed with neighbors, was serious—even a little hostile. I later learned from Vera that the Russian-speaking TV moderator had claimed it was fake: the event was staged somewhere in the desert in the United States.

I was a kid who had barely been out of Omaha, Nebraska, but I started to realize how much I had taken for granted about my stable, peaceful life back home. I was never in personal danger while in Vera's country, but I was witnessing life in a conflict zone. And I have often looked back with regret at my own behavior at the end of my stay. Vera's family were generous, dignified people. Her father was particularly proud that his daughter had come to the United States to study, and he was grateful to my family for having taken care of her and making her feel welcome. He announced that he was going to take me and the family out to dinner to say good-bye. I didn't think much of it, although I could see that Vera was not comfortable with the idea. She tried to discourage him. Milos insisted.

We went to a restaurant that was nearly empty. Vera was uptight. I had been operating at a state of low-level hunger almost the entire trip. (I was far from starving, but I was too young to have much perspective on that.) In my self-absorbed, adolescent mode, I thought, "Great, finally I can have a good meal."

We sat down and looked at the menu. Vera's father told me to order anything I wanted, while Vera shot me concerned looks. At this point, I was annoyed at her, and, for want of a better word, I was being a jerk. I saw something on the menu that was translated to me as involving steak or hamburger, and I said that was what I wanted. I really didn't consider or even understand what it cost. Vera told me, "You don't want that. That is not what you think it is." Her father told her to be quiet; he said that I could have whatever I wanted.

The rest of the family ordered modestly from the menu, and when my meal arrived, it turned out to be steak tartare. Yes, raw meat. I took one look and announced, "I'm not eating this." Of course, I had not intended to order raw meat, and Vera had tried to warn me. She was upset. The others at the table ended up sharing what I had ordered. I'm not sure they liked it much either, but they were not about to let that much protein go to waste.

All of us make mistakes because of youth or ignorance or both. We can't do much about youth, but we can do something about ignorance. That trip was the first real solo adventure of my life. What I saw and experienced would come back around later and fuel my desire to help people who find themselves, like Vera's family, on the wrong side of events beyond their control. I remember the fear and unease I experienced watching the secret police beating people with their billy clubs, and the shocking and visceral realization that I was not in Omaha anymore. I was in a realm where you couldn't count on the law to protect you, where the police could not be trusted and rules were capricious, where there was a fundamental disorder that could endanger you or your loved ones.

In 1968, the Soviet army occupied the streets of most towns in Czechoslovakia. I learned to take covert photos for the first time, and it was the first time I had my film confiscated. *Photo: Howard G. Buffett*

Years later, in the mid-1990s, I would be arrested and detained briefly in Bosnia for taking photographs. This was toward the end of the bloody, three-year Bosnian conflict, which pitted Croatians against Serbs in former territories of Yugoslavia. I remember feeling helpless in a situation without any obvious rule of law. Police officers with unclear motives and intentions sat in front of me, considering actions that would determine my future, and I had no say in what they would do and no recourse. Eventually I was released. In these and other brief periods of feeling powerless, fear about what comes next has never lasted more than a few days or a few hours for me. But it is daily life for millions of people in the world. And one constant is that where there is poverty and conflict, there is always food insecurity. It's not only physically uncomfortable but also degrading and dehumanizing.

I first learned these lessons because we had an extra bedroom in our house and a mom who made sure we knew that the world was a much bigger and more complicated place than we might realize. And a dad who sensed that I was ready for an adventure. The memory of that trip where I never got enough to eat, and of that steak tartare dinner and all the complicated emotions at the table—Vera's father's pride, my ignorance, Vera's loyalty and concern for her family—continues to remind me that food is a basic ingredient of our humanity. Hospitality is universal; nourishment, fundamental.

From Bulldozing Dirt
to Building Soil

The knees of my pants have always given me away. I was that little kid with a truck that you see in every sandbox in every crowded playground: growling engine sounds, rolling the truck up a slope, crashing it down, dumping a load of sand. I'd go into our backyard in Omaha and play with Tonka trucks for hours. It was best after a rain, when there was water and mud, and I'd grind the knees of my jeans into a filthy oblivion. To this day, when I return from a trip to visit agricultural projects around the world, my wife, Devon, laughs at the state of my stained and ripped pant knees. The first thing I always do at any location is kneel down, grab a chunk of soil, and roll it through my hands to check the structure and organic matter, and I pick through the roots of whatever is growing.

I had to learn the difference between dirt and soil, however.

Many people assume that because my family is from Omaha, Nebraska, we are farmers, and my dad just broke the mold by going into finance. Not the case. My great-great-grandfather started a grocery store in Nebraska in 1869, but I never had a conversation about farming with any relative that I can recall until the 1980s, when my dad volunteered to invest in four hundred acres north of Omaha that I rented back from him.

No matter where I am in the world, if I am talking to farmers, I end up on my knees inspecting the soil. *Photo: Trevor Neilson*

And yet I consider myself first and foremost a farmer. I am never happier than when I'm sitting in a tractor or a combine during planting or harvest season.

When I graduated from high school at age eighteen, I wasn't ready to jump on the college track. I had excelled in high school. I got good grades. I starred on the debate team. I became a black belt in Taekwondo. But I started college with no real sense of what I wanted to do. I first attended a small, private college in South Dakota because two of my friends went there. One year was enough of that. I then decided that I wanted to go to Japan and learn a form of karate called Shotokan to complement my Taekwondo training, but the look on my dad's face pretty much ended that plan.

I was restless and curious, and then I heard about the World Campus Afloat run out of Chapman College in California. Now called Semester at Sea, the program offers students the chance to steam around the world on a cruise ship, taking classes but also visiting ports of call in countries such as Morocco, South Africa, India, and Taiwan. That experience affected me in many ways that would inform my later travels and interests, but when I got back, I still didn't know what I wanted to do. I went to Chapman College itself for a while and then I came back home. I was not interested in learning finance or investing. Near as I can remember, what set me on my course in life was watching a guy in Omaha operate a big front loader doing construction work. I thought, "Now, that is something I would love to learn to do, and maybe somebody will pay me to do it."

When my curiosity is engaged, I am a man possessed. I knew a businessman named Fred Hawkins, who owned a large construction company in Omaha. I called Mr. Hawkins and asked if I could come talk to him. He was a gruff, self-made man who had built an impressive company. I walked in, introduced myself, and said that I wanted to learn to operate bulldozers and other big equipment. He looked me square in the eye and said, "Kid, you were born with a silver spoon in your mouth. You wouldn't last five minutes with my union guys. Get the hell out of my office." The Buffett name got me in the door, and then it got me tossed right back out again.

I don't think he meant any offense. Over time, as the child of someone like my dad, you just get used to people reacting in pointed ways to the *idea* of who you are, rather than figuring out who you *really* are. I guess children of famous Wall Street financial executives and Hollywood actors can find plenty of company among other kids going through similar experiences, but being Warren Buffett's son in Omaha—not so much. Omaha is full of great people, but it's a place where you figure out what people think or expect of you. Sometimes it's fair, and sometimes it's not. A little needling is an irritation that pales compared to the struggles and challenges that billions of people on the planet contend with, but it can frustrate you when you're young and would like to be considered on your own merits.

I left Fred's office with an "I'll show you" chip on my shoulder. I went to see another construction guy I heard about from a friend. He was named Frank Tietz, and this time I said, "Look, I want to learn to drive a track loader." He replied that he could not hire me because I did not have any experience. I asked, "How can I get any experience if no one will hire me?" That wasn't his problem.

"Okay, I'll work for free for a month," I suggested. After that, he could decide if it was worth it to pay me. I thought I had a surefire plan.

"Nah, can't do that," Frank replied. "My guys wouldn't like that."

"Why would they care?" I asked.

"Well, they'll see you working for free on jobs they would have made money doing. That won't work."

I hadn't thought of that, so I was frustrated leaving his place too. Then I called a friend of mine named Bill Roberts, who owned an excavating company. I asked him, "If I buy my own equipment, will you let me work on jobs you don't want?"

Bill said yes.

My half-baked adventure gained speed: I scoured the paper and found a CAT 955K front-end track loader for $16,500. I thought that sounded cheap compared to other Caterpillars advertised. (It won't surprise you that there was a reason for that!) I talked a bank into giving me a loan for $20,000, because I knew my dad would never loan me the money.

Bill Roberts helped me out again by hauling the CAT to my first job site: a lot where a friend needed a basement dug. I figured that was a good place to start. Within a day, I was sitting in a hole in the ground with slanted walls and a ramp so steep, I was lucky I didn't pitch the CAT over forward. I stopped working. I knew where Bill was digging a basement, and went and studied him for several hours. I then came back and, through trial and error, figured out how to get the walls straight. Thank goodness I was pretty good at getting the floor level.

Bill was a true friend, passing on small jobs to me and hauling my CAT to the site on his trailer. Next, I figured that I wanted my own trailer so I could haul the CAT myself. I visited a guy named Harry Sorensen, who also operated heavy construction equipment and had drilled for oil in Texas. "Can you build me a trailer?" I asked him.

"Yes. Can you give me a down payment of $3,500?" I had made some money by then, so I gave it to him.

Six months later Bill was still hauling me around, and I kept going back to Harry, who would say, "Not done yet; come back in a couple of weeks." Finally, I said, "Okay, Harry, I need my thirty-five hundred back." He replied, "Well, I don't have it."

"What do you mean you don't have it?"

"Well, I got something else for you that will help you out. I got this tractor you can sell, or you can use it yourself grading or doing other jobs." It turned out to be a 1958 Minneapolis-Moline 5-Star tractor. Even *I* knew that it was not remotely worth $3,500, but what was I going to do? He had spent my money, and I was not going to get my trailer, so taking that tractor was the only way I could salvage anything. Bill just laughed when he learned I now had two pieces of equipment and still no trailer.

I started using the tractor for a few jobs, and the transmission went out. I went to a distributor for the parts to fix it and found out they'd cost $3,500. Spending $7,000 on a tractor worth $1,500 tops was nuts.

I started asking around and ended up meeting a genius at equipment repair named Otto Wenz. I told him, "I've got this tractor with a blown transmission, and I can't spend a lot of money." Well, he fixed it, and fast. He wouldn't take any money, so I asked what I could do to help him. He said he needed some cornfields disked. Disking, or disk harrowing, means pulling a tool with concave blades on it that chops up the crop residue and the soil. Many farmers do it before planting to loosen up the clods of dirt and bury weeds. I'd never done any farming, but I was grateful to Otto, so I showed up on his farm. His son Wayne was there, and we hooked up a disk to his old John Deere 6030 tractor. I was out in the sun driving that big tractor, and I was enjoying learning from Wayne about all the different steps of farming. Best of all, I was not in a hole in the ground trying to make dirt walls straight. It hit me: "This is more fun than digging basements."

In 1976, I bought a trailer I could pull behind my dump truck to haul my CAT as I expanded my business. *Photo: Unknown source*

Farming took hold of me. Later that week, I was the last one in the fields, and it was getting dark. Otto's old tractor had no cab and crummy lights. We'd been working on some land with terraces. When I finished the one I was doing, it was dark, but I thought, "Okay, just one left, and I've got time; I might as well finish that one too." I was about five minutes into working on it when I saw a pickup truck speeding at me with its headlights flashing madly. I stopped, and Wayne jumped out and ran over. "*Stop!* You're disking a field where my dad's already planted corn! I'll go grab the planter and replant, and maybe he won't figure it out."

It's funny how often the path to where you need to be in life can be littered with foul-ups, setbacks, and mistakes, but anything worth doing or learning involves those elements. Otto, Harry, Wayne, a farmer named Francis Kleinschmit, and another group of guys I would meet a few years later all stand out as characters who one way or another nudged me down the road to becoming a real farmer. If Harry had built me that trailer, I might have become the bulldozer king of Omaha and never gone near farming. If the tractor hadn't broken down, I wouldn't have met Otto or had a patient guy like Francis to show me the fundamentals.

In talking to people all around the world, it is striking how many successful people admit that they just jumped right into whatever they decided to do. They never let fear of making a mistake paralyze them. They even may have tried several careers before they landed in the one best suited to them. To make the most of your forty chances, from time to time you've got to do things you don't necessarily know how to do, make some mistakes, call an audible, and try again. It's a simple concept, but so many people are afraid of change. (Farmers, in fact, tend to be among the folks most resistant to change.) When you feel yourself drawn to do or try something, don't overthink it.

After this introduction to farming, I moved away from Omaha for a few years, but I thought about these experiences a lot. By the time I moved back, in 1982, I had a wife and four stepdaughters to support, and the first thing I did was find some land to rent so that I could farm it. I am never so happy as when I'm on a farm, and I've talked to thousands of farmers on every continent except Antarctica.

When HWB was very young, he would come in the cab with me with a pillow. I'd put the soundtrack of his favorite Disney movie on the tape player, and we'd spend hours together. I'd let him steer, and I'd point out to him animals or features about the fields. Today he is farming the Omaha acreage my dad still owns. HWB doesn't love the big motors and the dirt as much as I do, but he is a whiz with the onboard computers and GPS systems that increasingly enable most large-scale farming today. He's got the high-tech gear so dialed in that he once, while on a flight from Washington to Omaha, sent me an email saying that he had just turned on his irrigation pivots from thirty-five thousand feet using his BlackBerry and the plane's on-board Wi-Fi! I was the kid in the sandbox with the trucks; HWB was that kid you count on to reprogram the VCR after a power outage.

FARMERS ARE MORE DIVERSE THAN THEY MAY APPEAR

Obviously, my personal path to farming was not typical. My son enjoys it for different reasons than I do. But I'm not sure that most people in the United States—or even in governments and organizations trying to set agricultural policy or work on global hunger issues—understand just how diverse the farming experience is for hundreds of millions of farmers around the world. I have rarely seen a farmer who is a great economist, an outstanding academic, or a successful politician, but the inverse is also true—not that it seems to stop some of those folks from popping off about agricultural production in a particular geographic area or circumstance, often without a clue about what it means to farm there or how farmers think.

American farmers are unique in the world for several reasons. They have access to vast, flat regions of our country with good soils within what I call the "fertility belt," or the region in the Northern Hemisphere between the 30th and 45th parallels. That region comprises most of the lower forty-eight states, and it holds the most temperate climate, the best soils, and the most productive agricultural lands in the world.* But we are blessed not just geographically. US agri-

---

* The northern farming belt includes the American Midwest, the Black Sea region of Russia and Ukraine, and the North China Plain. Farms in the southern fertility belt, including those in Chile, Argentina, and southern Australia, are also highly productive, but there is a lot more ocean than land at those latitudes. Very little of Africa is in either fertility belt.

culture also benefits from incredibly solid infrastructure, waterways, and access to vast information resources and research data.

As a country, we began investing in our agricultural infrastructure in the 1700s, when 90 percent of the population depended on agriculture to make a living. Our early presidents, including George Washington, were farmers, always interested in improving their yields and supportive of farmers' concerns. Early on, the US established a land tenure system that connected individual farmers to their land in a reliable and stable way, inspiring them to invest and develop it, allowing them to use their land to obtain credit. The US Department of Agriculture (USDA) was established in 1862, the same year that the Morrill Act created land-grant agricultural colleges. By the 1960s, decades of investment by the government in these programs—plus wide-scale research and other key infrastructure elements such as rural electricity, roads, and railroads—created the conditions that propelled an almost tripling of productivity over the next four decades.[1]

Ongoing research and technology development now allow farmers to produce on a scale unimaginable even a few decades ago. Satellites steer tractors, and combines and fertilizer applicators can vary the amount released in one-square-foot patches based on taking an automatic assessment in real time of what the plants *within that square foot* require. In 1926 every American farmer was feeding 26 people; today every US farmer feeds 155.[2]

These farmers have the expertise and resources to use the most sophisticated and complex technologies and inputs—and we must support that. The food ecosystem is complex and multifaceted; a disappointing US corn crop one year may exacerbate starvation globally by driving up worldwide corn prices, while surpluses another year might enable us to quickly and efficiently ship lifesaving aid after an earthquake. As the world's population grows, so must our productivity. US farmers already produce about one-fifth of the world's grain for consumption. What is not so clearly understood is that when the United

States maximizes the productivity of its farm acreage, it saves fragile ecosystems elsewhere.

Even in my hometown of Decatur, a Midwestern city surrounded by lush farmland, people don't realize how much farming here has changed in the last thirty years. We have hundreds of thousands of acres of corn and soybeans, yet I still meet people around here who think of farming as a little-red-barn enterprise. Several decades ago, the area had lots of medium-sized farms of maybe a few hundred acres, each employing a farmer, his family, and maybe a few others. Now these parcels are thousands of acres in size, but they are farmed by fewer and fewer owners, who employ a handful of workers and rely on larger and more sophisticated machines. Drive by agricultural land, and you'll see tall poles holding GPS receivers. Those enable farmers to operate their equipment hands free, their coordinates beaming to and from space. They may pick up some extra hands at planting or harvest, but the level of automation and mechanization is significant.

That's one extreme in the United States. At the other end of the spectrum are the growing ranks of small-production organic farmers who are using various lower-impact, green techniques and fueling the organic and "buy local" movements. There is a lot of important research and technology developed in that area. I'm all for it. I believe we need diversity in every sector, at every scale. One of the most impressive demonstration farms I've seen is the Rodale Institute in Pennsylvania, where for decades scientists have been testing and developing higher-yield organic methods that protect and enhance soil quality.

I am a relentless advocate of better soil management, and we'll get into more detail about that later. I will speak a sometimes unpopular opinion, however: with hunger afflicting nearly a billion people every single day, I do not believe we can feed the world with organic farming. The overall challenge is too big and the conditions in the areas hardest hit are too extreme to rely solely on these methods, which require considerable training, restricted use of fertilizer and seed, and intense management. I agree with the sentiment that attention to soil quality *everywhere* is essential—from the largest US commercial corn farms to the smallest patch of land around a poor farmer in Guatemala or Ghana. That effort involves the use of cover crops, crop rotations, and reduced tillage techniques that I do believe can be implemented by any size farmer almost anywhere. But in the end, improving food security for almost one billion people will require the use of the best practices at many different scales, tuned to local conditions, to achieve success.

THE PYRAMID OF SMALLHOLDER FARMERS

When it comes to global hunger, every farmer has a role to play. The commercial farmer's role is different from a smallholder's role, obviously, but the worldwide food ecosystem needs good, smart actors at every level, in every region. The farmers I am most focused on are ones I feel have been misunderstood and underserved by a lot of well-intentioned efforts to address global hunger: subsistence farmers.

In 2008 I met a woman in southern Ethiopia, a country racked by drought and famine.[3] Her name was Adanech Seifa. As always, I carried my camera, and the photograph I took of her sitting on the ground with her twelve-year-old son, Negese, at the Misrak Badawacho distribution site remains a haunting reminder of the people we must figure out how to help in a long-term, sustainable way. In the photograph I took, her eyes are hollow and tortured. Her son's chest is concave. Narrow ridges of skin hang off his ribs. His legs are so thin that his knees look like oversized knobs.

Adanech told me she had 1.25 acres that had not produced enough to feed the eleven members of her family for two seasons. She was there to try to get food assistance. She once had chickens, but they died from disease and probably the drought. She had no way to store her crops, and, when I met her, she had already sold her last goat and sheep to buy food. But due to the ongoing drought there, local food prices were high, so that food was gone too.

I knew food aid could get her through the next week, maybe the next month. Food aid is essential to keep people alive in extreme circumstances like these. But everyone knows that food aid is not a long-term solution. The question is, how do we create long-term solutions? How can we help farmers like Adanech create a sustainable food source and income?

I felt unsettled when I photographed Adanech and her son. As she spoke and I photographed, I realized her child was dying. *Photo: Howard G. Buffett*

There are hundreds of millions of people like Adanech on the African continent and elsewhere in the world who do not have an even remotely funny or unlikely story about how they "chose farming." Those farmers, perhaps half a billion according to the FAO, provide 80 percent of the food consumed in the developing world using rain-fed systems. They couldn't possibly relate to the nostalgia of the little red barn. Most will never drive a tractor or a combine, and they don't think of themselves in romantic or noble terms as stewards of the earth. They barely grow enough food to survive, and a drought or infestation of pests or a virus can mean the death of one or more of their children. They farm in conditions inhospitable and extreme, with the most rudimentary of tools and inferior seeds. They have no other option.

Unfortunately, there are governments and investors and well-intentioned philanthropists who have been advocating systems well suited to the high-output farmers of America's breadbasket, to areas of the world where there are millions of farmers like Adanech. Subsistence farmers cannot benefit from these approaches. To put the conditions in place so that large-scale systems allowing for modern mechanized agriculture could take hold would demand trillions of dollars of investment in infrastructure and decades of training and capacity development. In Africa, just creating a functional system of roads and water management to fuel large-scale farming across the continent would require the support of fifty-four different governments, most of which to date have not seen fit to invest even 10 percent of their annual expenditures in agriculture, even though it is the primary support of their populations.

At our foundation, we conducted an analysis of African farmers in which we divided them into three groups. We realized the situation was well represented by a pyramid. At its peak, representing less than 5 percent of all African farmers, were the elites: commercial farmers who have enough land and production to hire laborers and who can afford high-quality seeds, herbicides, pesticides, and fertilizers. Some have irrigation, they can obtain credit, and they have some kind of path to market so that they can sell what they grow. They also have a unique designation in Africa: they eat three meals a day, but grow little of what they eat.

The second tier, only slightly larger, is made up of what we call "stable" farmers. They mostly eat what they grow, although in most years, they sell some to supplement their income. They may have some small storage system so they can withhold some crop to sell when prices are higher than at harvest. They usually eat at least twice a day, and some of their children may go to school.

About 90 percent of African farmers (more in some areas) are what we call "fragile." Adanech would be in this group. The families eat two or fewer meals per day. They tend to bring in more income from off-farm work but still live on less than $2 per day. They have no equipment, no large animals. They reuse seed (which diminishes in productivity over time) and often have no access to inputs such as fertilizer or pesticides. They eat almost everything they grow, and if they do have some food to sell, they don't have storage, so they have to sell during harvest, when prices are lowest. They rely on rainfall for their crop production. Most of their children don't go to school and tend to be less healthy, and the primary farmer in the household is often a woman.

Millions of farmers like Adanech are starving to death right now. Their energy is low. They have never been trained to use effective and efficient farming techniques. They do not have access to a farm extension agent to teach them how to use new methods. They usually do not own their own land. The gulf between their capabilities and the resources and infrastructure needed to implement large-scale, high-tech farming renders the whole idea unworkable. Technology on the scale that increases yields on rich, irrigated fields that are serviced by smooth roads, logical rail connections, and giant grain elevators cannot solve food security for fragile farmers. Millions of people live in isolated regions with dirt paths for roads and limited commercial options beyond carrying one bag of food at a time to a trader to sell, or one bag of seed or fertilizer back to their farms.

People are farmers for various reasons. Some farmers are sixth or seventh generation, and they have been doing things a certain way in a particular place for a very long time. A few others, like me, take a circuitous path to agriculture. But the vast majority of farmers in the world farm because it is their only option. In many cases, it is a failing option. The global food ecosystem is complex; we need to develop a deeper understanding of where food comes from and what the people who grow it have to endure. I approach it like a farmer, because that's what I am. My pant knees can vouch for that.

There is an old saying that the difference between men and boys is the size of their toys. My days in the sandbox never left me, but today I use my tractor for serious work. *Photo: Doug Oller*

Story 4
Devon's Gift

The moment that I realized the situation had turned life threatening is burned in my memory as a white streak, intense and slashing, like a teacher underlining a key word on a chalkboard with a harsh swipe.

I was in Senegal. The air outside was stifling hot and still. I was sitting in the backseat of a Toyota Land Cruiser with the motor running and the air-conditioning vents all blasting at me. I had not expected any of the events of the last half hour, and I was having trouble believing that they had happened. People from this village were milling around outside the gates of a compound I had just left, their conversations growing louder and more hostile. The two people who had been with me inside were trying to back their way to our vehicle as well. The local people surrounded them, glaring at them, gesturing at me. The reason was sitting in my lap: my camera.

A half hour earlier, this had been a calm, quiet scene. It was a scene so unremarkable that I had been focused mostly on taking portrait shots of a beautiful little girl in a vibrant green and purple scarf. I was on a trip that had been organized by the international

NGO World Vision. We were exploring agricultural conditions. This part of Senegal was mostly desert, so we had taken a break in this town for water and to stretch our legs. World Vision's local staff person had made a point of going over to speak with a man standing by a brand-new Mercedes-Benz. He was a powerful figure in this town. There were children milling around him, and when this little girl in the scarf saw me holding my camera, she came over and started posing, her eyes locked on the lens. The other children would swarm around as I took photographs, and then she would slip out of the back of the pack and materialize somewhere else. She wanted to be the star and be photographed alone. Like so many people around the world, she wanted to be seen, remembered, and validated.

It was the most extreme contrast I could have imagined, a beautiful young girl in a barren street of sand. *Photo: Howard G. Buffett*

For purposes of this story, I will call the World Vision staffer Charles. If I were to identify him more precisely, even today his life could be endangered for the risk he took on my behalf. Charles finished speaking to the man with the Mercedes and herded us back to the Land Cruiser, and we took off. As he drove, Charles explained that the man was a marabout, or a powerful religious leader. The designation "marabout" refers to Sufi Muslim teachers who run schools that teach the Quran. My NGO contacts in the area told me that these marabouts had very extreme practices that were rejected by mainstream Muslims; communities like theirs could be found only in small, isolated areas of North Africa.

I could see that Charles was distracted and a little upset. Suddenly he could not hold back his frustration and anger anymore. He shook his head and said that inside the compound where we had been parked, there were children in chains.

There was a US colleague from the NGO with me, and we both snapped to attention. We insisted that Charles turn around. As we drove back, he explained that one aspect of this sect was that men had many wives and created large families, but often they did not have the resources to feed them. Therefore, they would send some of their children to the marabout's compound to be indoctrinated into the religion—and fed. To support his operation, meanwhile, the marabout would send them out to beg for money. Often the children hated doing that and tried to run away. So the marabout ordered that they be shackled or chained to each other or to trees so that they could not escape.[1]

Charles pulled up and parked near the wall around the compound. The Mercedes was gone, so he got out and walked up to a man standing by a gate. Charles came back, looking nervous: the man was the marabout's son. We could go in for a few minutes, but I could take only one camera and no extra film. (I was not yet using digital cameras.) We drove through the first set of gates and then got out and walked through the second. We were shocked to see at least fifty young boys in shackles, some chained to trees, some to each other. I'm not sure how Charles pulled this off, but the marabout's son said that

I could take a few photographs. I tried to make a show of focusing on the grounds and the structures, but I was trying to get as many photos of the children as I could. There were adults inside. They watched me with some concern, and then they began to gather. Their voices got louder, their looks more menacing. Charles sensed we'd crossed some tipping point. He told me to back out of the compound while he and my other colleague distracted the crowd. I made my way to our vehicle and climbed inside. One other man from the NGO who was traveling with us was sitting in the far backseat of the car waiting.

It was a lot to process, and I was drained from the heat. When you are looking through a camera lens and see children in chains, you have to keep reminding yourself that this is the twenty-first century, and the scene is not some surreal nightmare. Their faces were haunting: mostly sad and tired, and yet intrigued that someone was paying attention to them. Sometimes these schools claim that they are giving children the "experience" of living like poor beggars to reinforce the importance of giving back later in life. It was hard for me to imagine any such positive outcome that day. How could this be? How could parents turn over their children to such a situation?

Then I saw the white streak dash by the front of our vehicle: a young man, probably in his late teens, dressed all in white, with a wild look on his face, yanked open the front door. He jumped into the driver's seat and reached for the gearshift. I hooked his arm from behind so he could not shift from neutral into gear. Meanwhile, the other member of our party sitting in the far back jumped out, yanked open the driver's side door, pulled the boy in white out, and pushed him away from the car. Charles and the US World Vision person had reached our SUV by now and got in. The mob surrounded us, and Charles began driving forward slowly—but not braking, even as they yelled and approached, some slapping at and pounding on the car as we finally pulled away and drove off.

According to Charles, based on what he had heard from the crowd and knew about this group, he believed that the boy in white intended to drive the vehicle head-on into a wall. If he crashed our vehicle and injured or killed us—and even himself in the process—he would be treated as a martyr by extremists in this angry group.

Our time in that compound was short, and I got to take only one film roll of 36 photos. The most poignant one to me is that of a sad boy with a shaved head sitting on the ground in shackles, reading a religious text. He had old socks pulled around his ankle bones so that the crude apparatus did not rub them raw. I sent hard copies of the photographs back into Senegal, and my contact took the photo of this boy and some other photographs and brought them to a local govern-ment official to report how children were being mistreated in this facility. At first the official denied it, but the photos didn't lie. We were told it led to doctors being allowed in to examine the children.

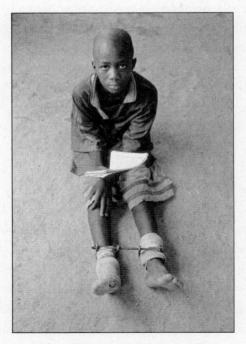

I could barely believe I was looking at children in chains, but I had to concentrate. I had one camera, 36 frames, and I had to get the best proof I could in only a few minutes. *Photo: Howard G. Buffett*

I can no longer count all the times my camera has put me in dangerous situations, either because I was seeing something people did not want me or anyone else to see, or because I was daring various animals or terrain or the elements to get in my way. But sharing what I learn on my travels is so much a part of me now that I almost can't separate the photography from my philanthropy. I have produced several photographic books about endangered species and habitats and the experiences of the poor around the world. I use photography to explain what I'm doing and why—to share the nobility and dignity of people I see even in horrifying or neglected situations; people who are defiant against tyrants and resolved to survive against the odds. I try to use photographs to get across not only the unique, detailed, and personal aspects of suffering that I see, but also the vast scale: refugee camps holding tens of thousands of people nobody wants to think about or deal with, or slash-and-burn agriculture encroaching on rain forests. The irony is that my now decades-old passion for photography did not begin as a high-adrenaline hobby. It began as a gift from my wife, Devon. She thought that photographing nature seemed to speak to my patient side.

OUT WEST

In my twenties, during some of my first adventures in big-equipment wrangling and farming, I was briefly married to a woman from Omaha named Marcia Duncan. Despite our good intentions, we discovered that we weren't compatible. I was young and restless and still trying to figure out how I would spend the rest of my life. I asked my father for advice about a business I could try to learn that was run by individuals that he respected. We discussed several companies Berkshire owned outside Omaha, and he said he would help me find an entry-level job—"You will start at the bottom." That was fine with me. Eventually, I went to California to work at See's Candies.

One of my first jobs was to hit the road with a longtime See's employee who was a trusted maintenance engineer. See's candy stores had a stylized look, with a black-and-white color scheme, including black-and-white-checkered tile floors. Most of the sales clerks were women in white dresses with black bows. Once a year the maintenance engineer would travel from California to Texas and all the Western states to inspect scores of See's stores, making sure that everything was in good repair and giving them an extra sharp once-over cleaning. At the time, he seemed to me to be eighty years old, but I'm sure he was much younger. Still, it was a good lesson to be around somebody who took pride in doing a good job. I moved into production and packaging, where I ordered the boxes we needed to fill daily orders.

Ordering boxes sounds simple, but it had to be aligned with production. Mistakes with those boxes could have significant consequences for the business if you couldn't fill orders properly. Also, there could be a problem if you ordered too many: we had periodic fire marshal inspections, and if the halls were cluttered with piles of unused boxes, that could get the plant shut down.

It was no secret to me that some employees at See's were not keen on having Warren Buffett's son working there. Once a coworker ordered two or three times the number of boxes we needed for an order just to create that fire hazard. My supervisor called me in and threatened to fire me for being so incompetent. He showed me the purchase order for the boxes: my signature had been forged, which I immediately pointed out. After they looked into it, they discovered that the guy responsible resented how I'd gotten my job.

My dad wanted me to commit at least two years to learning a new business, and I agreed. I liked the business fine, and over time I made some friends at See's. But then I met Devon.

Another option for an entry-level job for me had been at the *Buffalo Evening News* in New York. After I met Devon, I remember thinking, "Thank God I didn't go to Buffalo!" I have never met anyone like Devon before or since. She already had four children and was a terrific mother. We had a lot of fun my last year at See's, but I also enrolled at the University of California, Irvine, this time trying to focus on discovering what I might need, what I might use, to shape my life into something rewarding and worthwhile.

But I missed Omaha. And despite enjoying my courses at UCI, I wanted to get married, and I needed a job to support this instant big family. It didn't make sense for me to try to establish myself in Southern California. So we moved back to Omaha. I still had contacts from when I was learning how to operate heavy equipment, and I picked up a contract mowing miles of levee along the river. Within two months of our getting married, Devon was pregnant with HWB.

Once I moved back to Omaha, I started farming much more seriously. And for the first time in my life, I felt like I was calming down inside. Farming does that for me, especially planting and combining. Although it can be monotonous or overwhelming for people who aren't used to it, I feel reassured and recalibrated by spending time driving equipment in the fields, doing the basic work of farming.

When you're sitting in a tractor or driving a combine, you have to pay attention to what you're doing, but you simplify your visual world. I started to see things I had never paid attention to: Hawks and coyotes. Sunsets and moonrises. The yellows, oranges, and other colors of the cornstalks, depending on the different times of year or the time of day. Soil after a rain, sparkling when the sun comes out, going from black to brown as it dries. Foxes darting into the cornfield. The bright green geometries of John Deere equipment against golden, windblown grain.

I did not even own a camera at the time, but I wanted to show Devon and the kids what I was seeing out there all day. HWB was still young, but we had four girls in the house who all loved animals and nature shots. Devon's daughter Erin had a basic 35-millimeter camera—not fancy. I asked her if I could borrow it to try to capture some of these moments I was experiencing in the field so I could show the family all these striking scenes.

Somehow Devon knew that photographing these sights was opening up something in me. I've since heard her tell people, "For the
first time, maybe in his life, I think Howie was pretty serious, and
for a lot of the day, he was quiet. He wasn't joking around telling
stories or focused on other people, and the light and the colors and
all these images from nature were resonating with him. People say
they feel like they see Howie's soul in his photography."

Devon went to the Nebraska Furniture Mart and bought me my
first nice camera. It was a Pentax 35-millimeter single-lens reflex.
I was hooked. Photography eventually played a huge role in what I
came to understand about hunger. I could not "look away."

Early on, when traveling, I would photograph nature. But even
when my mission was to get shots of gorillas or polar bears or cou-
gars, I'd often turn and take pictures of the local people too. It was
almost like a quiet muse nagging at my conscience. In so many endangered habitats, those people would be visibly poor and hungry.

I learned a lot I never could have if I was not in pursuit of a shot.
You pay attention to factors such as light and air quality. In many
villages in the developing world, there is a noxious, smoky haze low
to the ground that people are exposed to, which damages their lungs
over time. It might be from garbage burning, or it might be the residue of charcoal fires. Whatever the source, the smoke and fumes are
unhealthy to inhale, particularly for young children, and unpleasant
to smell. It is present because people are poor, and whatever is burning is somehow keeping them going.

Another element to taking people's photographs that always fas-
cinates me is that even if they are extremely poor, they often have
some item they treasure, some element of their identity, that they
want to show me. In refugee camps, I have had women bring me
cooking pots with bullet holes in them or a dress stained with blood
that they carry so they can have tangible evidence of something
horrible that happened to them. Or children will want to show
you a special little toy or doll, or a little car. They are proud when

you photograph them with it. It validates them and what they care about.

Pursuing a shot can put you in harm's way as well. Sometimes you get so intent on framing the picture you forget that. Photojournalists talk about how once they have their cameras in their hands, they have a sense of being on a mission, with their camera a truth gun of sorts. The problem is that despite the illusion of holding a weapon, the truth gun is not going to protect you from anything real. My search for a powerful photograph has landed me in some precarious situations: freezing cold at fourteen thousand feet in a Blackhawk helicopter above Afghanistan, for example; getting charged by a polar bear; even confronting angry men holding pickaxes around a diamond mine in Sierra Leone.

The boy from Senegal in chains embodies one of the many faces of hunger to me. What happens to a child raised in chains who must rely on a cruel teacher for food and shelter? Questions like these have haunted me over the last decade. At times, I am driven to the depths of despair by the tragedies I've seen and the human anguish hunger causes. When I am behind my lens, I tell myself how much it matters that I collect evidence, and that those images stand to someday turn hearts and minds in the right direction. That is my emotional coping mechanism in real time. But it weighs on a person.

A few years ago I had back surgery, and Devon was by my side as I came out of the fog of anesthesia, talking while still half-unconscious. She later told me she felt like she was hearing "a breaking heart." I was moaning, "They are all going to die, the people in Sudan. The mothers can't help their children. Nobody understands. People are dying all the time . . . I can't help them . . . nobody cares . . . the man in Chad . . . They're all going to die. I can't save them fast enough. No matter what I do . . ." Devon was startled at what the medications had unleashed—we realized it was a part of me that had been hiding behind the lens.

I've come home from one-week trips with five thousand or more images—many which carry a unique meaning from my journey. I find in telling any story that the ability to share the image of a child in distress, or an aerial shot of a refugee camp or a deforested hillside, is a powerful part of trying to get others to understand what I have seen. Photographs have come to represent one dimension of how I try to maximize my forty chances.

Story 5
Because "Al Called"

Dwayne Andreas was a brilliant man but not a tall guy, so the day I looked up and saw him walking a little clumsily toward my office carrying a heavy stack of books and articles and reports about two feet high, I knew something unusual was going on. It was 1994. I was at my desk at Archer Daniels Midland Company, a multibillion-dollar corporation and the largest corn and soybean processor in the world. Dwayne was the CEO. He didn't often play mail clerk. He plopped the whole stack on my desk. "Howie, Al called!" he barked. "We need to help him out on this. Get the ag guys turned around on this biodiversity thing—fast!"

I had been working for ADM for two years, and I was also on the board of directors. I'd had a number of different responsibilities, including scouting for new businesses in Central America, being the official company spokesman, and also consulting on public policy. I had an office next to Dwayne Andreas's nephew Marty, who was a senior vice president. Dwayne told me he wanted me to read the material and then write an op-ed piece we should try to get printed in a major newspaper by the following week. Then he turned and left.

I knew that Marty had overheard Dwayne speaking to me, so I went around the corner and asked him, "Al who?"

Marty smiled. "Al Gore. The vice president."

As I write this book, it's the twentieth anniversary of the Earth Summit, the first conference in Rio de Janeiro, Brazil, on the subject of climate change, development, and biodiversity. In 1992 then-senator Gore was in Rio promoting biodiversity and warning about climate change.[1] Two years later, as vice president, he was still getting pushback from many sectors of big business and that had prompted his request for help from Dwayne. The US Senate had just recessed without agreeing to ratify the Convention on Biological Diversity that 168 countries had signed during and after Rio.[2] The livestock lobbies in particular were set against the United States signing on to this convention. Gore had called Dwayne, who had a talent for seeing right to the heart of complicated situations, and he figured out that ADM and all of agriculture should get behind the idea of protecting ecosystems. Dwayne was famous for having good friends in politics. He knew how to keep them.

I now look back on the experience that started with that stack of papers dropped on my desk as a pivotal moment. Farming is my hands-on, practical connection to the challenge of hunger. Photography is my emotional connection. But this project created for me an underlying intellectual framework for understanding and working on global food security. It was the beginning of my seeing the big picture of how conservation and agriculture related to each other in ways I had never imagined. Frankly, most people don't realize these connections today.

THE ADM YEARS

Devon and I had moved from California back to Omaha in 1982, and I began making my living and supporting the family by farming and working at the Essex Corporation, a diversified construction company in Omaha. I loved farming, I enjoyed Essex, but I also got a little restless, and I felt a small tug from my grandfather's legacy.

My grandfather, Howard H. Buffett, was a Nebraska congressman from 1943 to 1949 and again from 1951 to 1953. His family had been in the grocery business, although he started his own stock brokerage before he went into politics. He was a Republican to the core, devoted to the belief that freedom should be the paramount value that Americans treasured and protected. My dad, Warren, has surprised many people in his life by being both a successful capitalist and a Democrat. Neither my mom nor my dad began as a Democrat, but they switched to the Democratic Party during the civil rights movement. I'm fully aligned with my parents' convictions about civil rights, but I'm also a throwback to my grandfather. I like smart, lean, compassionate government. The idea of leaving people alone for the most part appeals to me.

I'd always been interested in politics. One day in 1988 I read in the *Omaha World-Herald* that for the first time in decades two seats were open for election to the Douglas County Board of Commissioners—without an incumbent running. I called Devon and told her I wanted to run.

"Do you even know what the county board does?" she asked. I did not.

I called my mother and ran it by her. The county board seat represents a large constituency, not much smaller than the local congressional district. "You should run for school board first," she advised. "You should work your way up to county board."

Despite this logical input, I focused on the idea that with two vacant seats, I had a better chance of winning. That opportunity might not come again for a long time. So I went to my dad and said, "If someone runs for office and they lose, do you think people think less of them?"

"Absolutely not," he said.

If he had said yes, I would not have done it. On two words from my father, I embarked on my political career.

I wasn't sure how the campaign process would go. I went into it with a lot of apprehension, but I do like meeting and talking to people. I tend to be upbeat and straightforward, which seemed to appeal to voters as well. One night I was supposed to go to some kind of ice cream social event for candidates hosted by a group in an area of Omaha that was almost all registered Democrats. I asked my dad whether I should bother going. I'll never forget him looking at me a little puzzled and saying, "Howie, just don't be a jackass, and they'll think you're great." Watching some of the antics that go on today at even the national level, I wish more candidates would follow his advice.

In any event, it was fun running for the board. I used to take the kids out on the campaign trail with me. Once I was standing in front of a church handing out leaflets with HWB when he was about five years old, and an elderly man walked up and said, "Howard! It's so great to see you running again!" HWB was confused and started to ask me what he meant. I whispered I would explain later. I just smiled and thanked the gentleman for his support and later explained to HWB that the man had probably voted for my grandfather forty years earlier, and when he saw "Howard Buffett" on a sign again, the man confused me with him.

My dad was supportive of my efforts in the campaign. His involvement was a tricky situation. If he didn't support me, that would look odd. If he gave me too much in campaign contributions, that would not look good either. He settled on matching $1 for every $10 I raised. When people asked him about my running for office, he joked that my signs should spell Buffett with a "small *b* because Howie's the one with no capital."

I had to campaign hard to win. It happened that while there were no incumbents involved, three of the four of us running were all sons of people with significant name recognition. In addition to me, there was US Senator J. James Exon's son and also the son of the popular mayor of Omaha Bernard Simon, who had passed away while in office. Our only female opponent, Lynn Baber, came up with a clever campaign slogan: "I'm nobody's son."

Election night arrived. I was nervous. There was a funny story in the family about how my grandfather went to bed the night of his first congressional election before the votes were tallied. A reporter called first thing the next morning and asked for a quote. He replied, "I'm sure Chip [Charles F.] McLaughlin will do a good job for the people of Nebraska for the next two years." The puzzled reporter replied, "But you won!" Those kinds of stories are a lot funnier when you're not a candidate sitting around watching all the other races in your election year tilt in favor of the other party.

My dad and I stayed up watching the late returns. Around one in the morning, we gave up and went to bed. It was looking good for me, but I refused to declare victory until the votes were officially counted. The next morning, I learned I pulled it out. I enjoyed my time on the board and felt that we did some good work. Governor Kay Orr appointed me to the Nebraska Ethanol Board soon afterward, an experience I also found fascinating.

As my four-year term neared an end in 1992, there were new wheels in motion, and they weren't attached to my tractors or combines.

THE BIG BUSINESS PERSPECTIVE

I had joined the ADM board in 1991, in part because of my experience and understanding of ethanol, which the company produced. The odd turn of events that landed me at ADM was Dwayne Andreas's trying to recruit me to run for governor of Nebraska. It was tempting, but I realized that I preferred my smart, lean government to be run by other people; I did not want to give up time with my family, or farming, or my other interests to embrace a full-time political career at that level.

Less than a week after I turned down the suggestion, however, ADM came back with an attractive offer: the chance to learn big agribusiness from the inside as a company executive. I had to move to Decatur, Illinois, where ADM was located. At first I considered that a nonstarter. But the company kept recruiting me, and I realized there was plenty of land to farm around Decatur. Devon and I decided that it could be an exciting adventure, and we could afford a larger house with more room for the kids on the bigger salary ADM was prepared to pay me. So in 1992 we moved to Illinois.

Those three and a half years at ADM would turn out to be important in our lives in large and small ways. I loved Omaha, but in Decatur, the family enjoyed operating below the radar. Also, Marty Andreas was a passionate amateur photographer, and we encouraged each other's interest in photography. We used to talk about lenses and techniques and bring our cameras whenever we traveled on business. I became very involved in buying businesses in Central America, and I made lifelong friends in Mexico. Also, because I was always meeting outsiders who wanted to influence ADM to support them on policy or other nonbusiness initiatives, I became much more aware of the complexity of politics and markets and regulations, both domestically and internationally.

My education about biodiversity was one of the most important of my life. Today many more people are familiar with the importance of biodiversity; most were not then. And arguments about biodiversity in the media at the time tended to be explained through the lens of pharmaceuticals, as a large portion of medicine's array of drugs originally came from plants from around the world. The idea that the next plant to go extinct could be the one that cures some form of cancer is a compelling one, but I began to realize that biodiversity plays a much bigger role in everyday life.

When an important crop develops an infestation or becomes vulnerable to a new virus, agricultural scientists often combat the problem by interbreeding the existing crop or replacing it with another variety from the same species to resist the threat. In the nineteenth century, for example, grape growers in France were plagued by a root

louse called phylloxera. Their solution was to import a so-called rootstock from America that was resistant to the louse and graft grape
varieties such as chardonnay or cabernet onto that rootstock.[3] In the
1970s, the availability of diverse varieties of corn helped stave off disaster in the United States when existing strains fell victim to southern
leaf blight fungus.[4]

But the element of biological diversity that became of paramount
concern to me involved land use. As a farmer, I know that you can't
just grow anything anywhere. The connection I had never thought
about before I dug into this subject was that not maximizing production in fertile or well-irrigated areas of the world such as the
United States threatened the ecosystems in more fragile areas.

Established rain forests and other ecosystems are home to millions of species that play a critical role in the overall health of the
air, water, and soil. They work together to provide the diversity that
ensures survival at many levels. Rain forests sequester a lot of carbon. Grazing lands in the African savanna are arid for much of the
year and, therefore, not well suited to agriculture, but they allow
migration and perpetuate important species' survival. At the time
I began investigating what was happening to forests globally, I had
an awakening. While nearly 50 million acres of prime farmland lay
idle in the United States in 1993, I discovered that Indonesia cleared
1.5 million acres of tropical forest to grow soybeans. Ecuador was in
the process of expanding cropland and depleting forest at the rate of
2 percent per year. Large areas of the Amazon rain forest had been
torched to make room for cattle grazing.[5]

One of the misconceptions about tropical rain forests is that they
grow out of rich soil. Rather, these regions have evolved in a complex
web that often results in roots of living trees growing up out of the
ground and into dead trunks and other vegetation because the underlying soil lacks nutrients. The nutrients are in the plant matter, and
it's best for the health of the region and the planet if we leave them
there. Instead, too often slash-and-burn agriculture creates a brief

few years of production from these soils, and then the soil is so depleted that little will grow. What's more, without the trees and other vegetation, the remaining soil is subject to erosion at a much higher rate, leading to mudslides, sedimentation, and contaminated water.

As we flew over the rivers of El Salvador, the water looked like chocolate milk due to soil erosion. *Photo: Howard G. Buffett*

I was in El Salvador in 2012, and we flew along the west coast on our way to visit an agricultural project. This country was once covered in lush rain forest, but by some estimates, 85 percent of it has been lost to farming and other uses since the 1960s.[6] In some areas, farmers have cultivated every inch of the soil on steep slopes: they tie ropes around their waists and anchor themselves to trees so they can plant and harvest without falling down the face of the hillside. Unfortunately, they have not used cover crops to keep the soil in place, and the frequent rains wash so much soil down the slopes that the rivers look like chocolate milk. As we passed overhead, there were huge mushroom-shaped dark areas where the rivers emptied into the Pacific Ocean. Productivity for these farmers is declining. Every day, the ocean claims tons of topsoil that will not be regenerated in their lifetimes.

This was once a healthy forest on this Guatemalan hillside, but it's now permanently scarred from slash-and-
burn clearing, vulnerable to severe soil erosion.
Photo: Howard G. Buffett

"NOTHING TO FEAR"?

American farmland, on the other hand, has the potential to produce cereal grains without doing serious damage to the larger environment. We
have the climate, geography, and technology to increase yields dramatically in our farming regions in a sustainable way. In my opinion, American farmers have neglected preserving the health of their soil for too long,
but we know how to protect soil and increase yields, and that is what we
must do. The most striking equation I came to understand during my
research on biodiversity was that the US government was spending billions of dollars idling fertile cropland to support prices, while developing
nations were subsidizing efforts to intensify production on fragile soils.

Another historical event had compounded the problem. Thanks in
part to President Jimmy Carter pursuing a grain embargo against the
Soviet Union in 1980, we had unintentionally created circumstances that
took a heavy toll on rain forests. Brazil, Argentina, and other countries

that previously had no ability to sell grains in volume into the worldwide market suddenly saw an opportunity when Carter decided to punish the Soviets for invading Afghanistan. They jumped at increasing production to sell into those markets and began converting forests at rapid rates.* Meanwhile, we were sitting on excess production capability on our fertile, healthy, productive cropland, and we had taken ourselves off the market.

I started checking in with some of the other sectors in agriculture: food processors, farm associations, and companies that provided various agricultural products. Although they were not anxious to get involved in the public debate, they were willing to remain neutral. What made sense to them was to increase yields and market penetration for American farmers on rich soils that, if farmed properly, did not damage anything else. If fragile ecosystems could be protected, so much the better.

I wrote an op-ed piece for the *Washington Post* headlined "Nothing to Fear from Biodiversity" in September 1994. I said we'd been foolish to fail to sign the convention and lose a seat at the table of world leaders discussing this critical issue. "If the world's food supply is going to keep pace with population growth, the emphasis must shift to producing more on fertile, well-managed soils and less on fragile acres," I wrote. I then went into some detail about different contributions that plants from abroad had made to the health of US agriculture. My fundamental argument was that because twenty species made up 90 percent of the world's diet, it was essential to maintain diversity.

Dwayne liked the article. Not long after, he walked back into my office and said, "The US Senate committee wants you to come testify on biodiversity." I said, "You don't want this. They'll rip me to shreds because I'm not a technical expert on any of this. Let me do a written statement." So we went with that. Professor Ray Goldberg, an agriculture expert from Harvard University, was on the ADM board at the time. Ray read my statement and called to ask if he could publish it in his

---

* As you'll note in part 5, Brazil has adjusted its policies over time to reduce rain forest destruction in the Amazon.

next book. I plunged back into the research and rewrote the statement into a report: *The Partnership of Biodiversity and High-Yield Agricultural Production*.

The gist of this paper's argument is simple, but it represents the core reason I so often stress the productivity of American farmers as essential to a comprehensive, sustainable approach to reducing global hunger. It's not because America needs to feed every hungry person in the world with food grown on our soil. (I'll explain later that I support shifting food aid strategies to use more local purchase from farmers in food-insecure regions.) However, efficient, high-yield agricultural production in the United States has saved millions of acres of habitat, helped stabilize prices, and created the food storage needed to support food aid in situations where that is the only option. At the rate that China, India, and other areas of the developing world are growing, their food needs are increasing dramatically too. When we increase our yields to help supply those markets, we diminish the pressure on fragile ecosystems elsewhere. We also maintain a valuable surplus for emergencies.

ADM was my first, but not last, experience inside a huge global corporation. I also joined the boards of Lindsay, ConAgra Foods, Coca-Cola Enterprises (formerly the largest bottler of Coca-Cola products), and then later the parent Coca-Cola Company. And I have sat on the board of Berkshire Hathaway since 1993. It is true that corporate agendas have shaped a lot of agricultural research to focus mainly on large-scale production, and we need to broaden our horizons, as we'll talk about later. But just as I often cringe when economists or political scientists write about farming without understanding it, I also cringe when I hear activists and environmentalists treating all big corporations as greedy monoliths that must be regulated into submission. There are smart, open-minded people in every sector who care about addressing human suffering, responding to critical needs, and protecting the environment.

Like our global ecosystem, the food economy benefits from diversity. Farming conditions, markets, and local tastes and needs are different all around the world. We need everybody at the table to fight hunger.

Story 6
The Ovarian Lottery

When my mother, Susan Thompson Buffett, did the first, last, and only television interview of her entire life with PBS's Charlie Rose in 2004, she had recently recovered from oral cancer. Some who saw the interview noticed her slight speech impediment and thought that perhaps she'd suffered a stroke, but that was not it. She had made great strides in learning to speak again after her surgeries, but it was still a struggle. Fortunately, it did not undermine her sharp but never unkind sense of humor. She was talking about my father and some of the dynamics of their relationship, and she said with a mischievous smile: "I thought I'd marry somebody like a minister or a doctor—somebody who would do some valuable service for human beings. Marrying somebody who makes piles of money is sort of the antithesis of what I thought I'd do. But I know what he is. There is no finer human being than who he is . . . so I overlooked the money."[1]

My mother passed away later that year from a cerebral hemorrhage. She and my father were visiting friends in Wyoming. They were together when she died. Our friend the great rock star Bono of U2 sang at her funeral. And for a woman who "overlooked the money," *Forbes* magazine listed her as the 153rd richest person in the world in 2004. Her Berkshire Hathaway stock stake was worth around $3 billion.

Our family's involvement with philanthropy has been a source of curiosity to reporters and others for a long time. My dad said famously that he would never consider giving his children the bulk of his money, and people would sometimes talk about this statement as if it hinted at a rift between us. That was never the case. He had seen the children of other successful executives develop an attitude of entitlement that he did not want in his children. He is practical. Just as when he made me present a plan that would yield him a profit on the farmland he offered to purchase, he always wants the numbers to add up. My mother, meanwhile, had a lifelong interest in empowering people and especially in helping all children reach their potential. She loved hosting exchange students from exotic places, but she also worked with low-income children in Omaha. She was appalled and offended by any kind of discrimination. She had a bumper sticker on her car that read "Nice people come in all colors." To her shock, someone once scratched out "all colors" and wrote "white" over it.

In large part due to my mother's interest and inspiration, my brother and sister and I began our first efforts in philanthropy in the late 1980s. My parents brought us together, and my dad said he was starting a family foundation. Each of us would get to determine where $100,000 a year should be donated. It was aimed primarily at giving opportunities locally: everything from the Nebraska Game and Parks Commission to the Big Brothers Big Sisters of America to the Chicano Awareness Head Start Program. I dubbed it the Sherwood Foundation, as an allusion to Robin Hood and his merry men distributing the money they took from the rich.

I think each of us ended up appreciating that low-key introduction, which was enough money to help these organizations without tempting us to get ahead of our own ability to analyze and make sound philanthropic investments. Soon we each wanted to do more.

In 1999, my parents decided that it was time for us to start working with larger amounts of money to have an impact in the philanthropic areas we chose. Soon after, Susie, Peter, and I each received roughly $26.5 million to launch our individual foundations. It was during this period that I made some initial forays into wildlife conservation, and not long after that we purchased a large fenced parcel of land in the Limpopo region of South Africa to set up a cheetah habitat and research center called Jubatus.

Around this period I had my epiphany about how I was never going to make a significant difference in wildlife conservation if I wasn't willing to make a difference in the lives of people who were starving. My mother and I traveled in Africa together in 2002, and she and I talked frequently about philanthropy. I think she was happy with the impact that my travels and my photography were having on my larger sense of responsibility to contribute to the world.

Traveling to South Africa in 2002 with my mom and HWB was an unforgettable experience; we enjoyed sharing her passion for people and for life. *Photo: Paul Laing*

Her cancer diagnosis came as a shock in 2003, and we rallied round her. As she said to Charlie Rose, she was putting a little more heat on my dad to free up more of his wealth for philanthropic causes.

My mother had her own shares of Berkshire Hathaway, and in January 2004 she made her second gift to all three of our foundations: this time, shares valued at $51.4 million. I can't imagine a more loving gesture. My mother had seemed to make a good recovery from the cancer, and so her sudden death in 2004 rocked us all. We all knew the world had lost a real force. But she had found yet another way to inspire us to do good in the world. She had made provisions in her will for our foundations, and her estate gifted $51.6 million each to Susie's, Peter's, and my foundations in 2005.

My father was devastated by my mother's death—she was his best friend and partner in life. As many accounts have noted, he was so distraught that he could not bring himself to attend her funeral. We all felt a little more alone, but my father felt it deeply. I think he had always enjoyed the thought of being able to give my mother significant funds to make a difference in the world. He always thought she would outlive him. What would happen now?

Well, I think he sat down and looked at the numbers. Giving away money is a complicated business, as I appreciate more and more all the time. I have met so many decent, optimistic, generous people who want to make a difference, but they become disillusioned with the difficulty of finding the right fit for their philanthropic interests. Almost by definition, the causes that need the support the most often do not have the infrastructure, management talent, or strategic plan needed to deploy large amounts of capital efficiently. It's tempting to pick projects that are straightforward and "doable." There is nothing diabolical about that. The problem is that those kinds of projects are one-offs. The gains may not be sustainable, and the impact tends to be local or limited. Meanwhile, there are some global organizations that do good work, but they have grown to a size that limits their ability to innovate, and administrative costs and approaches seem to produce fewer and fewer returns.

I think my father looked around at the philanthropy sector and, without my mother to take the lead, understood that he needed an organizational structure capable of handling a gift at this scale. That shrank the universe, and he realized that the existing foundation with the broadest and most robust structure for handling a large gift was the Bill & Melinda Gates Foundation. At this point, in 2006, it was already managing $29 billion and employed more than two hundred people.[2] The foundation was going after global challenges where it hoped to have a broad impact. That mission appealed to him.

However, he also liked what Peter, Susie, and I were doing, and he decided on a generous course of philanthropic investing with us as well: his commitment to Gates was worth about $31 billion at the time. As with the Gates commitment, his gifts to us were based on the conditions that we personally would be alive and active in our foundations and that we followed certain legal requirements such that his gifts were charitable. He pledged the equivalent of more than $1 billion to each of our foundations to be distributed over many years. This decision was a dramatic change in the scope and resources available to us, and it has fueled our exciting journey. As a gift to the three of us on his eighty-second birthday in August 2012, he announced that he was going to double his commitment.

To me, perhaps the most inspirational element of this experience has been my dad's expressed wish that we tackle the hardest problems. Unlike many NGOs, we are not dependent on demonstrating "success" to our benefactors during fundraising drives. We can jump into difficult situations and help people who have no other option and no other resource. We also have the luxury to learn from our mistakes and recalibrate.

As he mentioned in the foreword, my dad has a concept he calls the "ovarian lottery": the notion that the degree to which you are likely to prosper is determined by the circumstances of your birth. He has described this concept in different ways at different times. He sometimes says, for example, that if you had the choice to be born in Bangladesh and pay no taxes or be born in the United States and pay some taxes, what percentage of your income would you be willing to part with to be born here? He believes that the opportunities available to a person with intelligence, drive, and spirit in the United States are different from what a person with the same profile, born into a Chad refugee camp or some remote village in El Salvador, could possibly hope to leverage.

Until fairly late in his life, he left it to my mother to figure out how to have that impact. My mother worked on a lot of community projects when we were young, but in later years, she focused on just a few larger areas. She was a passionate supporter of civil rights, and she advocated for family planning and reproductive rights for women globally. She wanted to work to raise the standard of living for people who found themselves in difficult, often extreme situations. It was about basic freedoms and fairness.

The ovarian lottery is not just a clever way to explain how fortunate we are. It is the reality for these Ethiopian mothers and their hungry children—and for hundreds of millions of others born into difficult circumstances around the world.
Photo: Howard G. Buffett

If you knew my mother, and even if you just watch the *Charlie Rose* segment, I think you can imagine why my father never worried about what would happen to the bulk of his fortune. As she said, making money has always been part of the "scorecard" of my father's life, but he's pretty indifferent to spending it. He just isn't interested in the luxury items and displays of wealth that some in his position embrace. He loves the competitive aspect of investing—the idea that he can read the same material as anyone else and figure out a strategy that creates an outstanding return, when many others lack the patience and discipline to consider how a market is likely to develop in the short, medium, and long term. But he knew that my mother had a beautiful, giving spirit and that she was smart and unselfish. He trusted her completely to do good things for the world with his fortune.

I'm driven to honor my mother's legacy as well, and it's one reason I am working so hard on my thirty remaining chances. I think of her every day, and I am grateful that she launched us all on such an amazing and important course.

Story 7
Reality Has a Nutty Taste, Especially When Fried

If I had a stronger stomach, I might never have gone to Malawi.

On a map, the small African nation of Malawi looks like an elongated cornflake. It is a narrow, landlocked country in the tropics of southeastern Africa, next to Zambia. Its dominant geographic feature is Lake Malawi, which runs about two-thirds of its length along its eastern borders with Tanzania and Mozambique. Despite that huge body of water, most of the country's arable land rises up from the lake, so the agriculture there is mostly rain fed and often subject to droughts. Malawi is a densely populated and extremely poor nation, and its population has one of the lowest levels of protein consumed per capita in sub-Saharan Africa.[1] More than 80 percent of the population live in rural areas, and the vast majority of homes have no electricity. The World Bank estimates the steadily growing population at roughly fifteen million people, and that has put profound pressure on the agricultural land, which is hampered to begin with by sandy, highly acidic soils.

In many parts of central and south Malawi, as in other parts of Africa, the villages seem to grow out of the earth itself. The rural houses tend to be made with bricks fashioned from the reddish soil. The roofs are often thatched grass. If a family saves some extra money, getting a corrugated metal roof is desirable and a bit of a status symbol. The fences and animal enclosures are made from sticks and branches interwoven and lashed together with cords. The women wear *chitenjes*, large pieces of bright cloth that they use for skirts and for baby carriers. In rural areas, many people go to local markets to buy used shirts, pants, and shoes that enterprising locals buy from traders. Also, many items of clothing collected in charitable aid drives in the developed world find their way to Malawi. It's odd but not uncommon to see children in remote areas wearing T-shirts promoting American television shows or sports teams.

There are many Americans who had never even heard of Malawi before 2006, when Madonna visited the country and adopted a little boy and, later, a little girl. But in my mind, Malawi will always represent something that has become fundamental to the regard and respect I have for those working in development and hunger reduction around the world. To appreciate the unique conditions in any location where you want to make a difference, you have to spend time on the ground. You can read a library full of books, but until you venture beyond the airports and the conference hotels and the NGO offices, you will not understand the nuances of what's at stake and what people face.

Around the same time that Madonna drew attention to Malawi, I was watching a television news show that said many of Malawi's people were starving. The reporter claimed they were so hungry that they were eating termites. There was even a video showing people with sticks plucking the bugs, half a thumb length long, out of dirt mounds.

I am not afraid to do unusual things. But when it comes to food, I am a meat-and-potatoes guy. If the local food isn't something I recognize, I don't eat it. The thought of eating bugs pulled out of the ground was horrifying to me—talk about desperation!—and I figured I needed to do something. I booked a trip to investigate.

We made arrangements to meet up with the United Nations World Food Programme (WFP), which was working in the country. A friendly, capable country director named Dom and a driver named Douglas met me at the airport in Lilongwe, Malawi's main city and capital. Malawi is an especially friendly place. Its tourism bureau promotes the country as "the warm heart of Africa," and many people I know who have traveled there remark on that warmth and hospitality, even in the face of the country's extreme poverty.

The agricultural areas we were scheduled to visit were near the larger city of Blantyre, four hours south. Blantyre is named for the hometown of Dr. David Livingstone, the Scottish adventurer and missionary who explored all over Africa in the midnineteenth century, and was famously found in Malawi by explorer-journalist Sir Henry Stanley.

The poverty was obvious. One striking image was lots and lots of people walking at a steady pace along the road, often barefoot, or women carrying water buckets or sacks of grain or bundles of charcoal on their heads. This sight is common in rural Africa, but no matter how many times I visit, it always takes me some time to readjust to seeing small children who appear to be alone, or a child who looks to be four or five with a baby strapped to his or her back, walking along a two-lane road where cars zoom by at fifty or sixty miles per hour. Thanks in part to the high population density, I recall peering into what looked like an empty forest and realizing there were people resting and walking among the trees.

Douglas had the steady nerves needed to drive these roads. The main route to Blantyre was paved and not bad, but the road was chaotic. Bicyclists and oxcarts and children and goats would veer onto the road or head straight toward you like waves of attackers in a video game, and drivers always seemed to react by dodging rather than slowing down.

It is common in rural Africa to see children walking together carrying heavy loads on their heads. *Photo: Howard G. Buffett*

We headed south through rolling hills and the landscape became more savanna-like, with more low brush and grasses, eucalyptus and acacia trees, and the occasional baobab trees. Baobabs are odd looking, with huge trunks and small leaves and branches. They have nicknames that reflect that, such as the "upside-down tree," and, because of their unusual fruit, the "dead rat tree." The trunks have a bulgy, almost skin-like texture, making them resemble giant elephant legs.

There are only a few places to stop on the road. Various vendors gather around the gas stations, where it's also common to find grain traders paying cash for individual bags of maize or the root vegetable cassava, which poor farmers bring in during harvest. Where there is cash, you'll also see men drinking beer, prostitutes, bicycle rentals, and sometimes tires for sale. And then there are guys leaning into the road offering those driving by what look like shish kebabs. I'll get back to that.

FRESH OR FRIED?

As we happened to be passing one of these truck stop market areas, I asked Douglas about the termites and mentioned that I had been shocked to see the CNN report. He smiled and pulled over. He pointed to a roadside stand with pans heating on a low grill. "Try some yourself," he said, going on to explain that termites were a seasonal food considered a great delicacy all over Malawi. The poorest (and probably hungriest) people could not afford to eat them fried from vendors, but they happily grabbed them right out of the ground when they emerged from the termite mounds.

Alongside the roads in Malawi are an abundance of small shops and individuals grilling food. It's a good idea to ask exactly what kind of meat is on a shish kebab. *Photo: Howard G. Buffett*

I had come a long way to investigate a local delicacy that had nothing to do with poverty. I could not bring myself to try them but am told they taste like nutty carrots.

As we went back to the car, I took a closer look at the men selling the skewers and noticed what looked like black strings hanging off the sides. Douglas grinned again. "Boiled mice," he said. It turned out that boiled mice are a regional delicacy savored by the Chewa tribe in the southern and central areas of Malawi. They are consumed whole: fur, tails, and all.

I am not trying to ruin your appetite. Time and again I've learned that you have to be on the ground to understand the fundamental dynamics of agriculture and food. What seems like a great solution to you may fail for reasons you could never have anticipated. As I learned more about Malawi, for example, I came to appreciate the role that the "mouse hunters" play in the rural communities. They are part of a unique ecosystem. As you travel the countryside, you will see puffs of smoke rising from the savanna or near villages. Many are small fires set by mouse hunters. Mice burrow holes in the ground underneath brush and crop residues, often near cornfields. The mouse hunters clear brush and plant residues—or what the locals call "trash"—with the fire, which prompts some mice to run into their grasp. And then they dig down into the holes to collect the mice hiding there, all the while on guard for the snakes that have outsourced their home building to the mice and also set up camp in mice tunnels.

Mouse hunters are part of the fabric of agriculture in areas of Malawi. Members of my team visited a seed development project sponsored by the Clinton Foundation in 2012, and they discussed this element with farm manager Brave Simpuki. He runs the Mpherero Anchor Farm Project, and he explained that in the region are so-called customary lands, or property owned by the tribes, not by individuals. According to local tribal practices, mouse hunters have the right to go into planted fields that they do not own and burn the crop residue on the ground. The tribe not only considers mouse hunting a legitimate use of the land, but the entire community has an interest in keeping the mouse population under control so that the vermin do not overrun the village and eat all the stored food saved for home consumption.

Understanding this is important, because Brave is trying to promote soil improvement practices in these rural communities. One component of that is leaving crop residues on the ground after harvest to improve the soil's organic matter and retain moisture. Brave explained that part of his job involves talking to mouse hunters and villagers about accommodations. His team was trying to convince chiefs to ask mouse hunters to replace the crop residues they might burn in a given field. This can be done by bringing in residues from another area when the hunters finish harvesting mice.

The unique situation involving the mouse hunters illustrates a common thread in development projects. A "recipe" developed in one country or context may not work in another. You may give clear information to farmers about the importance of leaving crop residues, and you may have a stack of papers and material to back it up, but if you are in southern or central Malawi and don't factor in the mouse hunters, you're going to have trouble. You will have created conflict not easily resolved. That will prompt the tribal chiefs to get involved, and you don't know how they will view the situation. This is not something that will be apparent from geography books or economic models developed in an American think tank.

It's not even a situation that some people from northern Malawi can fathom. "If you tried to give a boiled mouse to a member of my tribe to eat," says a Malawian friend of ours who works with a prominent NGO in Lilongwe, "we would vomit."

I confess I felt a little better when I heard that.

Every year I think about cutting back on some of my travel, but I have to see situations for myself before I understand the value of these initiatives. And sometimes it takes more than one trip to absorb it all. I've gone back to Malawi several times. The need is great. The people are poor but have great dignity and warmth. The availability of good land is limited, and the extraordinary population density increases all the time. I no longer pay much attention to the termites, but I never underestimate the tenacity of the mouse hunters.

Where Hunger Hides

It was an October evening, brisk but not yet cold by Midwestern standards. Shortly before midnight, we pulled up in front of a small wooden house on an otherwise quiet Decatur street. I called in the 10-60 code that we had arrived in the area. The Macon County sheriff and I both were in uniform. His weapon was holstered, as was mine. I had been trained that it's best not to treat any dispatch as a "routine" call, but we were not expecting trouble. We had a warrant, and we were meeting a deputy sheriff there to arrest a woman in her mid-forties. She was accused of stealing clothing and then returning the same items for cash.

We rang the bell, and the suspect opened the door. She looked exhausted and began crying as the deputy explained that she was to be arrested and would have to be handcuffed. The scene inside was not violent or dangerous, but it was grim. A girl who looked about fourteen was sitting on a stained couch; a boy around twelve was lying in bed in a nearby room, his leg in a cast. The deputy took a statement from the young girl while we waited for her aunt to come get her and her brother. I spoke to the boy for a few minutes. He seemed despondent and said his father didn't care about him. He was upset that he would have to leave his home.

As we prepared to transport the mother, she told the deputy she had heroin in the house that she was holding for someone else. She wanted to "cut a deal." I heard the young girl tell the deputy, "I am never going to do this to my kids." Clearly, this mother's decisions were creating terrible consequences for her children. I happened to look over at the kitchen table. On it sat a box of food from a local food pantry. I thought, "What would these kids have been doing for food without that resource?"

About twenty hours a month, I work shifts as an auxiliary deputy sheriff in Macon County, where I live. This position is voluntary and unpaid, but it is not honorary or ceremonial. I completed forty hours of state qualifications and passed my weapons proficiency test. I carry a firearm while on duty, and I am a sworn law enforcement officer with full powers when I'm with a full-time officer. There are a dozen such positions in the county. As in many places in the United States, sheriffs typically ride alone in Macon County, and the program is designed to provide backup for its officers in an age of strained budgets and resources. It's also giving me new perspectives on hunger and food insecurity in my own hometown.

THE SMELL OF MONEY

Macon County is in the center of the state of Illinois, the heart of the American Midwest. Unlike many areas of the developing world where our foundation supports food-security projects, the surrounding farmland has excellent soil. There are no civil wars raging in Decatur. We have good roads and extensive rail coverage, storage capacity, and plenty of huge grain elevators to take in corn and soybeans year-round. Farmers control what and when they sell. We don't have corrupt agricultural ministers or tribal uprisings that displace landowners.

I always look forward to coming home to Decatur. It's a low-key, unpretentious city with a small-town feel. My foundation is headquartered in a three-story brick building downtown. For a long time, we didn't even have our name on the door. One time an electrician came to fix some wiring, and the only identifying decorations we had in the lobby where he was working were framed food aid sacks, including one made to carry rice for Liberia imprinted with the words "World Food Programme." The next week, we received a bill from the electrician made out to the World Food Programme. We broke down and put up a small sign.

I live in a comfortable house in a quiet neighborhood. I like walking into my own kitchen and checking the door of our refrigerator when I grab a Coke. It's sort of Devon's and my own low-tech Facebook page. There's barely an inch of surface showing. Devon keeps it covered and updated with snapshots, school photos, team pictures, vacation images of our children and now nine grandchildren, cousins, and close family friends. Unlike those in many of the photographs I bring back from my trips, the faces in these pictures are almost always happy and healthy.

Decatur recharges my batteries in part because it's near where I farm; most of my fields are about twenty-five miles south. As planting or harvest gets closer I always feel a familiar nervous anticipation. There is so much to do on a farm, so much you'd like to do, so much you'll never get to finish. There is always a grain bin to improve or some low-yield spot in a field you're trying to figure out how to fix with drainage or fertilizer. There is the weather report to check almost hourly during key planting or harvesting periods. Compared to working on global food insecurity, focusing on farming here feels doable and immediate.

Decatur is also the headquarters of Archer Daniels Midland and the world's largest corn processing plant. The ADM plant is Decatur's most dominant feature. Its big, white, blocky buildings loom large on the eastern side of town, with giant chimneys spewing steam. ADM's total of nine corn processing plants here and globally can process 2.6 million bushels of corn per day. ADM also owns 26,000 railcars to ship grains, 1,500 trucks, 1,700 barges, and even 8 oceangoing vessels.[1] The plant perfumes the air with a tangy smell that some people describe as "corn cooking." Others describe it less politely. ADM executives I worked with used to call it "the smell of money." And yet each day, the smell of corn processing wafts over approximately 18,500 people in Macon County who cannot count on where their next meal is coming from.[2]

I wasn't oblivious to the fact that Decatur's fortunes have been sliding since we moved here in 1992. It had a population of about 85,000 then, and that's shrunk to about 76,000.[3] Like a lot of small and medium-sized cities in the Midwest, it prospered as a manufacturing town but suffered when companies such as Firestone closed down old plants and moved jobs to other regions of the country or the world. Decatur has had a harder time than some of our neighboring cities. It never developed a significant white-collar component to its job base. Nearby Springfield, for example, is the Illinois state capital. Bloomington-Normal has Illinois State University and State Farm insurance, in addition to a Mitsubishi Motors assembly plant. Champaign has the University of Illinois at Urbana-Champaign, plus a number of high-tech companies.

ADM, where I worked previously, is the dominant employer in Decatur. Another food processor, Tate & Lyle, and Caterpillar have significant operations in town as well. Those companies have done well, but others have moved on. As people lose jobs and leave town, it pushes down property values, which yield fewer taxes to support local services and at the same time draw in people from other regions trying to make ends meet. My friends in community organizations tell me that the only population segment now growing is those over sixty-five. Once this kind of dynamic takes over a region without a diversified economy, it's hard to reverse.

Yet for a long time, as I was focused on global issues, I drove past some of the small rural communities near my farmland where it was obvious that whoever was living there had slim resources. We did invest in community projects, but I realize now that I used to think of Decatur as my refuge from food-insecurity issues. That was an illusion.

In 2008 I happened to be in our foundation office downtown the day after Christmas, and so was one of our staff members, Molly Wilson. Molly and her husband, Mike, have lived in Decatur for quite some time and found it to be a great place to raise a family. For years Molly had volunteered at a local soup kitchen called the Good Samaritan Inn. She was seeing the growing numbers of people coming into the soup kitchen, especially children. I had been hearing from local folks that Good Sam was trying to do good work out of a run-down facility. It had just announced a capital drive to finance a new building to expand its services, and it seemed like a good day for us to check it out.

There were people of all ages lined up outside in the cold. Molly and I went in, and even though the facility was dark and cramped, there was a great spirit in the room among the people serving lunch.

Molly introduced me to a woman named Kathleen Taylor, who was directing the soup kitchen, and she was impressive. She had the peripheral vision and ears of a great mother, able to talk to you and give you her full attention, all the while aware of somebody carrying too heavy a load or putting something in the wrong place twenty feet away. She would look up and bark a quick correction without breaking conversational stride.

I was amazed at the number of individuals seeking a meal that day, and I asked standard questions: How many people do you serve? Where do you get your support? And so on. Clearly, it was a high-value service being run on a small budget and on the backs and sweat of the volunteers. Kathleen explained some of the dynamics that affected how many clients would be there on any given day. For example, attendance fell off on days when buses didn't run, but it shot up once a month when a bus from the state prison dropped off newly released inmates.

Hunger has been on the rise in Decatur, as in
the rest of the US. It's become more common
to see individuals on the street asking for help.
Photo: Howard G. Buffett

I talked to her for two hours, and then I asked her a question she
couldn't answer. It had to do with the operating budget, and she
looked at me, frowned, and said, "You know, I don't have that answer.
Hold on." She pulled out her cell phone and called a board member
and started asking the person my question and probing for more details herself. Finally, she said to the person at the other end, "I don't
know, I didn't get his name." She put the phone on her shoulder.

"I'm sorry, we'll have to get back to you. Can you leave your name
and phone number, and we'll call you?"

I told her my name, and she told the board member. He brought
over all the accounting books so that we could review some numbers.

Kathleen was focused on making the food bank work. We talked
about how services such as this one are so vital to a community, yet

often community leaders are not comfortable supporting them publicly or admitting that they even exist. It's kind of like having the NFL's leading punter on your football team but playing it down: because if he's getting a lot of time on the field, you have to admit that something is wrong with your offense. Our city should be proud of a soup kitchen that serves a large number of people who are food insecure, but its existence raises the questions: Are our civic leaders doing enough to create jobs and get those who are homeless and need meals back on their feet? Are the rest of us doing what we can to help our community thrive?

That day changed and broadened my thinking yet again. If my goal was to fight global hunger, and I was serious about the word *global*, how could I neglect the hunger and food insecurity in my own town among my own neighbors? At this point in my life, my mother had passed away, and I sort of felt the *whoosh* of her spirit in the air. She had always been a big supporter of the Omaha community, particularly anything to do with children. A high percentage of food-insecure people in America are children. There were kids running around Good Sam that day. I realized I had to embrace global food security.

I committed that our foundation would help them build a new facility, but on the condition that all the members of the city council work a volunteer shift at Good Sam so that they, too, got a more complete picture of food insecurity in their town. When Kathleen worried that they wouldn't do it, I told her to remind them that they were not going to want to face the publicity that a $1 million donation was being held up because the city council members wouldn't roll up their sleeves for one shift.

HUNGER IN THE US IS OFTEN HIDDEN

It's not that I didn't realize hunger was an issue in America, but I did not appreciate how widespread and yet hidden it was. I had spent some time in Appalachia, particularly in the poorest areas of West Virginia where people struggled with hunger daily. There I took some photographs of a man named Everett, who had a deep impact on me. We were driving by his home, and he came out on his porch to retrieve the mail. He was so thin. The image stuck in my mind. I went back later in the day, found him, and struck up a conversation. Then I took some photographs of him. Everett was a veteran and on his front porch flew a flag that he proudly saluted, but he was barely surviving. He had Parkinson's disease. After our visit, I sent him some of the pictures I'd taken. He told a representative of a local agency who had been with me and who delivered the photographs, "Tell that photographer to come back and take pictures of me in my uniform." I wanted to do that, but a few months later, we could not find him. I later learned that Everett had died.

As I was leaving, this veteran, Everett, squeezed my hand. He put his other hand to my heart and said, "God has blessed you." *Photo: Howard G. Buffett*

I was affected by this encounter. For a long time, it was hard for me to think about hunger in America without thinking of Everett. However, the local poverty of the region was so dramatic that I did not make the connection to hunger in the United States more broadly until years later, after my experience at Good Sam. It astounds me that one in six Americans is food insecure. I have learned that every county in the country, from the wealthiest suburbs to productive agricultural regions, is home to people who cannot count on eating three meals a day. Millions of families are a layoff, a personal crisis, or a serious illness away from financial trouble so severe that they could end up without enough to eat.

In the United States, food tends to be the most elastic of the monthly expenses for families. Rent, utilities, transportation costs, and insurance bills are not negotiable month to month, so for folks struggling to make ends meet, those get paid first. That's one reason you can end up with families living in relatively nice homes or apartments, driving cars, holding down jobs, and yet with little left for food. So when Dad is laid off or Mom gets her hours cut back, families dial down their food budget and buy less costly (and typically less nutritious) food when cash is short. Or they seek other ways of supplementing their pantries through food stamps or visiting a soup kitchen or a local food bank. Food insecurity is also on the rise among older people who may have thought they were in good shape but then must decide between buying expensive medicine, a car repair, or food.

Once the Good Sam experience focused my attention, I looked for other insights into hunger in my community. I spent a Saturday going on some delivery runs with the Decatur Meals on Wheels team. We went to three different homes. I was struck first by what these three clients had in common. Their homes were neat and well kept. From the sidewalk, it was clear that the home owners had pride. You would not drive down these streets and think, "Poor people live here."

And yet there were unique aspects to their stories and lives that I'd never thought about before. In one home, a husband and wife had moved to the area from a southern state to be near their son, yet once they arrived, he paid little attention to them. The husband never arose from bed during our visit because he was in the early stages of Alzheimer's. The wife was polite and hospitable, but she had a deep sadness about her. She and her husband had worked all their lives, but now their finances were strained. She had broken her ankle sometime back and had a lot of trouble getting around. She couldn't drive or carry much. The meal delivery was vital to them.

At the next house, the meal client was a rail-thin man chain-smoking on his porch in front of a space heater. He and his nephew and the nephew's friend were watching a football game on a small television. The client was gracious and grateful for the food. The two young guys with him looked to be in their twenties, edgy and glassy eyed, making sarcastic, smart remarks at almost everything the client said to us. The meal client was a veteran and had had some jobs in food service, and seemed to be a good guy who deserved more respect. When we left, I wondered how much of his own meal he would get to eat.

At the last stop, we met a retired school cafeteria manager. Her house was neat as a pin, lovingly decorated. She was ninety, cheerful, sharp, and funny, with bright, merry blue eyes. She reminded me of one of my favorite people from my childhood: my warm, kind Aunt Katie. This lady's challenge was shopping and standing to prepare a meal. She used a walker, and grocery shopping and standing at the stove to cook were physically beyond her capabilities. You don't have to be poor to be unable to afford to pay someone to shop or cook for you; Meals on Wheels was a huge help that kept her independent and in her own home. She did confide that the nutritional rules meant she was missing one thing: the simple pleasure of some fried chicken. I dropped off a bucket of KFC the next day. She looked so delighted that it made my day. Whether you're in Decatur or Armenia or Darfur, everyone likes to be treated as an individual and paid a little personal attention.

The foundation helped the Good Samaritan Inn construct a new building with a modern kitchen and storage capabilities, and it is an impressive operation. They have a committed and enthusiastic new director, Brenda Gorrell Pyat. Local supermarkets donate a large share of the food, so she is managing to serve three hundred people a day, on average, for about $8,000 a month.

When I last visited in 2012, Brenda said that the demand for services had been rising steadily. For roughly one-third of the guests, this meal is the only one they get all day. I visited with a few of the patrons, including a ninety-seven-year-old man named Bob who had driven himself there for lunch. "How are you?" I asked, shaking his hand. He quipped, "Still above ground!" and gave me a thumbs-up. Bob was a World War II vet. He wore threadbare clothing and had worked for many years at the old A. E. Staley corn processing plant in town. Life was not easy for him, and this hot meal made a difference.

Sitting at a table by himself was a man whom the Good Samaritan team calls "the poet." His name is Victor. Victor travels around with a backpack holding sheets of paper on which he writes poetry and songs. We talked for quite a while, and his story is yet another angle on hunger. He is a veteran also, and he was trained as an electrician. In fact, in the 1970s he was the first African-American electrician hired by the city of Decatur, to work on traffic lights. He told a story about how, when he used to show up to fix a broken traffic light, there would often be police directing traffic and a crowd around. When he would step forward to start to go to work, the police would often yell at him to get back. He rolled his eyes and explained, "They had no idea why a black guy would be coming at them with his tools." Victor said that he lived for a time in California and repaired Xerox machines and made $50,000 a year. But his marriage broke up, and he started using drugs and alcohol. Recently, he was homeless for some months, as he has been several times in his life. "Drinking and using drugs," he said. "That'll do it."

He showed me his poetry, and it was impressive. He was so proud of a poem he had written called "Decatur: Down But Not Out!" He was proud of his city. There was a lot of talent in this man.

Also at Good Sam that day were a number of thin, jittery clients who were likely meth users, based on the appearance of their damaged teeth. Since I began working my shifts with the sheriff's department, I've had more and more exposure to the toll that drugs take on people. I don't drink alcohol or use drugs, and I have always had trouble relating to those with addictions. Especially when they have children with them, I battle frustration and discomfort. I feel so bad about the difficult lives I imagine the children to be living, and I know this problem can affect people of all socioeconomic classes and situations. A cousin of mine died of a drug overdose. But I remind myself that staying alive long enough to conquer an addiction depends on having access to food. The children of addicts need to eat, regardless of the mistakes their parents have made.

I first got involved with the sheriff's department because I have a deep respect for American law enforcement. I have been to so many places in the world where the rule of law is not in place. There is a different standard of treatment for the rich as opposed to the poor. In those parts of the world, poor people often cannot trust the police to do the right thing and cannot count on them for help. I wanted to understand the training and the mindset that go into creating a professional law enforcement organization.

I now have a much better appreciation for how challenging "keeping the peace" can be, even in an organized, just, and free country. But it's also given me some new insights on how and why families are struggling, and how so many children bear a terrible burden when their parents stumble. About sixteen million children in the United States often do not know where their next meal is coming from, and a box from a food bank may be more important to them than many of us can possibly imagine.

PART 2

Bravery, Courage, and Hope

Possibly because I'm a photographer, it is always the individual faces of people that I see when I think about different facets of hunger and food security.

In this section are stories of some individuals I've met who make the themes and fundamental issues of food insecurity today real—some through their dedication, some through their suffering, all by their humanity. First, I'll talk about several individuals who have experienced the physical and psychological toll hunger exacts. Next are stories about some deeply committed heroes putting their unique talents and passions to work.

Battling hunger today is a complicated enterprise that not only involves producing and distributing food but also can mean fighting ignorance, corruption, violence, and apathy. It is always difficult, and it can be dangerous.

Story 9
Loved but Lost

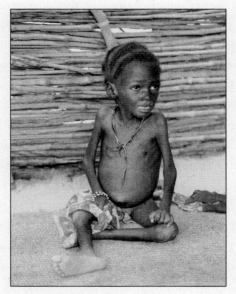

Photo: Howard G. Buffett

I never got her name. Her simple little string necklace and tiny bracelet made it clear that someone loved her and was trying to make her feel special even with the meager resources available in this im-

possibly poor village in northern Niger, one of the poorest countries in the world. The little girl's mother had died the year before.
The mood in the small, reed-walled home where she lived with her
grandmother was so somber that I could not bring myself to ask too
many questions.

But I did take her photograph.

It's hard to determine her age. She looked about four, but she
could have been several years older. Severe malnutrition from birth
stunts a child's growth. Her features were well defined, and the
look of suffering and discomfort on her face haunts me.

I'm told that there are two classic profiles of people in the grip
of starvation. This little girl had the swollen belly that we associate with protein deficiency, and it is a common sight in the most
chronically hunger-plagued regions of the developing world. It
can seem odd that individuals with such sticklike arms and legs
have these large bellies, but it is the result of fluid that is leaking
out of their bloodstream and into their tissues, resulting in edema.
Blood vessels require both dietary protein and salt to maintain a
healthy structure. When deprived of these essential nutrients, the
vessels can't contain the fluid, and it often gathers in the abdo-
men. (It also can build up in the feet or legs, especially when an
individual is too weak to move very much.) Ordinarily, a healthy
body clears the fluid buildup. But in these children, it remains
there because the body does not have the energy to pump it back
out. Because this little girl also lacked other nutrients in her diet,
she had hardly any muscles on her arms and legs, and had not
grown normally. None of her bodily functions performed properly,
including her immune system—the body's defense against disease.

There is another body type we associate with severe hunger,
and that is one I have seen more commonly in camps where displaced persons are living as a result of famine or conflict. This
body type is best described as emaciation. Photographs of concen-

tration camp survivors after World War II show these effects: you feel as though you can count the person's bones, and the skin can seem too big for the body. This is more common among people whose vasculature is stronger than that of children with the swollen bellies.

Both types of malnutrition are referred to as severe acute malnutrition (SAM).[1]

The good news is that today medical and aid personnel can reverse the damage of SAM in a child like the little girl in Niger. Modern procedures involve a simple intervention with a specially formulated food that contains the nutrients the body requires to recover and rebuild tissue. Refeeding, as it's called, used to be done with specially formulated milk that had to be prepared and administered in a clinic for a period of five to six weeks. But in 1996, French researchers developed a new type of nourishment called RTUF, or ready-to-use therapeutic food. It consists of peanut paste, milk powder, sugar, oil, and added vitamins and minerals, and can be squeezed out of a foil packet for consumption. RTUFs (the best known is "Plumpy'Nut") are reaching more and more children because administering them does not require trips to a clinic. Dramatic improvement typically occurs in just six to eight weeks. The nutritionists at WFP tell me that today the cost of saving a child from SAM is about $45.

The bad news is that this type of therapeutic feeding was not available to the people of this village in Niger. The little girl I photographed died a few days later.

It's difficult to grasp the enormity of a world with almost a billion food-insecure people. It is not at all difficult for me—and now I hope it will not be for you—to remember this face of hunger: the suffering of the little girl in Niger and the tragedy that she died from a condition we can prevent. Estimates vary, but perhaps 20 million children may be suffering from SAM in the world today, with at least one million children under age five dying from SAM every year.[2]

It is difficult to read about starving children. It is much worse to see this suffering in person. We can only imagine what it must be like to experience it. If we cave in to our own discomfort and look away, the pain of this little girl from Niger will continue for millions more.

Story 10
Empty Calories

The freshly picked, bright yellow ears of corn almost glowed against the dark, corrugated metal roof. Maria, an eleven-year-old Guatemalan girl, reached up high to drape them over the rafters. The family hung its corn in this manner to keep rodents from eating it and to keep air moving around it to prevent mold. By the window below, her grandmother looked out into the sun, wearing a bright green embroidered blouse made from a traditional fabric. The girl looked healthy and pretty and there was a serene expression on her face. She was focused on her task. There was no hint of a problem here. The eventual photograph I took shows a scene so calm that I feel a painful contradiction when I look at it. But I do look at it because it reminds me of a face of hunger that lives in the shadows around the world—even in our country.

In Totonicapán, Guatemala, where I met Maria, one of every sixteen children dies of malnutrition before reaching the age of five.[1] So was Maria's apparent health an aberration or the result of her family's being better off than others were? No. Like almost all the children in the village, she had a diet consisting primarily of corn and beans.

Throughout a trip I took to Guatemala in 2007 I would see many children with plump cheeks and even stocky bodies, yet I learned that they were not healthy. I would see ten-year-olds I originally thought were six-year-olds. They were not emaciated—often not even thin—but they had not had access to the right micronutrients and so were not developing in a healthy, normal way. While corn and beans are satisfying to eat, that diet does not include key micronutrients such as vitamin A, iron, and iodine.

As she hung what appeared to be plenty of food, it was easy to forget that like so many children in Guatemala, Maria and her family battled chronic micronutrient deficiencies.
Photo: Howard G. Buffett

Micronutrient deficiency is widespread. Roughly 2 billion people around the world suffer from iron deficiency, for example, and 250 million preschool children worldwide are deficient in vitamin A. Iodine deficiency, the most prevalent cause of brain damage in the world, is easily preventable, yet it remains a problem in fifty-four countries. Guatemala battles all these nutrition deficits. Almost 50 percent of children under five in the country suffer chronic malnutrition, and 30 percent of pregnant women have nutritional deficits.[2] Even when children such as Maria survive into their teens, they often are anemic and suffer painful thyroid disorders. What's more, their immunity is often compromised, rendering them dangerously vulnerable to otherwise survivable infections such as measles.

Undernutrition begins in the womb. Undernourished mothers cannot provide proper vitamins and minerals that a baby needs to develop normally. Unwell, undernourished children often lack the ability to concentrate and develop mentally, and later they lack the energy to attend school. They experience what is called stunting and never reach their full height potential. SAM victims need immediate calories and nutrients to survive a crisis, but food security is about the long haul, from cradle to old age. Childhood undernutrition ultimately leads to cardiovascular disease, immune disorders, and psychological and developmental disorders.

According to the experts at WFP, one misconception about global nutritional deficiency is that it's a fairly recent development, stemming from people falling out of harmony with their environment or abandoning traditional diets. Reality turns out to be much more complicated. Scientists say that the micronutrient issue appeared about ten thousand years ago when humans who had evolved as hunter-gatherers turned to agriculture. The transition shifted food consumption worldwide, and the majority of the human diet became cereal and tuber crops. While growing crops took less energy than hunting animals, grains possess fewer vitamins and minerals than meat. The human body hasn't adapted much yet (ten thousand years is brief from an evolutionary perspective), and so the lack of vitamins and minerals is problematic on a global basis.

Undernutrition is widespread in the developing world, but it exists in the developed world as well. If you aren't getting the amount of calories you need, you are unlikely to be getting enough of many different healthful components of food. In the United States, we have obese individuals who are malnourished. They eat meat but are not getting the exercise of the hunter-gatherers. And they also have diets high in fat, sugar, and processed foods but deficient in vitamins and minerals. These deficits impair their immune systems and lead to diabetes, cardiovascular disease, and other health complications such as weak bones and skin conditions.[3]

One member of my team spoke recently with a pediatric nurse in California who explained that among Hispanic farmworkers in California's famous Napa wine country, studies showed pervasive iron deficiency in the children. Iron deficiency at a young age can create lifelong deficits in brain development. "We need to educate these families—some of whom are sending home money to family members in Mexico or other countries—that they are unwittingly shortchanging their own children," she explained. "They are trying to spread their resources too thin and giving their own children instant soup night after night, but not enough protein or fresh vegetables for vitamins and minerals."

Undernutrition has unique elements that depend on the ecosystems and societies involved. There is no unchanging Garden of Eden anywhere. Anthropologists say that for as long as humans have been on the Earth, entire cultures have died out from all sorts of "natural" factors. The ecosystems on which we rely for our food are changing, influenced by weather shifts, new animal or plant species appearing or disappearing, or the emergence of pathogens. In response, humans have migrated around the world as famines or droughts struck, or herds died from extreme weather, or food staples developed diseases or were wiped out by pests. Consider the Irish who emigrated to America when the potato famine decimated Ireland's food supply in the nineteenth century. Some scientists believe that overworking and failing to protect soil played a role in the decline of civilizations, including those of the Greeks, Romans, and Mayans.[4]

In many regions of Central America, native people can but do not grow green vegetables packed with vital nutrients such as vitamin A. I'm told that generally speaking, the people do not have a tradition of raising these crops. They often have limited education in general and almost no exposure to health and nutrition advice, and they grow what feeds the most people. They often have plenty of tortillas and beans, so they have sufficient protein, and they eat until full. Yet the lack of micronutrients leads to their children developing blindness, thyroid problems, and other metabolic disorders. In these situations, families have to be educated about nutrition, encouraged to diversify their diets, plant more green vegetables, and sometimes receive nutritional fortification—in the form of supplements to correct imbalances.

Nutrient fortification is an essential intervention to address malnutrition and micronutrient deficiencies in children. WFP distributes bags of fortified meal in Guatemalan villages.
Photo: Howard G. Buffett

Food insecurity involves not only a lack of calories needed to keep people going every day but also insufficient access to the nutrients that make a child grow properly at vital stages and that allow human beings to thrive at every age. My photograph of Maria is a constant reminder to me that living is not the same as thriving and that achieving food security is never a quick fix.

Story 11
Little Cromite

His gray shirt was unbuttoned, and the scar peeking out from the center of the young man's chest was about as wide as the blade of a bread knife. It was not a ragged wound—it was eerily neat. HWB and I were sitting in an empty schoolyard in the Sierra Leone countryside in 2008, and the young man we were talking with seemed both jumpy and vigilant, his eyes continually sweeping the open area around us. They showed little humanity or feeling. Twenty years old, surviving on the equivalent of pennies a day and occasional food aid, this particular face of hunger represents not the biology of insufficient food or nutrients, but the lengths to which starving children with no other options have been pushed to survive.

Hunger is always, to some degree, a companion to war. There is the famous saying "An army moves on its stomach," and in conflict zones, it's common to see combatants running people off their land, stealing food—even using starvation as a military tactic. Controlling whether an enemy or a captured population eats or not can be a powerful lever. Yet sometimes the perpetrators of the violence are victims too.

At the time of our visit, the issue of "conflict diamonds" had caught the media's attention. In part, it was due to the 2006 film *Blood Dia-*

mond starring Leonardo DiCaprio, which had caused a worldwide stir, drawing attention to the true cost of luxury extracted with the blood and lives of some of the poorest people on the planet. It centered on the story of a poor man who came across a giant diamond while toiling under armed guards in the miserable, muddy diamond mining pits of Sierra Leone. The man was a farmer, and his son was brutally taken away from him by the vicious thugs of the Revolutionary United Front, or RUF. The rest of the man's family ended up in a refugee camp, while he was sent to the district of Kono to mine diamonds to help support the rebels in the civil war. His son, meanwhile, became a child soldier.

The film's story is grounded in real events in Sierra Leone. The RUF was a mercenary rebel faction supported by powerful Liberian warlord Charles Taylor throughout the 1990s, including during his presidency. (In 2012 the International Criminal Court sentenced the sixty-four-year-old Taylor to fifty years in prison for the atrocities he ordered as president.) To gain control over the rich diamond mines close to Liberia's border, Taylor instigated civil war and terrorized the people of Sierra Leone. The rebel group abducted thousands of children like the boy in the movie and the young man in front of me at the schoolyard in Sierra Leone. The RUF moved through villages, systematically killing chiefs, village elders, government employees, and innocent civilians. Throughout the 1990s and up to the official end of the civil war in 2002, an estimated fifty thousand people were killed, and up to half the country's population was displaced, including tens of thousands to Liberia and Guinea.[1] In a terrifying scene from the movie, RUF soldiers holding machetes grabbed villagers and stretched their arms out over a stump or table. A soldier would ask, "Long sleeves? Short sleeves?" The meaning: Do you want your arm chopped above or below the elbow?

By the time we visited Sierra Leone, there had been a stable peace for a half dozen years. But the consequences of the conflict would forever haunt the people who had lived through it. We learned that many had been forced off their land so that the government could sell diamond mining rights to foreign corporations. There were thousands of widows trying to raise multiple children with no resources. In addition to the massacres and the displacement, the long sleeves/short sleeves torture had created an estimated twenty-seven thousand amputees.[2] In some cases, both their arms had been cut off. Many others, including huge numbers of former combatants with no skills and no other way to support themselves, now worked in diamond mines for pennies a day.

I toured the diamond mines of both Kono and Kenema, and saw that Hollywood had not exaggerated the horrors of this situation. In Sierra Leone, hundreds of millions of dollars—billions, even—in diamonds and other minerals are pulled from the ground by some of the world's poorest people. In 2012 Sierra Leone ranked 177th out of 187 countries on the United Nations Human Development Index, and per capita Gross National Income is less than $2 per day.[3]

Africa's resource wealth has long been a curse for its poorest people. A government funded mostly by oil, gold, or diamonds does not need to be concerned with taxes or votes. Corrupt leaders can sell off their country's assets. Misuse of resource wealth removes ordinary people from the political process and undermines any chance at democracy.

There has been some progress in Sierra Leone. But I realized in looking at the conditions at the mines during my visit that the years of conflict had severed any compassionate connection between the government and its people. Boys as young as eight, wiry from the exertion and without an ounce of fat on their bodies, carried bags of dirt and pebbles back and forth from the pits to a sorting and cleaning area all day long. The tension around the miners and the guards was thick. I wondered: If the last decades' leaders had needed to rely on a voting public for support, would this horrible, slavish labor for a few cents and perhaps a cup of rice per day in the diamond mines have developed?

Where hope is gone, life is cheap and violence is power. At one point, as we advanced toward the muddy banks of a pond where miners were working the pebbles, looking for diamonds, guards holding pickaxes and machetes watched us. I had my camera by my side and decided to squeeze off some shots from my hip to see if I could capture some of the conditions. The *click-click-click* was deafening, and the men began yelling and walking toward us, their weapons in hand. We apologized and backtracked with help from our government hosts. These guards and many of the miners had been soldiers, my hosts explained. Many were angry, aggressive men who saw little reason for hope. Later my hosts arranged a conversation between me and a miner out of the line of sight of his employers. "They are sending us to our graves day by day," he said.

LITTLE CROMITE

A contact from one of the NGOs connected me with a "convener," as they were called in Sierra Leone: middlemen who, for a small fee, would arrange meetings for foreigners trying to do business or gather information. This is not at all how I usually conduct business, but it was the only way to get access to former combatants here. I wanted to understand what these people had endured.

The convener insisted that we meet way outside town and in small groups to draw less attention. We met with ten former child soldiers, usually three at a time. We met boys who fought directly, and girls who were abducted to serve as "wives" of the RUF commanders and soldiers. The girls, now women, had lived in a state of relentless rape and slavery. They too, often for the amusement and sadism of their captors, would be ordered to torture or kill villagers that the RUF wanted to wipe out or intimidate.

The boy in the gray shirt would not say his given name. His jungle name, however, was "Little Cromite." Jungle names and operation names give some sense of the level of barbarism that shaped the lives of these children: we also met Spare No One. They had reported to CO-Blood, short for Commander Blood. Their forays included "Operation No Living Thing" and "Operation Demolish Everything." Chromite, spelled differently, is a mineral made up of iron, magnesium, oxygen, and chromium, a hard metal often mixed with iron to make stainless steel for knives. Little Cromite's experiences had hardened him.

Little Cromite said he was abducted from the town of Kabula at age six. He said the RUF killed his mother in front of him and chopped off her breasts. Unless he went with her killers, he would not survive. As a little boy, he was too small to march and carry his gun, so they let him tie a rope around it and drag it behind him as his group moved from place to place. From an early age, he was injected with cocaine during the day by his commander, to give him the energy to fight and kill and torture, and the commander gave him marijuana to smoke at night to keep him under control. At age nine, when he objected to taking more drugs, his commanders slit open his chest, creating the slot-like scar he has today, and rubbed cocaine in it, inches from his heart.

I was sitting in an empty and abandoned school-yard when I met "Little Cromite." He asked if we could help him get to Somalia to fight. He was hungry, he had no job, but he knew how to shoot a gun, something he learned at age six after being abducted by the Revolutionary United Front. *Photo: Howard G. Buffett*

Psychologists believe that any person can get used to killing and even torturing when his or her captors are skilled in the art of mind control. Little Cromite grew up in a drugged state, a horror show beginning with his own mother's murder. He was told to kill, or his hands would be cut off. He was part of roving bands that would lock a family in its home and then burn it down; his was a world in which snitches were punished by punching a hole in the upper and lower lips and threading a padlock through the wounds and snapping it shut. He described once cutting open the belly of a pregnant woman because two soldiers were arguing about whether they could predict the sex of the baby she carried.

I won't continue in this vein. I have not even included the most extreme stories. I will never forget the look on one woman's face when she said, "We have seen things that no one should see."

One of the reasons I remain so committed to paying attention to victims of conflict and postconflict situations is that when you hear these stories, you understand the lasting damage inflicted on individuals such as Little Cromite. The child soldiers were ripped from their families and subjected to unending brutality; their humanity was stripped from their souls by the acts they were forced to commit. They were and are victims. And when the fighting was over, what was left? They were uneducated, unskilled for anything but war, traumatized, and, in many cases, permanently brain-damaged from drugs.

A few organizations have gone into Sierra Leone to try to train some of these former child soldiers to work in farming or in other sectors, but it is difficult to overcome the psychological damage. During a series of meetings we had in a half-finished school building outside town, a former soldier who had found out about our meetings decided to crash the session. I could see that even the other former child soldiers were nervous about talking to us in front of him. His eyes were wild, and perspiration rolled down his face. "I can show you!" he bellowed repeatedly at one point, recounting the rampages he and the other ex-soldiers would carry out. I was not the only one in the group who worried he meant that literally; that he lusted for a fresh kill to demonstrate the techniques he had learned from the RUF.

I spoke to more than one former child soldier who seemed disoriented and uncomfortable with his "freedom," if you can call it that. I suspect it's not unlike criminal offenders who have spent twenty years in prison and, upon release, have no idea how to act in a world where they have to think for themselves instead of following prescribed rules. Many re-offend, sometimes within days of release. Another child soldier said, somewhat quietly, "I had three meals a day, a gun, and a woman. That's more than I have now." When you are starving and have no hope, life gets basic.

Despite all he'd experienced as a child soldier, Little Cromite asked me before we left if I could help get him to Somalia to fight there as a mercenary. A child who experienced hunger but also a loving family would not, I believe, turn to murder or torture to keep himself alive. But the diabolical reprogramming that life as a child soldier involves has pushed many of these young people into a moral twilight state.

Our foundation has supported projects to try to educate and reorient former child soldiers to productive activities, such as farming. This is challenging: often local people understandably hate and fear them. When we were touring the diamond mines, I recall thinking that the thousands of workers were a ready-made army, already trained, willing to do anything for food. And yet if we ignore them and make no effort to bring them back into the mainstream of life, the anger and evil of their childhood experience may keep exploding in new ways.

Wherever people are starving and fear for their future, terrorists and fanatics will use food to lure some to the darkest corners of human existence. Food is power.

Story 12
Sex and Hunger
in Timbuktu

When I was a kid, you would hear people refer to the West African city of Timbuktu, a name that is both exotic and fun to say. It was used in the context of "in the middle of nowhere." If someone seemed to be packed for a long, arduous trip, you might say, "Looks like you're off to Timbuktu."

In 2003 I visited Timbuktu, located in the nation of Mali at the edge of the Sahara. It is an oasis in a barren, vast desert. Its primary sources of income are trading salt, mining gold, and growing rice and cotton. I was there in part because I wanted to talk with locals about some of the issues around agricultural price supports and efforts by the World Bank at the time to liberalize the economy and push it toward free markets. Mali is extremely poor and barely grows enough rice to feed its own people. Unfortunately, what I learned on the ground was that the World Bank's efforts were likely to have two brutal impacts. The first was farmers trying to convert fragile land to growing cotton, which would ruin the land and not provide any long-term benefit. The second consequence was that the existing system was at least returning some funding to support local education and health care there, which would change if the market was liberalized.

Timbuktu is a walled city and not at all modern. The streets are covered in sand, and the buildings are sandstone. Timbuktu is located where the Niger River flows north into the southern Sahara. Although isolated, it has long been a crossroad for local tribes and traders. Gold from the south mines at Boure and Banbuk was brought to the city and exchanged for goods and salt. When I visited, traders and farmers still were using camels to move around and transport their goods.

Camel trains were still a common sight in Timbuktu when I visited in 2003; unfortunately, so were signs of poverty and the lack of options for so many people around this remote, walled city. *Photo: Howard G. Buffett*

The Tuareg people founded Timbuktu in the fifth century. They are nomadic herders who for centuries have roamed the Sahara looking for grazing lands and water for their animals. Timbuktu also became an intellectual center for scholars of Islam: the city's historic mosques and extensive collections of manuscripts led to its being designated a World Heritage Site by the United Nations Educational, Scientific, and Cultural Organization, or UNESCO. There are many explanations for the city's name, but the most memorable one I heard there concerned an old woman who lived near a well near the Niger River. She would watch the Tuaregs' possessions while they moved on with the animals during rains. Supposedly the area became known for a variation of her name, which referred to the protrusion of her navel!

But when I hear the name Timbuktu spoken today, it has no connection for me whatsoever to these historical references or as a fancy way to say "far away." Instead, I am reminded of the tragedy of a young woman named Mohair, whom I once photographed there. She lived in what is called the "belt of misery." And to me she will always be a vivid face of the close connection between hunger and sexual exploitation around the world.

I have seen many heartbreaking examples of the sex trade that flourishes in areas of extreme poverty and hunger. At a landfill outside the city of Tegucigalpa, Honduras, I once visited an area where dozens of children spent their days picking over rotting, discarded loads dumped by trucks onto steaming piles. After only a minute or two out of the car, my eyes were burning and my throat closing from the intense stench and the methane gas. I cannot imagine the state of these children's lungs and sinuses from living in this environment all the time, not to mention that many sniff glue to get through it.

I photographed Carla, a thirteen-year-old girl who earned about fifty cents a day sorting through the garbage hauled there all day and selling the occasional salvageable scrap. Her eyelids were heavy and her eyes glassy from the glue she inhaled during the day to try to blot out the stink and deaden her suffering. Carla and her friends could not make enough from their scavenging, so they would sell their bodies to the truck drivers dumping the garbage to pick up a few dollars for each encounter.

Carla and others would sniff glue through a bag
to pass the time and deaden the pain of hunger
and abuse. *Photo: Howard G. Buffett*

This kind of scene is repeated all over the world, in slums, red-light districts, truck stops, and other places where those with few options gather. Hunger and sex also are connected by the sinister characters who watch and lie in wait to exploit vulnerable, starving people however they can. We funded a well-drilling project in Ethiopia once. The engineering was excellent, and it appeared to be a positive development for the community. But six months later we received a report that a man had arrived in the town and gone from home to home holding papers he claimed were issued by the government allowing him to demand a tax on the water from the new well. (Many people couldn't read, so the papers could have said anything.) If they could not pay the tax, he explained, he would be willing to take the "use" of one of their daughters for, say, a month. Water is a life-or-death proposition. By the time we found out, a number of families had supplied their daughters, who were forced to work as prostitutes for this man. When our partners discovered what was going on, the NGO in charge went to authorities, and we were told the man was arrested.

In the developing world, dumps attract homeless, desperate people looking
for scraps to eat. I have to stuff my nose with tissues and breathe through my
mouth just to spend an hour photographing landfills like this one, or else I
cannot stand the burning stench. These children experience hell on Earth.
Photo: Howard G. Buffett

No country has a corner on this market, and no country is immune. The US State Department estimates that 27 million people
are trafficked worldwide, and human trafficking in the United
States has been on the rise. An estimated 14,500 or more people
kidnapped in other countries are brought into the United States
every year[1]—many of them women and girls forced to work in mas-
sage parlors and bordellos. There are runaway teens who fall prey
to pimps. There are even elaborate networks of kidnapped, often
drug-addicted American teens and children who are transported
over state lines and forced to work as prostitutes. Many people don't
think of young US runaways as faces of hunger, but you can be sure
that having no resources and being at the mercy of those who control whether you eat or not is a fundamental part of this equation.
These children are victims of a variety of kinds of exploitation at the
hands of criminal adults. Sometimes they are running from terrible,

dangerous circumstances at home. Whatever has driven them to the streets, they are often hungry and vulnerable.

THE DEFINITION OF MISERY

The belt of misery exists right outside Timbuktu in encampments where former nomads huddle together to try to get access to shelter and water. There is some farmwork, and "mud workers" help build structures for a small wage, but the people here generally live on pennies a day. Temperatures during the Mali summer can top 110 degrees. Thick dust storms cover the urban landscapes in a monochromatic powder.

There still exists a form of slavery in the region, which once was a supplier to the Africa-US slave trade. And according to the US Agency for International Development (USAID), in some areas of Mali, 92 percent of women have undergone female genital mutilation and cutting. Most are excised before reaching the age of five, following the cultural belief that removing parts of the female genitalia will keep a young girl chaste and improve her chances of finding a good husband.[2] In addition to increasing the potential for complications during birth, the negative health consequences of the practice can include hemorrhage, HIV infection, infertility, and death.

It seems ironic that at the same time such a practice exists to uphold the "chasteness" of some women, there is no concern for so many others who must participate in the sex trade because they are out of options. Timbuktu is so far from any other place, in a sea of barren, hot, dry desert, that to be born into poverty there is to be doomed. My local NGO hosts told me that by religion and local custom in Timbuktu, a visiting man can select a young woman from the streets and declare that she is his wife and must sleep with him. When he's ready to leave, he can declare, "I divorce you" three times, and he then sheds any obligation to her or to a child that may result.

I visited a training class in Timbuktu where women were learning how to sew. Mohair's beauty and quiet dignity drew me to photograph her. *Photo: Howard G. Buffett*

Before leaving Timbuktu, I photographed a girl named Mohair, who was born into the belt of misery. She was fifteen when I met her, and she already had a child. It is painful to think that a young woman who displayed the same poise and dignity in person as she does in this photograph is forced into circumstances that result in a child from imposed prostitution. We met a number of pregnant teenage girls forced to do the same. These circumstances guarantee a self-replacing class of uneducated, poor, starving people who have no option to leave.

Story 13
Loss in Armenia

For decades, Armenia's economy relied mostly on heavy industry and bureaucrats in the former Armenian Soviet Socialist Republic who managed the country's entire agricultural system. They issued orders to plant and harvest, and they distributed seed and fertilizer to farmers. When that structure vanished after Armenia won its independence in 1991, many farmers had no way to access inputs or equipment. Many just walked off the land and tried to find work elsewhere. Squatters moved into abandoned properties and tried to figure out how to grow food. Food shortages erupted throughout the country, and ongoing conflict with neighboring countries sapped resources. Yet the country needed agricultural production more than ever.

In 2005 I went to Armenia to better understand what was going on and to see if we could help rebuild these broken agricultural systems. We traveled to different areas of the country to investigate. But the searing images I brought home from this particular trip had less to do with agriculture than with the intense pain of loss. I was especially touched by the situations of a number of elderly people in the province of Lori and a small village in the countryside.

So many of the people I met said they felt betrayed: by family members, by their government, and even, some would complain, by God. I reflected that the capacity of individuals to manage hunger varies based on physical condition, social circumstances and personal history, personality, mental health, and even cultural norms. I once spoke with a woman from Somalia who had fled to Ethiopia with her four children. She told me, "Here we die by hunger; at home we die by bullets." She was not at all emotional, and she immediately returned to the daily challenge of finding food and caring for her children. But in Armenia, I met a man who was despondent because he had been unable to afford a vaccination for his son, who later died. He described his circumstances by saying, "This is no way to live, but there is no way to leave." Part of his agony came from being aware of modern medicine and knowing that money he once had—or perhaps even the old Soviet health system—might have prevented his son's death.

At the time of my visit in 2005, World Vision told me that 40 percent of Armenians were living in extreme poverty as defined by the United Nations threshold of living on $1 a day. About another 30 percent of the population were twice as well off yet still below $2 per day. Those are staggering poverty rates, but not the worst that I've seen. What was so striking in Armenia was that so many poor people had once possessed some control of their lives and some confidence in the future. When Armenia was part of the USSR, it had built up a significant industrial sector, and it traded goods among the other republics. After independence, the country got tied up in conflicts with Turkey and Azerbaijan that led to those countries cutting off trade and isolating Armenia economically. Russia's own economic struggles translated to smaller markets for Armenian goods, and the country tried to develop agriculture again, with mixed results.

Many Armenians toiled under a grim Soviet system, it was true, but at least many had access to enough food and decent services. Some people I met were even living in what were once at least middle-class apartments or homes—although in several cases, they were empty of possessions (which had been sold) except for one room where everyone living there would sleep and gather to try to stay warm. A small quantity of food might be kept on an outside porch, with someone assigned to keep an eye on it. The sense of loss was overwhelming.

In many ways, these circumstances were luxurious compared to the gutters of Calcutta, India, or refugee camps in Ethiopia, but we saw little reason for optimism anywhere. The disbanding of the Soviet Union had brought democracy to Armenia, it was true. But the people experienced democracy as the freedom to live without health care, the freedom to go hungry, and the freedom to be forgotten. Many older people, many of whom looked as if they could have been neighbors of mine in Omaha or Decatur, indicated that their lives had been lived in vain. This despondency was a stark contrast to evenings I have spent in a poor African village, where there can nonetheless be a sense of joy and hopefulness even among incredibly poor and hungry people.

In one Lori neighborhood, after we had finished with a scheduled visit, an older woman walking with a cane and shaking slightly got our attention. She asked us to come into her home. As we followed her up a set of decaying steps, we saw her sister in the doorway, a disturbing sight. She was clearly not well physically, and later we found out that she was also mentally ill.

We learned through our interpreter that these two women lived alone. The younger one who beckoned us in, Anna, was eighty-two, and the sister, Maria, eighty-four. Anna was wearing many layers of clothing and a tattered head scarf. Her bright blue eyes darted back and forth, and soon we would learn that she spent much of her waking hours with her guard up. The house was dirty and cluttered. We stepped over human waste on the floor. The first thing that Anna showed us was the rope she used to tie Maria's door shut at night. It seemed that Maria became paranoid and violent at times and had tried to strangle Anna in her sleep. So Anna locked Maria in her room at night and slept on the porch, which was also their kitchen.

Anna went into a small closet and pulled out some papers, including a passport. She spoke of her family and began to cry. Her tears ran down her weathered, wrinkled skin, and it was difficult for her to stay composed. She was lonely, scared, and hungry. Among the papers were documents showing that Maria fought against the Germans in Russia during World War II. She operated an antiaircraft gun. Suddenly Maria began to speak for the only time, shouting, telling how she was never afraid, how she never left her post no matter how close the enemy got, and how proud she was to fight. With a wild-eyed intensity, she told us that she was one of the best shots. Then she fell silent, and Anna talked numbly about how Maria had become dangerous and insane.

I have never been anywhere in the world where more people opened their homes and their hearts than Armenia. This is Anna, a woman whose daily struggles deeply affected HWB and me. *Photo: Howard G. Buffett*

I am still moved by the thought of Maria clinging to her glory days as a soldier. I can't help but think that for all the chaos and stress of war, she valued her emotional memory of that time as organized and civilized. Perhaps wearing a uniform, following orders, being part of a unit, being fed, might all have seemed like a privileged existence compared to freezing at night in that sad, unkempt room as she grappled with hallucinations and violent urges, fearing her own sister.

Anna spoke with some despair about the idea that they had done their duty to their government and fought for their country but had been forgotten.

"BE CAREFUL, HOWARD, IT IS PRECIOUS FOOD"

On a trip I took to Tavush Province, I visited a mother with four children living in a one-room shelter originally built for their animals. They could not finish building the house after fighting broke out among warring ethnic groups in the region, so they had been living in this shelter for years. At night in winter, the temperature can drop to the teens or lower. The heat was from an archaic wood and dung heater that caused the children to cough heavily, and it barely raised the temperature to survivable.

My first memory of this visit was that there was a single ear of corn on the floor near the door. Like a lot of corn farmers, when I travel and see local corn, I will strip down the husk to check the kernels; or if I see an ear of picked corn, I will snap it in half to examine its structure and health. I picked up this ear and asked the mother if I could remove the husk to check it. She took it and stripped off the dry outer casing and handed it back; it was only about five inches long and only half pollinated. It had twelve rows of kernels, short of the eighteen that our farm at home would have. The in-country host traveling with me whispered, "Be careful, Howard, it is precious food."

My second vivid memory was that the family had an eight-year-old son named Tatul. My colleague remembered him from an NGO camp the previous summer. He asked the boy what he liked the most about camp. Without hesitating, Tatul said, "The food." I had the odd thought that such an answer would sound strange in the United States, where ridiculing the "chef's surprise" and other aspects of camp cuisine is as much a ritual of the summer camp experience as bug bites and tipping a canoe. But as we talked, it was clear that camp was the only time in his entire life when he received three meals a day.

My final vivid memory of Armenia was when HWB and I met Shakhik. She said she worked forty years for the government on a large Soviet-style communal farm. She quit school at age ten in the fourth grade because her government needed her. She was now seventy-six and partially blind. Shakhik said she was devoted to her country but now had to make do with a pension of only about $26 a month—less than $1 a day. The communal farm had 350 families, and at least there she had help and companionship. As we got ready to leave, she felt it important to tell us that she would rather have cancer than be blind because then at least she would have died. Her eyesight prevented her from getting around well, but she clutched my face as we left and kissed me on the cheek. She thanked me for listening, for taking time to come see her.

HWB was with me and he was moved by Shakhik's situation. He made sure that our contacts in Armenia got her a pair of glasses. There are times when you know you can only do one small thing for someone, but you feel that you must do it. At least, *I* must do it, and HWB has become the same way. It can cause problems. Dropping in and doing something specific for one individual can incite jealousy among others, or create discomfort for local NGOs we have asked to help us.

After this trip, I paid more attention to elderly people who are food insecure—wherever they are. I think again about Bob, the World War II vet from the Good Samaritan soup kitchen in Decatur. His corduroy pants were nearly worn smooth across his thighs, and his yellowed T-shirt was frayed and falling apart. His face was sunken and thin. But he seemed delighted and grateful to come to this place and get a meal. "I can cook," he confided, "but I really hate to clean up." His whole affect was so different from that of the two women in Armenia, although he clearly was very poor and probably would have battled hunger without Good Sam. How can we possibly calculate the psychological damage to an older person who does not know if someone—perhaps *anyone*—cares whether he or she eats or not? The older people I met in Armenia remind me of the importance of nourishment, real and psychological, to all people, of all ages, in all circumstances.

After the Soviet Union broke apart, poverty increased in many nations of Eastern Europe. That threatened the future of children like this young girl in Romania and broke the hearts of many elderly people. *Photo: Howard G. Buffett*

Story 14
Farming Under Fire

I have my sister, Susie, to thank for how I met Ed Price. For all the grief and teasing she and I have lobbed at each other over our lifetimes, this favor was one of the best she ever did for me—even though it could have gotten HWB and me killed.

In 2009, at a dinner in Sun Valley, Idaho, Susie sat next to General David Petraeus, who at the time was tenth commander, US Central Command. He told her about his efforts to try to bring agricultural assistance to farmers in Afghanistan. Susie is not much interested in agriculture, but she told him, "You ought to talk to my brother."

Several months and phone calls later, and against the advice of almost everyone else in my family and other sane people in my life, HWB and I were suited up in heavy protective gear, sitting with Dr. Ed Price of Texas A&M University on a bench in a cold, drafty waiting room in a US Army base in Kabul, Afghanistan. We were waiting for the low ceiling of fog to lift so we could get into a Blackhawk helicopter to go east to Jalalabad. For two days the fog was too thick for us to fly. We were going to meet with some local farmers trying to rebuild their agricultural systems after years of neglect and, more recently, occasional fighting as the United States and allies tried to root out the remaining Taliban forces in the area. You didn't need a travel agent to remind you not to pack a bathing suit in Afghanistan in February, but even in our winter gear we shivered. What's more, the day before, all of Kabul was on high alert after the Taliban had launched a series of suicide bomb attacks on Kabul hotels, killing a number of civilians. We had seen the flash in the sky while driving out to the base.

The only safe transportation to visit farmers was Blackhawk helicopters.
Photo: Howard G. Buffett

After seventy-two hours of cold, stress, danger, and boredom, the three of us had talked about everything from microcredit to shoulder-fired missiles to cassava, a vegetable that is a favorite tool of Ed's personal war against hunger. Dr. Price is an agricultural economist by training who at the time was director of the Norman Borlaug Institute for International Agriculture at Texas A&M. But what caught my interest is that he is one of the world's foremost authorities on a most unusual aspect of agriculture: namely, how you do it when you're getting shot at, bombed, and otherwise tormented and threatened.

Sometimes you meet a person who can teach you
more over one dinner conversation than you'd
learn in a year in school. It usually happens where
you least expect it. Ed Price, pictured on the right,
is one of those people. *Photo: Howard W. Buffett*

Ed had already made over a dozen trips to Iraq and Afghanistan
by the time I met him. He's taught agricultural economics at Texas
A&M for many years, and he has an extensive background in agriculture and development, beginning with his first job out of college
in the 1960s in the then-British colony of Sarawak. On the island
of Borneo, Ed worked with hill tribes who were seeing their land
degraded by the way timber companies were cutting down the surrounding forest. He became convinced that the violent conflict that
erupted could have been avoided if the tribes had been empowered
to harvest the trees themselves, since it would have been in their self-
interest to do it in a sustainable way.

Ed later went to a number of conflict hot spots. In 2002, while working on a project to try to improve the yields of rice in the Ivory Coast, he was caught behind the lines of a rebel insurgent force. He was held in a hotel under conditions where he was not at all sure he would make it out alive. But that experience, he says, changed his attitude toward risk in an odd way: "You're always affected by it. I was really shaken up. But after that, I started to realize that perhaps being willing to go into these situations is what I have to contribute. Maybe there is a better mathematician, or someone else is a better theoretician, but this is something I can handle."

He would get more chances. In the months and years after the US military moved into Afghanistan, Ed started receiving letters from former students. Texas A&M has two thousand students who are uniformed members of the armed forces, and it graduates more military officers than any school outside the service academies. Because of their training in agriculture and technology, a number of graduates who knew Ed served on so-called civilian affairs teams that were deployed just behind the soldiers fighting to wrest control from the Taliban. These units' job is to win the "hearts and minds" of the local people.

Oftentimes, however, the units are not necessarily expert in the problems the locals find most onerous. "They sometimes joke that they're there to hand out volleyballs," Ed says with a laugh, "but I started getting letters from former students describing a number of different agricultural problems, such as irrigation canals that were clogged with weeds. In one case, I got an email from a former student asking me how he should go about determining the value of a cow. Somebody from his unit had accidentally shot a cow and wanted to compensate the poor owner, but no one had any idea how to put a value on something like that.

"I realized that it might be important to have agricultural expertise involved in some of the efforts over there to not only help hold these communities from a military standpoint but also get the people back on track and organized to be able to feed themselves and their families." He responded to his students' inquiries, but he also made some calls to Washington, and he met Paul Brinkley, deputy undersecretary of the Department of Defense in the George W. Bush administration. Brinkley needed Ed's expertise for yet another hot spot.

Brinkley was leading a group of military, government, and private sector interests that were trying to help Iraq recover, not only after our invasion but also after years of neglect. Iraqi agriculture had all but collapsed during Saddam's expensive war with Iran in the 1980s. Roads were in terrible condition, irrigation canals dysfunctional, irrigation pumps broken. The system for getting seed and fertilizer was increasingly squeezed to the point where farmers just gave up, so food shortages were a growing problem. Ed made a series of trips there and even lived in Iraq for six months trying to help the local farmers reorganize and rebuild capacity.

General Petraeus, Paul Brinkley, and others understood the can-do spirit for which the Afghans are legendary and that some good expert advice could yield big dividends. So, Paul asked Ed to go help Afghan farmers establish some pilot projects. Our foundation ended up helping to fund the construction of an agricultural college, some center-pivot-based irrigation to try to get two crops grown per year, and a processing plant for a women's co-op that I'm hoping will become a model not only in Afghanistan but in other parts of the world.

In that freezing cold Quonset hut in Kabul, we forged a relationship that has produced some other exciting projects too. I am always impressed with people who are not only analytical and strategic but also practical. For example, I still remember our conversation about cassava, a tan, bulgy root vegetable that looks like a bouquet of potato bugs. But it has particular value in conflict areas because it is fairly rich in carbohydrates, calcium, vitamins B and C, and essential minerals, and it can grow in harsh, dry conditions. Best of all, Ed explained, the nutritious payload is underground. "It makes it harder to steal, and it means a farmer harvesting it is less exposed."

Knowing the difference between planting a crop that you can harvest when you need it versus planting something like corn—which rebels or an occupying army can easily burn or steal (or more easily attack you while you harvest it)—is information that can have life-or-death consequences. After our initial collaboration, Ed became the first Howard G. Buffett Foundation chair in conflict and development at Texas A&M, and his team is producing some important research that I am convinced is essential to helping craft more realistic and practical solutions for conflict-exacerbated hunger.

Story 15
Seeds of Change

Joe DeVries is a wiry, blunt-speaking guy who was born in Ada, Michigan. As a college freshman, he was inspired by a traveling missionary's talk. It helped him prepare for a life helping the poor in the developing world. He studied agriculture, and his first job was working at Disney World's Epcot theme park as a researcher in the Land pavilion. Next, Joe volunteered to work for the United Nations, which sent him to build irrigated rice systems in northern Mali. It was important but fairly tame stuff. That changed in 1989 when Joe joined the relief organization World Vision. The NGO sent him to Mozambique, the former Portuguese colony on the east coast of Africa that was in its second decade of a brutal, complicated civil war.

Mozambicans were starving, but it was too dangerous for food aid convoys to travel on the rural roads. So Joe's job was to get packets of seeds to farmers displaced by the war so they could grow their own food. He and his staff, flying in tiny Cessna bush airplanes, ferried thousands of tons of seeds, hoes, and machetes to farmers, often dodging gunfire. His teams would land near a village, and, after unloading their cargo, the locals would bring out fresh victims of land mines to be flown out for medical treatment. Joe's stories of the time are harrowing: the planes he flew in were often peppered with bullets. One local farm extension employee he worked with was tied to a tree and beaten to death for trying to help farmers.

Flying behind the front lines made Joe a hero to thousands of farmers who depended on his efforts to keep their families from starving. When he'd visit a village to check on the crops, the local people would surround him. But on one visit in October 1989, as he endured the long speeches by local leaders in his honor, he saw a lone farmer at the edge of the crowd trying to get his attention. Finally, the ceremony ended, and Joe let the persistent grower drag him away to see his farm about a kilometer outside the village.

Joe walked into a field for which he had supplied cowpea seeds two months earlier. The plants appeared healthy, but they hadn't flowered, which meant that there were no pods filling with the protein-rich beans. Joe asked to see other plots around the village and saw more of what no one but the one farmer had been willing to tell him: none of the lush plants had pods. The crop was a failure. The seeds had been imported from Zimbabwe, and the farmers had planted them according to instructions. But the seeds were the wrong variety for that lowland tropical area. The plants never got the right cues from their environment to start seed production.

Looking into the eyes of the hundreds of farmers who had trusted him, he realized that some people in the village would starve because of how naïve relief organizations can be about agriculture. Joe resolved to take on the mission of making sure that the seeds he gave poor farmers would be the best possible variety. "It was a tragic learning experience," he says, looking back, "but that is where my fascination with matching new seeds to Africa's agro-ecologies began."

Joe and I have traveled around the world together in the last decade. He is one of the most determined and passionate guys working in agricultural development that I know, and once I heard this story of his having stood among those farmers I understood why. Talk about a life-changing experience.

Joe returned to the United States, and in 1994 he earned a PhD in plant breeding and genetics from Cornell University. Dr. DeVries then went back to Africa.

THE SEEDS AFRICA NEEDS

After a few years more with World Vision, in 1997 Joe joined the Rockefeller Foundation, which was then one of the few philanthropies working on seeds for African farmers. He became a corn breeder in Nairobi, Kenya, but quickly came up against a problem when he developed new varieties designed to improve yields in local conditions: there were no government or other local seed corn producers who could multiply the seeds so there would be enough to give farmers. Under pressure from the United States and other donor nations to get their fiscal houses in order, African governments had slashed spending on many services, including state-run seed production. The conventional economic wisdom in the West at the time was that the private market would do a better job at such things in Africa. But the lack of infrastructure, scientists, and bankers throughout much of Africa in the 1990s instead meant that vital functions such as seed production had collapsed entirely.

Joe felt that Africa was facing a vacuum when it came to seeds. The governments were retreating from doing seed research and development, and the private market wasn't interested either. Multinational companies did not see subsistence farmers as potential customers. The result was that the vast majority of smallholder farmers in Africa couldn't access new seeds, and so were condemned to reuse tired varieties that lost their potency over time, as insects and diseases found their vulnerable spots. Some African farmers have been handing down the same seeds for decades, even as the weather and pests changed. Little wonder that Africa's grain yields are a quarter of the world average.

Creating good so-called hybrid seed is time consuming and hard work in any part of the world. Hybrid seeds should not be confused with genetically modified seeds, where the plant DNA itself is manipulated in the laboratory. Hybrids are created through traditional breeding techniques that involve selectively choosing traits to combine from both parent plants such as increased yield or drought resistance. Crop breeders have to be willing to work under a hot sun in their plots as they jot down data in their books and decide which plants to mate together, a process that in the case of wheat can involve surgeon-like skill with tweezers. Creating one new variety that resists a new disease or makes more kernels takes years.

Joe DeVries would describe himself as a maize breeder; I describe him as a modern-day hero. He is a crusader against hunger. *Photo: Howard G. Buffett*

And Africa is probably the most challenging place for a crop breeder to work. Unlike in Asia, where one miracle seed can be planted across huge expanses of irrigated land, growing conditions and topography in Africa change so dramatically over short distances that monoculture is largely impossible. The vast majority of Africa's farms depend upon rainfall, which means that the availability of water varies widely. A variety of corn that thrives in one village might not adapt in another just a few hours down the road, thanks to everything from changes in elevation to differences in the soil. And the crops that Africans want to eat change across the continent as well. Bananas are a staple in Uganda, but in Sudan, it's sorghum; in Kenya, it's corn; and across much of Ethiopia, the favored food crop is teff, a cereal grass used to make bread with a spongelike consistency.

To get the seeds it needs, Africa requires an army of crop breeders to account for changing growing conditions and diverse tastes. The solution that the Rockefeller Foundation devised with Joe broke from the way that NGOs had long tended to work in Africa. Joe was convinced that aid in the form of bags of free seeds to farmers was not the answer. With the government out of the picture, it would have to be the private sector that got better seeds into farmers' hands. Working out of Nairobi, Kenya, Joe took it upon himself to become a breeder of seed *companies.*

In 2004 he helped to organize the $7 million African Agricultural Capital fund with money from the Rockefeller Foundation and London's Gatsby foundation. But just as the Rockefeller team in Africa was trying to find more donors to expand its agricultural work, new leadership at the foundation back in New York was mulling its future in agriculture. The Rockefeller Foundation had ended its agricultural work in Asia. Fortunately for Joe, at about the same time, a few officials at the Bill & Melinda Gates Foundation were beginning to think about making a big push into agricultural development. With three out of every four of the world's poor people living in rural areas, they had identified agricultural development as the key to fighting poverty. The Gates Foundation knew that my father was preparing to make a big gift, enough for them to embark on this new direction.

Roy Steiner at the Gates Foundation sent an email to Joe asking for some game-changing ideas that the foundation could support. In June 2006 my dad's gift was announced. By the time the dust cleared months later, the Gates Foundation would put $100 million into a partnership with the Rockefeller Foundation, which put up $50 million. Joe was at the center of their Alliance for a Green Revolution in Africa, or AGRA. He had a budget for giving fellowships to African agricultural scientists and research grants to fledgling seed companies.

Joe and I are friends, but we do not agree on everything. I have an allergic reaction to the term "Green Revolution" in Africa. Many of Africa's farmers are too poor, their soil too degraded, and their markets too fragile to go this route on a fast track. I believe solutions have to be tailored far more specifically to the reality of rural life and social considerations that do not favor big development blueprints. In general, I focus more on the quality of the soil, while Joe focuses on seed. Both are critical parts of the solution.

However, I support Joe's strategy of using the private sector to build a seed industry. It creates value that is sustainable and has a chance of maintaining momentum after various funders have left. Joe is almost single-handedly driving a new energy through the seed industry in Africa with smart and locally appropriate support for entrepreneurs. Literally millions of small farmers all across Africa now get seed through Joe's Program for Africa's Seed Systems. PASS is working with more than seventy private, independent seed companies and is headed for one hundred. Joe figures that the African seed companies helped by PASS harvested about 57,000 tons of seed in 2012, or about one-third of all the commercial seed produced in Africa and enough to plant roughly two million hectares. His goal is for seed production to hit 200,000 tons by 2017.

In southern Malawi, members of my team recently met a recipient of one of Joe's PASS grants who brought to life the logic of his approach and the opportunity to pursue market-based solutions with a social conscience. In a beautiful though poor region called Monkey Bay, there is a farm called Funwe, which was named for a strangely camel-humped mountaintop that looms above the property and has become its symbol. There lives another veteran of the NGO world, Carrie Osborne, an optimistic, high-energy Brit who spent twenty-five years working with Save the Children on HIV projects.

"NGOs are great, but you go project to project, and for the communities, support comes and goes," she explained. "My husband and I wanted to create something for the communities—particularly long-term, stable work for the local workers. The question was, could we set up a small business with a long-term sustainable course? We could never have imagined what we have now."

Carrie and her husband, Jon Lane, a water engineer, got a list of farm properties in Malawi that had been foreclosed and were available. In 2001 Jon began visiting some of the properties. She recalled, "To me, I looked and said, 'Oh this is impossible.' He's an engineer, and he said, 'You can fix a road, you can fix a building.'" They found a former tobacco estate that was a combination of woodland and agricultural land.

From the start, they focused not on commercial crops but on producing corn and legume seeds. In 2007 they came to Joe's attention, and he gave them a four-year grant to work on a new Malawi maize hybrid called MH26, which Funwe Farm has started growing and marketing through agro-dealers. Their progress has been gradual but impressive. Carrie figures they are now producing enough seed for food to feed 350,000 people for a year. She calls that "thrilling."

Sitting in a thatched roof *rondavel* (outdoor round hut), Carrie explained to our field team that it is satisfying to her that Funwe is making a difference in the local community by providing employment with a sustainable business, not aid. Funwe has 220 local people on the payroll, and the farm provides day care and meals to its workers. "Where you are sitting now is the poorest area of the third-poorest district of the sixth-poorest country in the world," she observed. "For ten years we've paid people when they get sick. We cover their medical bills. We have a little day care center, and we take food to the little nearby primary school by ox cart." She and her husband don't expect to ever make a personal profit from the venture, although they'd like to get their personal investment back. "We've had disasters and successes. We are private sector although I can't really say we're profit making. Still, it's quite nice that we've been able to stick with it."

Private seed companies like Funwe are starting to gain momentum, Joe confirms. In Kabiyet, Kenya, Western Seed Company is one of forty-five seed companies set up in Kenya with AGRA's backing, and Joe says that by 2015, he hopes that half of Kenya's farmers will be using these homegrown products, up from about 10 percent today. In this case, a native Kenyan is driving the effort. In 2012 Saleem Ismael, Western's founder, planted two thousand acres of hybrid seed corn—the biggest such field that Joe had ever seen in Africa. Our foundation's 9,200-acre Ukulima Farm in South Africa, where among other projects we sponsor research in seeds suited to African soils and climates, provides some of the foundation seed to Western. Western provides maize seed for smallholder farmers and has been steadily increasing production. "I don't know of any other subsector of the African agricultural economy that is growing at a comparable rate to that of the African seed industry," says Joe, who adds that the program has led to countries seeing their first homegrown seed companies. These include Mali, Burkina Faso, Niger, Sierra Leone, Liberia, Rwanda, Ethiopia, and, particularly satisfying to Joe, Mozambique.

PASS is training local people in the skills and technologies that will long outlive its involvement. Joe is focused on how to breed improved varieties of Africa's indigenous, staple food crops which are so important to small farmers. He's focused on the infrastructure elements that can facilitate a seed industry, including: university research, training local farmers in seed use, assisting local dealers in distributing the seed, and developing policies for local governments that knock down barriers to improved seed trading.

Joe maintains that governments and NGOs shouldn't give away seed because the competition discourages local seed companies from taking root (literally). Thus, it dooms the effort to the failing temporary aid cycle from which Africa must emerge. As Joe told me, "Half of the battle is just convincing African governments to believe in their own agricultural scientists and entrepreneurs as viable agents of positive change."

A BETTER GOAL: PROFITABLE AND SUSTAINABLE LOCAL BUSINESSES

There is a good explanation of this dilemma about giving away so-called inputs such as seed or fertilizer or other materials in economist Dambisa Moyo's book *Dead Aid: Why Aid Is Not Working and How There Is a Better Way for Africa*. A native of Zambia who holds degrees from both Harvard and Oxford, Dambisa calls it the "micro-macro problem," and uses the example of a local entrepreneur in Africa who is making and selling mosquito nets. This entrepreneur may employ ten people, each of whom has another ten or fifteen dependents living off his salary. The company is enjoying good growth, although perhaps not meeting demand for the nets. Along comes a philanthropist who decides to send $1 million worth of nets to the local community, probably putting the local net maker out of business. Isn't it good to send more nets to meet demand? Well, in the short term, yes—except that in four or five years, when those nets are worn out and useless, there is no longer a homegrown company to provide them. The choice is then more aid or no nets. If the philanthropist had instead invested in helping the business expand local net making, the result could have been profitable and sustainable.

In 2010 our foundation gave Joe $1.6 million to bring his seed breeding program to two postconflict countries, Sierra Leone and Liberia. Later that year, we put in $5 million to bring Joe's seed breeding program to South Sudan and USAID matched our $5 million. Today Joe's operation is going strong in South Sudan, one of the most difficult places in Africa to work.

Joe has made a bigger impact on improving the food security of the people of Africa than just about anybody I know. He and I share a common frustration, one all the more interesting given that he has spent most of his life in the NGO world. Joe told me once: "The development industry is the only industry I know that over time can get more stupid." Joe is still part of the NGO world, but he's shaking it up from the inside. He's now helped to launch seed companies in sixteen countries and figures the reach of that effort has fed twenty-five million people.

Joe DeVries has made a clear-eyed, on-the-ground assessment of what has worked and what hasn't, and he's changed tactics and is seeing success from doing so.

Story 16
Shakira

Yes, *that* Shakira.

There can be a thin line between enthusiasm and mayhem. I've seen it in aid distribution centers around the prospect of food arriving. People in difficult situations often engage in a certain amount of dreaming and magical thinking: hoping that they will be rescued, imagining a miraculous end to their suffering, fantasizing about what would happen if only someone they admire or have heard good things about could see them. It's the plot of countless movies, from *Willy Wonka & the Chocolate Factory* to *Slumdog Millionaire*.

Shakira Mebarak has a deep interest in the plight of poor children. She and I became friends several years ago. She is a talented entertainer and a big-hearted philanthropist, with a great sense of humor. When she visited my farm in Illinois I let her drive the combine. I don't know if it was her performer's precise awareness of her stage or her dancer's coordination or what, but she managed to drive the combine better than 95 percent of the people I have let try it.

In 2008 we were with her parents, driving down a street in Barranquilla, Colombia. I was there to look at some of the schools her Barefoot Foundation had funded, because they make a point of including school lunch programs and the children of internally displaced families as a focus. Our foundation was helping support that effort. As local people and many children from the city began to realize that Shakira was in the SUV, they were so excited and happy they surrounded us. They peered in the windows. They banged on the glass. They yelled. I had never experienced anything quite like that before. Our driver grew a little concerned that we might have crossed over that line into mayhem and asked if we wanted him to get us out of there.

"No," Shakira insisted. "I need to get out and see them and meet them."

She smiled at me and said, "Okay, here we go!" She got out with such a smile on her face, you would have thought she was about to head up the red carpet at the Grammy Awards. She shook hands, she signed autographs, she hugged children, she posed for pictures. I can also tell you that she was exhausted, drained from the heat, and a little apprehensive to be surrounded by that many excited and agitated people.

To me, Shakira is not just a singer and entertainer; on our trip to Colombia, I saw how deeply she cares for children and that she has never forgotten her roots. *Photo: Howard W. Buffett*

Shakira is not just a face. She feels a connection to poverty and suffering. Shakira grew up in Colombia, and was aware of the plight of the poor from a young age. Although her early life was comfortable, her father declared bankruptcy when she was eight, and she was sent to live with some relatives in Los Angeles. When Shakira returned to Barranquilla, much of what her parents once owned had been sold. Her father took her to a local park and showed her orphans who lived outside in the park. She has said that the vision of those orphans stayed with her, and she vowed that she would do something to try to help poor children if she ever became successful.

She made good. When she turned eighteen, Shakira set up her first foundation in Colombia. She followed that up with the Barefoot Foundation, which supports six schools in the Colombian regions of Barranquilla, Altos de Cazucá, and Quibdó. She has added schools in Haiti and South Africa, too. More than five thousand children receive nutritious meals, education, and psychological support services from the schools. Ultimately, the programs benefit some thirty thousand vulnerable children, their families, and community members, most of whom have been affected by population displacement due to conflict in Colombia.

Linking hunger and education is one of the strategies for battling hunger that works just about everywhere in the world. School feedings can be adapted for the specific nutritional needs of a community. Getting children fed and sometimes even providing food for children to take home can create an incentive for parents who otherwise might not be inclined to make sure that their children, particularly their daughters, receive an education.

School feeding programs address another reality: undernourished children lack the energy to do well in school even when they can physically be there. There are so many fundamental benefits of an education and nutrition, but it's also true that schools convey other important—even lifesaving—information such as personal hygiene, dental care, and sanitation practices. Teachers can identify illnesses or conditions such as hearing loss or vision problems.

The United States established a National School Lunch Program in 1946, later adding a School Breakfast Program. Today these two programs reach more than thirty million students each year (54 percent of enrollment) in over one hundred thousand schools and child care institutions, at a total cost of more than $11 billion a year. In 2008 Congress added a Fresh Fruit and Vegetable Program, allocating another $1 billion for fiscal year 2008 through 2017 for school feeding programs.[1]

If we believe that a school lunch program is important in the world's wealthiest country, imagine its value in the poorest countries, where most of the hungry school-age children live. If American children deserve a healthy meal at school, so do children in other countries. In 2002 Congress launched the McGovern-Dole International Food for Education and Child Nutrition Program to provide agricultural products and financial and technical assistance to countries in the developing world that are committed to universal education. The point is to support school feeding programs, but it has been disappointing to me that the program's budget often is not fully funded.

Our foundation has directly supported school feeding programs in Burundi, Guatemala, Honduras, Colombia, Sierra Leone, Tajikistan, and the United States. Shakira's commitment to schools and to making sure that food programs are part of the package is a big contribution.

Shakira also understands the importance of hope to people who are struggling. She takes on the challenge of letting people who feel vulnerable and forgotten know that she cares, and that is what motivated her to get out of the car.

One of the transitions in my thinking over the last ten years or so has been the realization that we cannot move the needle on an issue like global hunger simply on a project-by-project basis or even by supporting research. We also have to pay attention to global awareness and advocacy. There is a saying I've heard in Africa that applies here: "You cannot play the drums with one hand." We have to leverage our financial resources and our ability to bring attention to situations, and we have to work on forcing a shift in the thinking of a critical mass of people.

Celebrities willing to lend their energy to important causes are powerful allies. I am pleased to work with several who have become friends. Benefit concerts, endorsements, and personal appearances on behalf of a project usually represent a lot of work and time. And these efforts can come at a personal price. I was in a meeting with the rock singer Bono once. He is a friend of our family's, and sometimes he is a target of aid critics and others who question his credentials, which I think is unfair. He is consumed by the challenges he takes on, and he is committed to getting measurable results. This particular day, an article had been published that jabbed at the sincerity of his advocacy work on behalf of the poor; even making fun of his cowboy hat. Someone else at the meeting expressed anger about it, but Bono just smiled quietly and said, "Look, let's not waste time on this. I asked for this; I put myself out there, and I have to be able to take it. It's not a big deal."

Shakira has talked about the faces of hunger that motivate her: "All I have to do is close my eyes, and I can imagine their faces. I know that each child has a name, a heart, a dream; I know that their lives are just as valuable as yours or mine. Yet many of these children die every day in total abandonment." Having spent time with her and having talked at length about some of the projects we've worked on, I believe that is truly how she feels. She is a person whose dreams came true, and she does not forget how important encouragement and hope can be.

A Franciscan Padre
in the Sierra Madre

Before I even saw him, I heard Padre David Beaumont coming down a hotel hallway in Hermosillo, Mexico, where our meeting was to take place. His low, husky cough was a reminder that he spends much of his time in villages where charcoal is burned for cooking and warmth. He wears the thinnest of robes: an almost threadbare brown cotton cassock with a rope belt over jeans and a shirt. His hair and beard are long. I suspect that he does not often see food of the variety and quality that the staff at the hotel brought to him when we met, but he appears to choose to live as his people do. He never touched the food, instead accepting only a cup of coffee after making the five-hour drive to see us.

In early 2012 I was in Mexico for several days of meetings with different participants in Mexican agricultural sectors: small and large farmers, grain brokers, food companies, activists, academics. I'm concerned about Mexico. I have many friends there from my days with ADM, and the country is in the grip of two situations that I'm not sure are appreciated by many Americans.

The first issue is a water crisis. Mexico has expanded its agricultural production inefficiently in recent years, and the water supply is dwindling in areas of agricultural importance. The rate of extraction from aquifers has exceeded their replenishment. Many large Mexican farming operations still use flood irrigation, the most inefficient of all methods. I visited several farms where I tried to talk up the value of center pivot or drip irrigation and other approaches that could cut water usage without lowering crop yields.

But the second and more immediate problem is the drug trade. Long before my trip there, I already had a good idea how deeply the drug culture had penetrated Mexico. For one thing, I'd spent a number of years riding with the US Border Patrol in Arizona. I'd also traveled throughout Central America interviewing migrants on their way to *el Norte*. I did not realize, however, what a dramatic impact the drug cartels had on agriculture in the most remote regions. Investigating that was how I came to meet this remarkable Franciscan priest.

Some try to escape poverty, hunger, and a lack of opportunity by going north to the United States. The "death train" is a dangerous way to reach the border. *Photo: Howard G. Buffett*

Padre Beaumont was born in New York on Long Island and educated in the United States. As a young man, he joined the Capuchin Franciscan order of priests. But for the last twenty years, he has worked in the most remote areas of the Sierra Madre in central Mexico—in small mountain villages between the states of Sonora and Chihuahua, where tribes such as the Pima and the Maqui live. He speaks several dialects, and he often travels between these villages by mule—trips that can take six or seven hours. The indigenous people in these areas have always been poor by our standards. However, Padre Beaumont described what had traditionally been a rich culture of people living in concert with nature in a beautiful forested region. They have grown wheat and corn for centuries and are by nature peaceful.

His diocese is centered in the town of Yecora but the population he serves is spread out over many, many miles. When he talks about Yecora, a happy, serene expression spreads across his face. He talks about the great love and faith his people have and their devotion to their children. But when he talks about what these people, mostly subsistence farmers, are up against these days, his expression darkens. An anthropologist who has been working with Padre Beaumont came with him on our visit and added, "The Pimas now feel they have no future. They say, 'Our legends are lies.'"

Drug gangs from the Sinaloa and Juárez cartels have overrun the region. The RAND Corporation says that Mexican drug cartels now export $1.5 to $2 billion worth of marijuana to the United States every year.[1] Padre Beaumont described a hellish phenomenon he says has spread from village to village. Heavily armed drug dealers move into town and order local farmers to switch their crops to marijuana, replacing corn and wheat, promising that they'll make more money. The farmers cooperate—what choice do they have?—but when the crop comes in, the drug dealers announce that they are going to pay in alcohol and guns instead of cash. The farmers are told that, with weapons, they can "protect" their crops better, and the alcohol serves to keep them depressed and submissive. If they object, the dealers may just shoot them on the spot. Occasionally the dealers shoot a local villager just as a reminder. He added, "Women are the heart of our community and our life, but so many women are growing up now with sexual, spiritual, and emotional abuse."

Padre Beaumont spoke of the lack of opportunity for the next generation of people living in the Sierra Madre, such as this young girl. *Photo: Howard G. Buffett*

Some farmers just give up from the stress and despair. "A good friend of mine, a wonderful mother of four children, had her husband come home one night and shoot himself in front of the family," Padre Beaumont told us. "That is the despair that is common now. I said to her, 'How will you go on?' She held her baby out to me. 'I have to do it. I have to keep going for this baby, Padre.' The people have such beautiful spirits; that's what keeps me going."

He brought a series of photographs printed out on copy paper to show us some of the effects on the children. Kids wearing clothing and hats depicting drug paraphernalia; boys playing with the same trucks and Tonka-style toy vehicles I played with as a kid—except a common game is "drug runner." The photos show a child grinning as he drives his toy with marijuana lashed to the truck bed just like the drug dealers he has come to idolize. "The police are the bad guys in these games, and the drug dealers are the heroes," Beaumont explained.

MORE CONSEQUENCES

This community is struggling with so many challenges. In part, I tell this story to show that sometimes our resources and expertise do not match the needs of a given situation. For example, the Padre said that drug lords sometimes pay the farmers who grow marijuana for them with alcohol instead of money. Therefore, there is widespread alcoholism among the men of these villages and that is undermining their ability to put food on their families' tables as well. The power of the drug cartels is so toxic in these regions, but rooting them out is a job well beyond the scope of philanthropy. The Padre also said that the local people were turning to harvesting trees to make charcoal to sell as an alternative to agriculture. That is a phenomenon we see in many impoverished rural communities around the world; there are a number of ways of trying to change that practice, but we could not recommend a course that would be well-suited to rural Mexico.

But then he brought up a concern where we may be able to help. Padre Beaumont said that local farmers had drifted away from planting a diversity of crops. Corn yields were dropping in general, and many farmers were no longer even bothering to plant the traditional blue corn that has been a staple in the region for a very long time. He is trying to help and encourage them to stay with the indigenous crops.

When we returned home, we began investigating whether any seed companies were working with improved varieties of native blue corn that might help the people of the region grow more food and improve their families' livelihoods. So far, we have not been success-ful in finding these resources, but we hope to keep looking and do what we can. This issue is broader than one community—it applies globally. Many large agribusinesses have moved away from the kind of research that benefits small farmers, and I am concerned that this trend will hurt farmers who already face significant challenges to increasing their crop yields. If the only option to upgrade seed is jumping three steps ahead to expensive high-tech seeds, smallholder farmers will continue to struggle with few good options.

I don't know much at all about saints. When I was young, my mother gave me a small medallion of Saint Francis of Assisi, and, from what I've heard about that saint, this Franciscan priest is living the same kind of simple life, devoted to the people he is serving and trying to protect the environment. Padre Beaumont represents an-other face of hunger I have encountered many times in my travels—that of the quiet hero who refuses to give up on some of the poorest people in the world. These individuals work out of the spotlight against difficult odds with limited resources. And they are truly an inspiration.

Story 18
Gorillas Versus Guerrillas

The gorilla ripped off my cotton surgical mask and then gently touched my face with his black, leathery finger. I was wearing the mask to avoid passing any human germs his way, but it can be dangerous to move quickly around a gorilla, so I had to stay put until he backed away. As I held my breath and grunted as deeply as I could to calm him, his sad eyes pored over me. Then he licked my chin. That was not even the most unusual experience I'd had that day.

It has been a privilege to have had the opportunity to see the mountain gorillas in their habitat. *Photo: Dan Cooper*

In mid-2012 I was in Virunga National Park, in the Democratic Republic of the Congo, or DRC. It is the continent of Africa's oldest park and home to over half of all mountain gorillas, the most endangered mammals in the world with an estimated fewer than nine hundred remaining. I have been traveling to the region for fifteen years. The Congo is one of the poorest, most poverty-stricken areas of the planet. Meanwhile, Virunga is a fantastic, frightening, conflict-plagued, vibrant jungle. It is a refuge for the gentle mountain gorillas as well as for vicious paramilitary guerrillas who terrorize each other, local people in small villages, and sometimes the animals.

It had been three years since I'd been to Virunga, but in May 2012 I was in neighboring Uganda and the Central African Republic (CAR), and we were able to arrange a plane and ground support to visit the park. I jumped at the chance. The man who runs Virunga, Emmanuel de Merode, I consider a true hero.

Getting to Virunga is never easy. The park is located along the DRC's eastern border with Uganda and Rwanda, two of many countries in the region with a complicated shared history. We flew over hillsides verdant and diverse, and we could see banana trees, coffee plants, and volcanoes in the distance and other signs of farming all around. Facilities are primitive. Our pilot had to execute a flyby when we arrived to make sure we had the correct landing strip, because we had been alerted that one was controlled by a rebel militia group that would have detained us with an unknown outcome.

As we landed, a good-looking guy in a khaki uniform walked out to meet us: Emmanuel, and with him a team of his armed rangers. I could see his mood was not light. After some quick pleasantries, he gave us a sobering security update. Shelling between rebel groups had been intensifying. He pointed to the mountain ridges around us to show where and how close the conflict was, although he also assured us that he had sufficient intelligence contacts on the ground that we would have at least twenty-four hours to evacuate if things got too close to his headquarters and the lodge where we'd be staying. He smiled and said, "It's not too late to turn around," knowing that I was not about to do that.

Emmanuel has a group of dedicated rangers to protect the park's resources. Every day he lives with the statement, "No one will starve to save a tree." *Photo: Howard G. Buffett*

We piled into a truck with armed rangers in the back and in another truck following us as well. Emmanuel drove. As we headed up to his command center, we passed houses made of mud. Townspeople and barefoot children wearing tattered clothing waved and smiled. Baboons and monkeys crossed the street nonchalantly, like little town officials.

Emmanuel is more like the governor of a small state than like a park warden. In addition to two hundred gorillas tucked away in the jungle region, he takes responsibility for an estimated one million poor people who live in several villages within and near the confines of the park. He has a security force, and when local conflicts displaced people in and around the borders of the park, he set up camps designed to shelter and feed several thousand people, sometimes while under military-type assault.

If that wasn't enough to keep him busy, one of the most impressive things about Emmanuel is that he always focuses on larger dreams of peace and prosperity for the local people. He believes that development is the key to protecting the environment as well. He has overseen the start-up of several local businesses designed to improve the lives of the people and create a self-sustaining path out of poverty. And he is pursuing a grand dream of turning the park into a world-class tourist destination. Talking about that subject tends to lift the serious furrows off his forehead and inspires the great investment of energy he makes in Virunga.

"It's a clean industry, a new industry. It creates jobs," he said intently. "Just look at what happened in Rwanda with gorilla tourism. They created 120,000 jobs and a $430 million industry. There is no reason we can't achieve the same over the next ten years. It's ambitious but achievable. There is no reason Virunga can't become a billion-dollar business. We'll have a new generation of Congolese, highly skilled, who will be the driving force behind peace and development. We will have setbacks, but we will keep progressing. This will also give us opportunities to develop local businesses such as hydroelectricity, creating tens of thousands of jobs. Our hope is to be the biggest employer in eastern Congo."

FRAGILE SAFETY

In some ways, our stories run parallel. Emmanuel began his career as a conservationist. He was born in Kenya, was educated in the United Kingdom, and always knew he wanted to work in conservation. He moved to Gabon in 1999. That's where he first started to work with gorillas. While in Gabon, he made plans to come to Virunga, "the most amazing site for a conservationist." There were no positions available, but he was determined. He resigned from his position in Gabon, bought a motorbike in Uganda, and drove it to Virunga, where he met the then warden and offered his services.

At the time, Virunga's rangers were untrained, undisciplined, and not even paid consistently. The gorillas were surviving on their own, despite constant threats from villagers, poachers, and militia encroaching on their turf. Emmanuel and his colleagues had a difficult time raising money to support what the park needed, but, ironically, they got their first grant from the US Fish and Wildlife Service and began building a network from there. He started working on the European Union for larger grants to rebuild the park, and the first came in 2005. But the world's attention turned to Virunga in 2007 when a number of gorillas were slaughtered in the park by illegal charcoal traders who resented the growing tourist business interfering with their activities.

The fragile safety of the gorillas hit the front pages.[1] In 2008 Emmanuel became park director, and that same year, Virunga was awarded a large grant from the EU to support his rebuilding plan. His immediate priorities were to cull and retrain staff, but then another conflict broke out, and the park was at the center of significant activity. The rangers themselves were attacked at their base of operations in the village of Rumangabo and forced to evacuate the families of staff. During the violent outbreaks, Emmanuel was two hours away in the city of Goma, working on camps for people displaced as a result of the conflict. Then there was a second attack, and all of his rangers were forced to retreat into the forest for ten days and make their way on foot to Goma.

During this period, the leader of one group battling the Congolese army, the National Congress for the Defense of the Congolese People, or CNDP, announced that he was going to create a new parks system. Emmanuel was overseeing three thousand people in camps for internally displaced persons (IDPs) and knew this would be devastating for the people and the park alike. So he went to the minister of the environment, who in turn appealed to the president of the DRC Joseph Kabila and got an exemption to operate outside the political fray and negotiate directly with the rebels and allow his parks people to come back and control Virunga. Eventually a larger peace accord was signed in 2009.

Since that time, Emmanuel has rebuilt the park and fought corruption. He had to arrest some of his own rangers who were involved in the gorilla killings, and that act helped set a new tone. He focused on institutional reform and on streamlining his rangers force.

The animals brought Emmanuel to Virunga, but he has embraced raising the quality of life for the local people as essential to his mission. Building the tourism industry brought new jobs and revenues that helped him build nine schools. He has transformed a charcoal problem (many acres of Virunga have been illegally deforested by charcoal collection) into an opportunity by importing equipment to compress charcoal dust left over from past activities into briquettes that can be sold. "You can't disassociate economic development from security in a situation like this," Emmanuel said.

We went to the new lodge that is the center of Emmanuel's vision of tourism for this region. It opened in 2008, and by 2011, it had hosted 3,300 tourists and generated nearly $1 million in profits. Visitors enjoy guided hikes through the diverse, lush rain forest and are able to come close to gorillas who have been habituated to the presence of humans. (Tourists do not have physical contact with the gorillas. Emmanuel asked me to appear in a video about why I have supported Virunga, which we shot in an enclosure not open to the public, where the staff has been raising some orphaned juvenile gorillas.) The lodge facility was terrific, and bookings had been growing. The food was outstanding: French press coffee, homemade bread and soups, steaks, and chocolate desserts as fancy as you'll see in high-end restaurants around the world. Best of all, 70 percent of what the lodge earns from tourism goes back to the national parks system, while 30 percent is returned to the local community for things like the schools they have built and water projects.

However, during our visit, there were no revenues. Emmanuel recently shut down tourism because renewed conflict made it too dangerous to risk having guests. As we sat with him and discussed the dilemmas he faced, the seriousness of the situation began to sink in. On the one hand, we were laughing at the idea that when the resort is open, it employs a full-time baboon chaser to keep the area's thirty to forty baboons from pestering guests. And yet the faint booms in the distance were actual skirmishes between rebel groups, endangering both human and gorilla lives in the eastern region of the park. Emmanuel has had to dip into cash reserves to keep the staff personnel employed and divert them to other projects.

The complex currents of this area, called the Great Lakes region of Africa, are hard to exaggerate. I lost track as Emmanuel recounted the different factions and Congolese forces that have made life difficult and dangerous for the local people and for his rangers—and that was just in the DRC alone. I was impressed with Emmanuel's calm, diplomatic way of assessing situations and never losing sight of his primary goal: protecting and benefiting local people and the park.

CHAOS DEMANDS COOL HEADS

He showed exactly that capacity just a few months after our visit. In November 2012 a faction of the original CNDP group, now called M23, took Goma by force. When the city lost power in the aftermath of the fighting, a million people living there instantly lost access to clean water. When a crisis like this erupts in a conflict region, it can be pure chaos. The government is preoccupied with military operations. Large numbers of people flee their homes and descend on cities or areas already struggling. Local officials may have no resources or authority to intervene effectively. There were probably seventy NGOs operating in the region, but each organization has its own mandates

and focuses first on protecting its own staff. When the spigots ran
dry and people began drawing unfiltered water straight from Lake
Kivu, Emmanuel realized that Goma could experience a rerun of a
2008 cholera epidemic that killed thousands of people the last time
the power went out.

As many as forty armed militias may be active
today in the DRC. *Photo: Howard G. Buffett*

He contacted us, and we were able to help by providing emergency funding within twenty-four hours. Emmanuel bought four
new generators to reactivate pumping, and his staff and other local
people worked thirty-six hours straight to return power and clean
water to Goma. One of my most satisfying activities as a philanthropist is to support and encourage motivated individuals like
Emmanuel, who find a way to work between the lines of their job
descriptions in times of crisis or opportunity.

M23 withdrew from the city, and there is a regional peace effort under way as I write. I have spent a great deal of my time in the region in recent years, visiting projects in the field and meeting with heads of state to support Emmanuel's vision for a "Marshall Plan" for eastern DRC. This area remains volatile, and we stay in close touch with Emmanuel as he balances protecting the park, navigating unpredictable conflict in the region, and making sure that the local people see an opportunity to improve their lives and feed their children by joining him in his big-picture economic vision. With the park he oversees under the control of rebel forces, Emmanuel's dream of high-end ecotourism is on hold for now, but he keeps pushing forward.

Our foundation has committed significant financial resources to several elements that we hope will be key to success: We've helped Emmanuel double the size of his ranger force and create the equivalent of an "army corps of engineers" to help rebuild critical infrastructure. We are optimistic, based on the success of a small pilot project, that we can help him move ahead on two hydroelectric power plants to harness the potential of local rivers. It's hard to overestimate what access to electricity could mean to the people of this part of DRC: it can enable light industry around local agriculture, and we are supporting initiatives to create businesses making soap from palm nut oil and extracting enzymes from papaya for pharmaceuticals. Collectively, these projects could bring as many as thirty thousand jobs to eastern Congo—jobs not involving guns or fighting.

PART 3

Hard-Learned Lessons

Philanthropists, NGOs, and nations investing in development face a fundamental dilemma: if we're invested in a situation that is not improving, are we doing something wrong, or would conditions be twice as bad if we hadn't gotten involved? For example, the economist Dambisa Moyo noted in 2009 that the developed world had sent more than a trillion dollars in aid to Africa in the latter half of the twentieth century, yet per capita income in Africa was lower than it was in the 1970s.[1] So: Did the aid make conditions worse, or would an even higher percentage of the continent be living below the poverty line without that aid?

That is a difficult question. But often—frankly, too often—we reward ourselves for good intentions and answer with the second option. There are many inspiring and committed people working on global hunger, and you've just met a few. But even terrific people can't make plans work that are fundamentally flawed or no longer make the best use of resources. People such as Joe DeVries and Emmanuel get that, and they change course as they go. That's not the case for some philanthropists and NGOs. And too many special interests in nations battling chronic poverty are exploiting the drawbacks of the status quo. In part 3, we'll look at some of the unsound approaches, misconceptions, and good intentions gone bad that I've seen firsthand in the last decade.

Can This Village Be Saved?

"Is that an axe sticking out of her head?"

I was in the backseat of an SUV traveling down a rural dirt road in Angola, which is in southwestern Africa along the Atlantic Coast. At the time, in 2006, Angola was still rarely mentioned in the media without an accompanying adjective such as *war-torn* or *war-ravaged*. The nation had been the scene of conflict for decades.

The Portuguese had been in Angola since the sixteenth century, and because of its Atlantic ports, the country served as a supplier to the slave trade that sent thousands of Angolans to work on plantations in Brazil. But Portugal pulled out of Angola abruptly in 1975, and after only a few months of independence, civil war broke out between the National Union for the Total Independence of Angola (UNITA) and the Popular Movement for the Liberation of Angola (known as MPLA, the acronym for its Portuguese name). Cold War politics dictated that Cuba and Russia back the MPLA, while the United States and South Africa supported UNITA. Not surprisingly, there was more at stake than ideology. Angola has vast oil and mineral reserves, including diamonds. Fighting went on for years, but as the Cold War ran down, foreign factions pulled out. Since 2002, the MPLA has been in power.

Millions of land mines, many laid by the Angolan army to keep rebels away from villages, crop fields, military camps, dams, and roads, are a horrible reminder of those years of civil disputes.[1] Civilians have always suffered the most land mine casualties. The vicious devices so prevalent in Angola are designed to mutilate and disable, not kill, and they've created tens of thousands of amputees. Ever since the end of active conflict, deminers in plastic head shields and armored jackets, and carrying metal detectors, have carried out the slow, excruciating work of identifying the mines for disarming or detonation. The late Princess Diana of Great Britain visited Angola in 1997, and she was famously photographed in a demining outfit walking along an Angolan road where mines were marked with red flags. She worked with the Red Cross as an advocate for children who had been maimed.

I was in Angola to understand the country's widespread food insecurity. Fields that had been mined were only slowly being reclaimed, and in 2005 and 2006, weather disruptions had ruined crop yields. I was reviewing some proposed agricultural assistance and irrigation projects that World Vision was developing and trying to raise money for.

I was with a small team on my way to meet farmers in several villages. We were driving down a dry, dusty road lined with sorghum fields when I spotted a woman with one leg. She was wearing a white blouse and a brown skirt, and she was moving along the road's shoulder at a steady pace, swinging her one leg forward between a pair of metal crutches. As we got closer, however, I saw a wooden handle about two or three feet long protruding from the front of her head. The visual effect was jarring.

"My God, is that an axe sticking out of her head?" I asked. But as we passed her, I could see the object more clearly: it was a farming hoe. She had made a furrow in her head scarf so that she could rest the handle on it, and the blade cradled the back of her head. The handle was shortened enough so that it was balanced as she swung along on her crutches.

"Let's pull over," I said.

An Angolan who worked for World Vision got out of the car with me. We did not want to startle the woman, so we waited until she caught up with us. My Angolan host asked if we could speak with her, and she nodded—all the while with the hoe balanced on her head and the rough handle protruding forward. She projected so much strength and grace that the effect was almost as if she were wearing a tribal battle helmet. She said her name was Augusta. She was thirty-six. She had lost her leg in a land mine accident in Cuando Cubango Province in 2001. Her husband had been killed in the civil war, and she had six children to feed. She was a farmer, on her way to her field.

The legacy of conflict can be permanent. Augusta demonstrates the courage and resiliency that farmers need to feed their families.
Photo: Howard G. Buffett

Augusta demonstrated the farming technique she used, propping her missing-leg side on a crutch while bending and striking the ground with the hoe in her left hand. It seemed like backbreaking work, yet I did not sense the slightest self-pity in the woman's outlook. Her only way to feed her children was to farm, so farm she did. I asked her if I could take a few photographs of her because I was trying to show the rest of the world the difficulties of life here. She agreed.

After I took some photographs and we said good-bye, I thought of the tractors, combines, GPS systems, and computer-generated planting and fertilizing I used back home in Illinois. I thought of the weather fluctuations and equipment breakdowns that cause farmers some inconvenience and might temporarily disrupt our plans. How trivial that now seemed. My dad's notion of the ovarian lottery means this impressive, determined, hardworking landmine victim in Angola will achieve only a fraction of what she might have in the developed world, simply because of the conditions of her birth.

Augusta's story was the kind that inspires philanthropy. And yet a few days later, I would leave Angola convinced that I had to stop funding a lot of what might be called traditional agricultural and food aid projects in Africa.

ONCE A BREADBASKET

Back in the SUV, we continued our five-hour journey from the city of Huambo to a series of villages in the remote areas of Huambo Province in Angola's central highlands region. This area has the most fertile soil and abundant water resources. Ironically, my hosts said that during the colonial era, this one region provided food for the entire country and surplus for export. Angola was once a major grower and exporter of coffee, for example, but the years of conflict decimated that sector. The region we were visiting was home to about 5 million people, or roughly one-third of the total population, and World Vision thought it had the greatest potential to contribute to pulling Angola out of poverty.

Clearly, the NGOs here were working against daunting odds. The baseline poverty was profound. The city of Huambo, where we'd started our trip in the region, was home to 450,000 people—and yet the municipality had no electricity. Angola had and still has one of the highest infant mortality rates in the world (overall child mortality from birth to age five was 66 percent at the time), and it has one of the lowest life expectancies. These days many point to Angola's economic growth thanks to oil revenues driving several years of double-digit GDP. But that has mainly raised the standard of living for its elites and politicians. When I was there, World Vision staffers estimated that at least two-thirds of the people made their living from agriculture.

The government was working closely with World Vision and provided about 70 percent of its budget for seed and the production of seed through cultivation. World Vision was trying to link credit programs with agricultural projects for rural farmers. These were all worthwhile goals. Among other challenges, however, Angola was a prime example of a country where the lack of land tenure posed a huge problem to agricultural development.

Rural farmers in Angola occupy land owned by the state but have no titles or documents formalizing their rights. Local government and tribal leaders have records of who is entitled and who uses the land, but these rights are vulnerable. Poor farmers can be displaced by people with more money or power. All sustainable agriculture, high or low tech, demands a long-term investment in the soil. How much will any given farmer invest in land that can be yanked out from under her or him at any time for any reason?

As we drove, the World Vision team explained that the current situation was dire. A combination of off-season rains and then drought had decimated crop yields for two years. What's more, malaria, diarrhea, and cholera were contributing to a high rate of child mortality. These largely pathogen-borne diseases were often lethal in children weakened already from chronic hunger and poor nutrition.

Before long, more signs of the famine appeared: as we moved deeper into rural areas, I began to see numerous newly dug graves, many of them just three or four feet long—the size of young children. I stopped to photograph a group of grave diggers. Then we traveled the short distance to a village called Iuvo, where about seven hundred people from that village and surrounding ones waited for us. We learned that the wetter valley regions, or *nacas*, where they planted crops during the dry season, had flooded and been washed out. Then a drought destroyed their usual wet-season crops in the highlands. The people were barely surviving on small amounts of sorghum and unripe bananas, and they were suffering.

I was sure many of the children I saw were not likely to survive. Many young babies and toddlers in their mothers' laps seemed listless, vacant eyed. Everyone was thin, with prominent and knobby joints—particularly the children. Cholera and malaria were ravaging many of these immune-suppressed children, and the World Vision team said that around one in ten people here were positive for HIV/ AIDS. A woman named Magdalena told me she had five children, and three had already died from the famine. Her son Julio was thirty months old, and I could see that he was ill and unlikely to survive without medical intervention. It seemed like a village of death.

A woman approached me clutching a baby. She told us that she had recently buried her three-year-old daughter. She motioned to her surviving baby, and her voice became stronger. "My body is broken," she said. Her milk had dried up, and the baby was starving. She pleaded with me to take her baby and she thrust the tiny child toward me, trying to force it into my arms. "It is the only chance for life," she said, eyes pleading.

This child would die. I could not take the baby. I felt an overwhelming urgency: these people could not wait for the next harvest. They were out of time. There must be something we could do now. I started thinking out loud with the World Vision team, including Jonathan White, its director of operations in Angola. If we moved and made a significant investment here, could we intervene and save most of the people in this village?

The chief arrived and addressed us. The tribal chiefs in rural Africa play a complex and powerful role. They are the arbiters, the decision makers, the enforcers. They can banish an individual from the village for an array of transgressions, from stealing to witchcraft. This particular chief explained that there were a total of eighteen villages under his authority, with a total population of around 1,600. What we did for any one village we would have to do for all to secure his support. With that, I realized the need I was starting to calculate had more than doubled.

I asked Jon to take this challenge seriously: What would saving these villages entail? What would we need?

TRYING TO MAKE THE MATH ADD UP

Jon explained that the first step was for a qualified medical professional to carry out an assessment of who in the villages needed general feeding support versus how many needed therapeutic feeding support. Nutritionists would need to be on hand to ensure the correct use of the fortified preparations for those suffering from severe malnutrition. Ready-to-use therapeutic foods were not yet readily available, and feeding even a bland "normal" diet to people in an advanced state of malnutrition can overwhelm their damaged metabolisms and trigger deadly consequences such as cardiac arrhythmias. Therapeutic feeding would demand intravenous tubes and monitoring vital signs during treatments. That meant more staff, equipment, and money.

Next, we would need to look at the larger issue of the failed crop, and we'd have to provide new seeds. They didn't have any to plant and no way to get any more. In a twist I hadn't considered, Jon explained that these two activities would need to be coordinated and timed carefully. If the seeds arrived before the food, the people were so stressed and starving that they would eat the seeds, not plant them. Also, people would need to eat and get their strength back before they could plant a full crop. Yet we would have to plant in the right seasonal window.

I asked the World Vision staffers if they could provide information on the financial requirements. They spent the rest of our five-hour trip back to Huambo on their cell phones trying to get me answers. By dinner that night, we were close to an estimate.

The good news was that they located a doctor working on a malaria project who could perform the assessment quickly. It would take $10,000 to $12,000 to cover the cost. I asked them to make the arrangements. However, the logistics of transporting in the equipment, food, seed, and staff to carry out a general and therapeutic feeding operation would be $580,000. The nutritional packs for the therapeutic feeding itself, which might continue for months, could cost as much as $1 million. Enough general food to get through to the next harvest for those in relatively better shape would require another $1.8 million. The seeds to restart the village's agricultural system would cost approximately $1.5 million.

On a mostly back-of-the-envelope basis, we figured that it would cost almost $5 million to "save" these 1,600 people. But a list of logistical challenges grew longer and longer. WFP did not have emergency funds or food on hand to send. And WFP could not commit to exactly when it could obtain and deliver the food even if we provided the funds. Jon felt he could get the government to supply the seeds, but perhaps the greatest challenge was the complexity of arranging the logistics. Without the vehicles, fuel, and trained staff to organize these relief efforts, nothing would take place. And the only person in the country who, realistically, could coordinate an entire emergency mission for World Vision was about to go on a two-week leave.

There is always a risk in having a bias for action. What loomed larger and larger for me was the realization that I had been touched emotionally by the situation of the people in this village, but they represented one cup in an ocean of hunger. World Vision had picked

Iuvo to show me out of hundreds of other communities suffering to the same degree. Perhaps we could spend $5 million, help this village, and do some temporary good. But whether we spent $5 million or $50 million or $500 million, approaching this kind of hunger as an emergency intervention, village by village, was not going to change the underlying issues preventing meaningful development here. The nation had to make investing in the health and welfare of its people a priority. No NGO could change the course of Angola's agricultural future, or this region's, or even this village's food security by going project to project. The government needed to invest in an agricultural system. The farmers needed roads, agricultural extension for training, the right to own their own land, access to credit, and help entering the market in order to generate revenues beyond their own subsistence needs and lift themselves out of this abject poverty and despair. We could deplete our entire endowment by sending in doctors, food, and seeds for starving people just in Angola and prop them up for a few years, but without those other foundational elements, the situation could slip right back into what I saw before me that day.

As I went to sleep that night, a slide show played in my mind: Augusta and her fierce determination and strength. The mother offering me her child. The small graves by the side of the road. The vacant eyes of the toddlers sprawled across their mothers' laps. The scramble by Jon and the World Vision team to try to make a difference despite the difficult odds.

There had to be a better way to use our resources to build the underlying infrastructure of agriculture here so that it could become sustainable. Faced with dying children, it was no wonder that organizations such as World Vision and many of the world's NGOs attack situations one project at a time. Of course, organizations divide up the challenges by region, and, of course, they respond to the most difficult situations where they feel they can demonstrate some success. The problem is that this well-intentioned approach does not change the underlying dynamics. The math still will not add up if the solutions are temporary.

We provided some emergency support to Iuvo, but we could not put the pieces together to "save the village," as I had hoped. And I realized that there is not enough money in all of philanthropy to "save" even half the villages in Africa like Iuvo on a project-by-project basis. Even when you're willing to spend millions, an emergency intervention is just a temporary painkiller.

Story 20
A Complicated Legacy

One of my biggest regrets is that I never got to meet Norman Borlaug. In the annals of American agriculture, or, for that matter, in almost any field, few individuals have made a greater contribution to the world.

In the early 1940s Mexico was grappling with a plant disease called stem rust that was decimating wheat crops. In 1940 vice president–elect Henry Wallace, who had been President Franklin D. Roosevelt's secretary of agriculture (and a cofounder of what became Pioneer Hi-Bred Seed Company), visited Mexico, in part to spread goodwill as world tensions were increasing. He saw the widespread troubles of farmers, and he saw the resulting poverty and hunger that the wheat crop failures had caused. When Wallace returned to Washington, he lobbied the Rockefeller Foundation to agree to send a scientific team to Mexico.

Stem rust weakens the stalk section of a wheat plant. The plants break and fall over, ruining the development of the grains at the top. Through a series of clever breeding experiments, a member of the team, Dr. Norman Borlaug, developed shorter-stalked wheat strains that were incredibly robust, high yield, disease resistant, and transportable—meaning that they could be grown equally well in different geographic regions. It took some years to work, but the accomplishment was enormous. Mexican wheat farmers' yields increased and set the stage for a vibrant wheat-growing industry in Mexico.

Borlaug's wheat strains proved vital and productive in other areas of the world as well. As the 1960s dawned, agricultural output in the developing world was not keeping pace with booming populations. Two devastating droughts in Asia killed millions, and the United States shipped massive amounts of wheat to India to keep hundreds of millions fed. But even as US government officials struggled to try to help Asia with aid, they encouraged government ministers in India, Pakistan, and other parts of the continent to consider Borlaug's hardy wheat developed in Mexico's Yaquí Valley.

Borlaug himself taught farmers in India and Pakistan how to maximize yields. He used demonstration plots to show poor Indian farmers that his new approach using the special hybrid seeds and fertilizer could produce five times more grain on the same amount of land than using traditional seeds and old methods. Borlaug also lobbied on behalf of the tools that farmers needed—such as seed and fertilizer—and also the credit they would need to buy the first two. Indian prime minister Indira Gandhi later even famously ripped up a flower bed and planted Borlaug's wheat. Aid came in from all over the world to help supply the needed seeds and fertilizer.

India's wheat harvest exploded. By the mid-1970s, the country was growing enough grain to build vast national reserves. In addition to pushing back the food shortages, this Green Revolution, as it came to be known, improved the quality of life more broadly because farmers now had extra crops to sell for money to pay for education, medicine, and other benefits. The Rockefeller Foundation and others supported research similar to Borlaug's to raise yields for rice, and, combined with wheat, many millions more in Asian countries were saved from starvation.

Dr. Borlaug won the Nobel Peace Prize in 1970. I have read a lot about him and his work, and I've spent time with his granddaughter Julie, who works at the Norman Borlaug Institute for International Agriculture at Texas A&M University. Dr. Borlaug was not an aloof scientist: he was out in the field every day, sleeves rolled up. He knew how to talk to farmers, in part, I'm sure, because he had grown up on a farm in Iowa. His personal commitment to the work, his understanding of the variables that matter in farming, and his larger appreciation of the political and socioeconomic factors that impact agriculture all added to his credibility and success. In the spirit of forty chances, it seems to me that he always learned lessons from previous harvests and refined and adjusted his approaches.

And yet the Green Revolution's legacy is complicated. The approach Dr. Borlaug pioneered involved using hybrid seeds and nitrogen-based fertilizer to dramatically improve yields of a single crop. As a solution to address acute hunger in India and Pakistan, it was brilliant. Focusing on one recipe for growing one crop, so-called monocropping, made it simpler and more efficient to produce, harvest, store, and distribute the wheat. However, I am frustrated when I hear the term "Green Revolution" tossed around like a surefire method for increasing all crop yields anywhere and everywhere. There is an assumption by some that we've already figured out this high-yield approach, and now if only we could find the money and cooperation from governments, we could make it happen wherever we need it. That is not true. There is never a single solution for permanently maximizing yields, even on farms in the developed world, or, for that matter, even for a single farm in the United States.*

---

* HWB uses different techniques on our Nebraska farm than I use on my fields in Illinois. I have fields whose soils have roughly 2 percent organic matter, while others nearby have 4 percent—that means I need to use different amounts of fertilizer on each. Other variables include slope, drainage, soil compaction, pH levels, and available nutrients.

A GREAT CONTRIBUTION BUT NOT A "SOLUTION"

In areas of the world experiencing extreme food insecurity today—particularly across the African continent but also in parts of Central America—critical Green Revolution conditions don't exist. The soils of Africa are some of the most weathered, abused, and challenging to farm on the planet. Many lack nutrients, some are so sandy that water drains right through them, and others are so heavy with clay that plant roots can barely penetrate. Africa's agriculture is largely rain fed, and droughts are common. Regions where subsistence farmers struggle to stay alive often lack roads and railroads, so it is difficult to transport seeds and fertilizer to where they are most needed. Tribal legacies control landownership, and fifty-four different governments have widely varying commitments to helping their own people. African farmers are vulnerable to plant diseases and pest infestations—therefore, monoculture puts their food security at even more risk. Traditionally, farmers have raised multiple crops so that the likelihood of all failing in one season is lower.

Finally, there are socioeconomic and infrastructure factors. India had already made a commitment to agriculture by the time Borlaug and the Green Revolution arrived. Agricultural extension existed throughout the country. The central Indian government could handle large-scale purchasing and negotiate with foreign governments for aid, and it could utilize the military to protect certain assets and equipment and move seed and fertilizer. Unlike the colonialists in Africa, who built railroads primarily to mines, colonialists in India built railways to agricultural areas, initially to facilitate cotton exports. That proved invaluable.

In the decades since the Green Revolution saved a billion people from acute hunger, it has also become clear that hybrid seeds and fertilizer did not solve hunger in India, and there was some environmental fallout. Today India has one of the highest rates of childhood malnutrition in the world, higher than those of many

African countries. UNICEF calculated in 2009 that 48 percent of all children in India under five years old suffered moderate to severe stunting.[1]

And in terms of the environment, overuse of nitrogen in some areas has polluted water tables and degraded soils, causing yields to fall. One problem is that nitrogen fertilizer supercharges the growth of various crops but does not replenish organic matter or replace other essential nutrients needed for productive soil. Merely fertilizing is like giving a sick man oxygen and caffeine, but not food. You can speed up his metabolism, make him more alert—even make him more energetic for a short time—but at some point, he will collapse from the lack of calories needed to retain body mass and fuel the brain and other basic functions. India's wheat yields increased for many years, but recently, many are concerned that as much as half the country's soil is degraded from overfertilizing.[2]

"WAIT, IT GETS WORSE!"

In early 2012 I took a trip to the Yaquí Valley in Mexico, where Norman Borlaug developed those hardy wheat strains. I spent a day at the headquarters of CIMMYT with the scientists who have continued his research. CIMMYT stands for the Centro Internacional de Mejoramiento de Maíz y Trigo, or the International Maize and Wheat Improvement Center. The nonprofit research and training center, which focuses on helping improve yields of these crops around the globe, has one of the world's largest research programs on wheat, and it is estimated that 75 percent of the wheat varieties grown in the developing world have their origins in the fields of the Yaquí Valley or come from CIMMYT research partners. Dr. Borlaug is a hero here: a giant portrait of him is painted on the side of a wall in front of the headquarters in Ciudad Obregón, and inside are photographs taken during his visit there shortly before he died in 2009.

We went out to the fields to discuss some of the techniques that CIMMYT is developing to try to increase yields and grow wheat efficiently and more sustainably. My hosts pointed out that we were standing just a few hundred meters from the original plots Norman Borlaug farmed in the 1940s, but they also talked about how one of Dr. Borlaug's last efforts was to encourage farmers to cut back on what had become excessive fertilizer use.

As we arrive at the CIMMYT Research Station, there is a large sign honoring Dr. Norman Borlaug. *Photo: Howard G. Buffett*

According to these researchers, the private farmers in the Yaquí Valley took to heart Dr. Borlaug's original findings that fertilizer was key to increasing yields. And the federal government helps farmers by subsidizing fertilizer and seeds. But a problematic situation has developed. Local wheat farmers have been overapplying and misapplying fertilizer to a staggering degree. The CIMMYT scientists explained to me that the efficiency rate of the nitrogen fertilizer being applied locally was about 31 percent, meaning that more than two-thirds of the applied fertilizer was not being taken up in the plants. Nitrogen uptake can vary based on a number of weather and soil conditions, but by way of comparison, in a typical year on my farms in Illinois, using a good nutrient management plan, we will usually get roughly two-thirds of the nitrogen taken up by the plant, and sometimes significantly more than that.

The CIMMYT scientists also explained the technique used by local farmers. First, they would apply the nitrogen in dry form; next, they would irrigate; and then they would plant. My reaction to that sequence was similar to what I imagine a dentist's would be upon hearing that a patient's nightly routine was to brush his teeth, suck on a sugary jawbreakers candy for an hour, and then go to bed. The order matters in farming! Applying all of the nitrogen before irrigation (in this part of the world, primarily flood irrigation, or what's called furrow irrigation), washes away much of the nitrogen from the planting beds themselves and drives it deeper into the soil or off the fields. It can't do much there but accumulate or make its way to the water table. The way that many US farmers fertilize is to use planters that drop fertilizer alongside the seed to make sure the seed directly benefits and the least amount is lost. These Mexican farmers used a technique guaranteeing that most of their fertilizer would be transported by the water away from the plants and their field.

Furrow irrigation can wash nutrients through the field and away from the plants, as seen happening here in Guatemala. *Photo: Howard G. Buffett*

"That nitrogen management is what I would call disastrous," I said out loud.

"Wait, it gets worse!" said a senior scientist from CIMMYT.

You've heard the joke by some doctors and nutritionists about how the only thing that people who take enormous amounts of vitamins accomplish is to produce expensive urine. To extend that analogy one more step, these farmers' nitrogen management approach is like peeing that expensive urine back into your own freshwater supply. Local wells around Obregón that have been tested (and most are not tested routinely) show that at least 25 percent of them are contaminated with more than ten times the maximum levels of nitrogen considered safe in drinking water. The CIMMYT scientists showed me a slide depicting another environmental impact of this situation: it's a satellite photograph of the Sea of Cortez, between the western shore of mainland Mexico and the Baja Peninsula, after planting season. So much nitrogen has migrated to the sea-bound water that a dramatic algae bloom is visible. A similar bloom occurs in the Gulf of Mexico, as a result of the Mississippi River washing a layer of freshwater above the salt water, with the nitrogen from runoff sparking a growth in anaerobic bacteria, which can damage native aquatic life.

CIMMYT attempted a project to try to persuade the farmers to use less nitrogen. As an experiment, the center took one acre and stopped fertilizing it for a season. The yield was essentially equal to that of the year before, due to the nitrogen still in the soil from previous years. That impressed some local farmers: fertilizer costs money, after all, and an equal yield without investing in it is money in the farmers' pockets. So CIMMYT went further and convinced a local farmer to run the same experiment on eighty acres. At first the farmer said yes. Then he called with second thoughts. It seemed that the local farming association offered its members a credit toward free fertilizer, and the farmer was told that if he didn't use the credit this year, he would lose it. CIMMYT intervened, explaining that it was conducting a one-season experiment, and the association agreed to make an exception.

Then the farmer called back again and said, "Look, I have a partner on the eighty acres who owns forty of them, and he's nervous about not fertilizing. He's going to fertilize his acres right next to the others, and I won't, and we'll see what happens." The yields were equal. The cost of the fertilizer reduced the partner's profits.

So here in the cradle of the Green Revolution, farmers grapple with this negative fallout from its approach. None of this was lost on Dr. Borlaug. A few months before he died, he visited the Yaquí Valley and implored local farmers to cut back on their fertilizer usage.

The good news is that researchers are working on solutions to these issues. For example, CIMMYT is trying to get farmers to use a technology for secondary fertilizer applications that is aimed at reducing total nitrogen applied in a field. GreenSeeker, developed at Oklahoma State University, falls into the category of brilliantly simple. Basically, when a plant is deficient in nitrogen, it turns yellow, or less green. By attaching the sensor to an applicator, a farmer can calibrate the amount of nitrogen fertilizer delivered to corn, for example, based on how green the leaves are. Another, less mechanized version of the technology for farmers with smaller operations allows them to make some of the same measurements and calculations with a handheld device. CIMMYT's educational outreach program is a forty chances moment for these farmers, and I hope they take advantage of it.

BORLAUG IN AFRICA

Dr. Borlaug never stopped working on hunger. Later in his life, he tried to adapt his original methods for Africa. In the 1980s

the Japanese philanthropist Ryoichi Sasakawa hired Dr. Borlaug
to spearhead an effort to bring Green Revolution approaches
to Ghana, Sudan, and other African countries, and Dr. Borlaug
worked to try to do that for two decades. He had some successes
in more developed areas, but in 2006 Dr. Borlaug gave a talk in
which he explained some of the difficulties of working in Africa—
from malaria to lack of transportation infrastructure—that were
significant impediments to progress. He said that Africa would
need the equivalent of a Marshall Plan—the expansive US aid program to rebuild Europe in the aftermath of World War II—for
development across huge swaths of the continent to make sustainable progress.[3]

As you look more broadly at the many countries of Africa where
agriculture is difficult and people are hungry and inject both internal and cross-border conflict and corruption into the mix, to me
the conclusion is clear: we need major initiatives in agriculture,
but they need to be designed around simple, basic technologies
and inputs for subsistence farmers, not large-scale farms. Generally, monocropping is not a good idea because it makes subsistence
farmers vulnerable to a species-specific disease or pests. We should
work on improving their access to appropriate equipment, higher-
yielding seeds, and storage facilities, because those elements will
help them to increase yields and better benefit from selling their
surplus crops into markets—the only sustainable path out of abject
poverty and hunger.

We can teach farmers soil management techniques that retain organic matter and build soil health. I call the emphasis on soil the
Brown Revolution approach. Today our Ukulima Farm in South Africa and our farms in Arizona are testing a number of exciting new
farming techniques and technologies that hold the promise of helping the people who need them most. They are low input, designed
for local capabilities and geography, and more realistic. Much as Dr.

Borlaug's Green Revolution helped Mexico and then reversed the tide on a horrible famine, a new Brown Revolution can carry his legacy forward with even broader impact.

Worms are powerful allies in the Brown Revolution. Here a Mexican farmer shows me soil he was improving with a revolving worm bank, a program we funded to help farmers become "soil nutritionists." It's a simple, low-tech approach that can improve soil quality almost everywhere. *Photo: Howard G. Buffett*

Story 21
For Yields to Go Up, We Have to Look Down

As I thumbed the machete blade with a flourish, I felt like one of those stage magicians who invites his smiling assistant into a box and then pretends to slice her into three pieces.

I was on a field visit in the Nampula Province of Mozambique. We were with a group from the international relief and development organization CARE, taking a tour of the Mogovolas District, where local farmers utilized what is arguably the simplest technology to improve soil quality available to many farmers in Africa. It's sometimes called a *zai* hole, or planting basin. There are different variations, but these farmers were using individual basin-shaped holes about two feet across with sloping sides. Someone in our group who was not a farmer asked what could possibly be so helpful about digging a hole in this field of otherwise rock-hard dirt.

I asked if anyone had a machete. A young farmer watching us grabbed one and handed it to me. I checked the blade and placed the tip in the hardpan (compacted, almost cement-like soil) between two basins. I pushed. Nothing happened. I put both hands on the machete handle and leaned all my weight on it. It penetrated maybe a half inch. Then I took two steps and put the tip a couple of inches from the base of a maize plant growing in the middle of the basin. I took two fingers and placed them on the top end of the machete. It slid easily into the earth all the way to the handle.

A subsistence farmer in Mozambique uses a *zai* pit to improve poor soil conditions. *Zai* pits work best where there is an abundance of labor and the opportunity to collect large amounts of organic material. *Photo: Howard G. Buffett*

I'm no magician, but these planting basins really do perform a little bit of magic: they turn dirt into soil.

Most of us take for granted the ground on which we walk. We even use expressions such as "dirt cheap" or "treating him like dirt" to suggest contempt and disrespect. Dirt is just the accumulation of what's on the ground. Dirt is the equivalent of inert

Play-Doh that we push around to create a base or foundation for other things we consider much more valuable: buildings, roads, canals, tunnels, walls.

Soil, on the other hand, is a treasure. It is any farmer's most valuable working capital. Soil fertility has the single largest impact on production capacity.

The difference between dirt and soil is that soil is alive: home to millions of diverse microbial organisms. The best soil for planting is soft and crumbly loam—a combination of sand, silt, and clay—and its surface is rich in organic matter, including decayed plant material and nutrients. The best soil has structural integrity, or tilth: neither so sticky with clay that roots can't penetrate it, nor so sandy that it can't hold nutrients and moisture. It is full of minerals that work their way up from the bedrock below. (Credit earthworms with a big assist.) Soil, like any biological system, is complicated. On just one of my fields in Illinois, there are four different class I (the best for agriculture) soil types of the A and B hydrologic groups: Flanagan, Catlin, Wingate, and Elburn silt loams. The hydrologic groups separate soil types by how water tends to infiltrate. To maximize productivity, I use a different seeding rate, or number of seeds planted per acre, for each soil type.

The soil in those Mozambique basins was no Flanagan silt loam. But in comparison to the surrounding rock-hard dirt, its looser structure and higher organic content were a huge improvement. After digging the pits, these farmers put in manure mixed with earth and plant seeds on top of that. That attracts termites, which dig tunnels in the soil, transporting nutrients from deeper layers to the top and aerating the mixture. Because of the bowl design, the basins collect and concentrate water around the plant roots, and they also trap blowing sand and other plant debris. The farmers also collect banana peels, peanut shell mulch, and other organic matter to keep "feeding" the organisms that decompose the material and improve the texture of the soil. It's like a mini–compost heap, and the practice increases yields, particularly during periods when water is scarce. Finally, the farmers plant legumes or nitrogen-fixing trees between the basins. The approach is used widely in dry West African countries such as Mali and Burkina Faso, where farmers have refined the technique and started teaching it to others working in difficult soil conditions. It has been spreading east to countries such as Kenya as well.

Basins are not *the* answer to feeding Africa. They can be labor intensive and need tending. But they are a clever, practical approach that requires no expensive tools or inputs. Locals told me that in the test plots in Mozambique, maize yields had *tripled*. The concept is a way to focus smallholder farmers' attention (and that of donors and government officials as well!) on soil quality.

SOIL AS A TOOL

Soil is the most important tool we have to feed a fast-growing world in coming decades, and I am referring to all soils everywhere. To meet the demands of the world's population growing from seven billion to nine billion by 2050, all farmers, large and small, must maximize their productivity in a sustainable way. It's not optional. While I sometimes feel a little lonely as such an outspoken advocate about global soil issues, I am far from alone. Jeremy Grantham, cofounder and chief investment strategist of Grantham, Mayo, Van Otterloo & Co., manages one of the world's largest investment funds, with assets in excess of $100 billion. He has said that soil degradation is one of the greatest threats facing humanity today.[1] In 2008 the FAO reported that land degradation is increasing in severity and extent in many parts of the world, with more than 20 percent of all cultivated areas, 30 percent of forests, and 10 percent of grasslands undergoing degradation. Further, the FAO estimated that 1.5 billion people—today a fifth of the world's population—depend directly on land that is being degraded.[2]

The challenge is clear: we have to conserve and improve the soil we have, and we need to turn dirt into soil wherever people need to grow food. That's true in America's breadbasket, it's true in the tropics, and it's true in the dry, hardscrabble, weathered soils that cover much of sub-Saharan Africa.

In the larger context of battling hunger, valuing soil belongs in the "hard lessons learned" category. This is in part because the importance of taking care of the soil growing our food seems to be a lesson that human beings have to keep learning. I'm not sure why. What many people throughout history have assumed is our most abundant resource is actually a thin skin. It takes five hundred or more years for an inch of soil to form when bedrock crumbles and earthworms and microorganisms refine it into black loam and transport it to the surface.

And yet entire civilizations have died out or had to pick up and move because they destroyed or depleted their soils through overfarming, deforestation, and other practices that waste topsoil much faster than it forms. The Mayans, the Aztecs, the Vikings, and the Easter Islanders all devastated their agricultural productivity by failing to protect and nourish their soils. One of the earth's current flashpoints for what I call agronomic bankruptcy is Ethiopia. Like those in much of Africa, Ethiopia's soils are considered "old" and weathered, yet the population has tripled in the last fifty years. As a result, on top of an infertile base, farmers have deforested and overgrazed cropland, depleting productivity. Soil acidity, salinity, and drainage problems—as well as the inherently low availability of the essential plant nutrient phosphorus—mean that large areas of its soils are literally dead, devoid of biological activity. They have reverted to dirt. Tossing fertilizer on dead soils would be about as productive as putting an oxygen mask on a cadaver.

The United States is blessed with some of the richest farmland on Earth, but we too have abused it. In the 1930s on the Great Plains, US farmers ripped away drought-hardy prairie grasses to make way for their crops. When dry weather killed the crops, there was nothing to hold down the soil against the wind. US politicians began to wake up to the danger when dust storms deposited dirt from the Great Plains on roofs in Washington, DC.

One of the most disheartening sights I confront in winter as I drive around my fields in central Illinois are the small hills on some of my neighbors' farms that lie fallow during the cold months. Their level fields' topsoil is almost black and several feet deep. But these neighbors are old school. They still finish off a harvest season by disking and chisel plowing: turning over that year's upper layer of soil, burying that year's crop stubble. They think this aerates the soil, helps it hold moisture better, and brings nutrients to the surface. As you drive around, their fields look clean and neat: just acres of empty earth.

But those small hills tell a different story. Invariably, the color of the soil is lighter at the top of the hills than it is on the flat land below. That's because tilling land on a slope causes topsoil to wash downward as soon as the rains come. There is nothing to hold it in place. And plowed flat lands also lose soil to blowing winds or to runoff when the fields flood from rains or snowmelt. According to one study, one hundred years after Iowa was settled, half the state's topsoil was lost.[3]

In contrast, I practice what is called conservation farming. Next to plowed fields, mine are downright messy looking. I don't remove the stalks of corn or wheat stubble after I harvest. I even plant annual rye or radishes and other noncrop plant species in between the harvested rows of corn. All winter, as the rains come and the snow builds up, those so-called cover crops help me hang on to my topsoil. And in some cases, they help my soil retain, or "fix," nitrogen so that I can apply less fertilizer for the next crop I grow. In the spring, when it's time to plant, I put seeds directly into the soil, never disturbing the dirt other than a thin strip where the planter opens up a slot to drop in the seed.

No-till farming systems always maintain cover on the soil. By planting directly into the previous crop residue or cover crops, this process builds healthy soil, sequesters carbon, reduces soil erosion, and cuts the use of fossil fuels. *Photo: Howard W. Buffett*

This approach falls under the category of "no-till" farming techniques. It's about an entire system of farming that uses cover crops, minimal till techniques, better nutrient management, and crop rotations. This is not "organic" farming. I do use genetically modified seeds that resist pests and are able to tolerate herbicides such as Roundup, and I do use nitrogen-based fertilizer. While I am convinced that soil-focused techniques are essential to our future, I don't believe that organic methods can produce the yields our planet needs to feed us all. And so I have settled on an approach that I feel is practical but also sustainable. I'm sorry to say that the United States has been slower to adopt conservation farming than countries such as Argentina and Brazil, where yields are just as good using these more soil-protective techniques.

Argentina's and Brazil's tropical climates create a unique issue for their soils: the warm, moist climate means organic matter decomposes faster. When farmers in the tropics slash and burn rain forest to try to plant food crops, as they did for many years, they get a few years of production at best before they deplete the soil of nutrients. Once that happens and they move on, they leave an ugly scar of empty ground behind them—ground that once nourished plants that contributed to the planet in many other ways, from housing animal and plant species, to producing oxygen, to sequestering carbon. In recent years, these countries have adopted much better soil nourishment and management techniques, and their farmers have experienced significant productivity gains in the process.

Farmers in many parts of Africa also practice a form of slash and burn. They find space on their tribal land for growing crops by using a machete to clear away the bush so that sunlight can reach through to the ground. After the harvest is gathered, the leftover stalks and leaves are burned to clear the field for another planting season. After two or three years, the exposed soil is so exhausted that yields plummet. Traditionally, farmers would then move on to hack out another plot and leave the depleted ground alone for several years so that it could recuperate. One of the problems in a place such as Malawi is that the population density is so high and the land available for agriculture so limited that fields cannot be left fallow to rejuvenate.

Farmers in Africa clear land for agriculture by cutting and burning brush, wasting valuable material that could build soil health. *Photo: Howard G. Buffett*

EVEN A POOR FARMER CAN MAKE SOIL RICHER

The first time I really understood the impact of slash-and-burn fields in Africa was from a rickety airplane as I photographed zebras and wildebeest migrating across the plains of the Masai Mara National Reserve near Kenya's border with Tanzania. After the shoot, the pilot said he wanted to show me something. His plane circled higher and higher to gain enough altitude to get over a towering escarpment. On top of it sat a forest. The pilot pointed down to where farmers were burning down trees to make room to grow corn. Local people were encroaching on the forest because they needed fertile soil. Later I learned that the rate of deforestation is often highest in the world's hungriest countries, which continues today. Togo and Nigeria had the highest rates of deforestation out of sixty-five nations, according to a 2011 study of deforestation rates between 2005 and 2010. Togo lost an average of 5.75 percent of its forests annually, and Nigeria posted a 4 percent rate.[4]

Much of sub-Saharan Africa's struggles are due to its having the most weathered and degraded soils in the world. Africa is an ancient plateau and the continent is worn out geologically. And as we've discussed, much of Africa lies outside the fertility belt of climate and ideal soils hardwired to produce the cereal grains that feed the world. Only a small portion of Africa's soils are fertile to start with, but then slash-and-burn techniques degrade those even more.

At our foundation's Ukulima facility in the Limpopo region of South Africa, the best ground has just a few inches of topsoil, if that. We have a number of projects underway that focus on soils. But one of them, spearheaded by scientists from the Florida-based nonprofit Educational Concerns for Hunger Organization (ECHO), features a series of over five thousand *zai* basins. ECHO is trying to determine how to coax even more productivity out of this technique.

"This soil is like beach sand. The water just goes right through it," says ECHO scientist Brandon Lingbeek, toeing the dry ground.

He explains that he and his research partner have been planting legumes such as cowpeas, pigeon peas, and lablab in between the *zai* holes planted with sorghum, a grain grown widely throughout Africa, as it's more drought tolerant than corn. The technique is called intercropping, and they hope not only that it will add more nutrients and organic matter to the soil, but also that the legumes themselves can be consumed by both people and animals. "The baseline nutrients in this soil are next to none. Weeds produce biomass, but they don't improve the nutrients of the soil the way legumes do. It's sort of 'grow your own fertilizer,'" Brandon says, laughing. "We're trying to not only find cheap options for poor farmers, but options that are sustainable. What sets our research apart is it starts with what these farmers are already working with."

A fence that runs along the *zai* pit plots demonstrates another challenge to these difficult farming conditions. One section has been reinforced with steel rebar rods and big rocks piled up against the base. Local porcupines love the legumes and wage a relentless assault at night. At one point, the guys pitched a tent and set up floodlights to try to scare them off. "As fast as we fix it," explains ECHO's Chris D'Aiuto, "they tunnel through."

This work could have important consequences for farmers coping with depleted and damaged soil, particularly in semiarid and arid regions of Africa such as the Sahel, where desertification has become a major issue. The effects of increasing droughts and the removal of trees from the landscape are exposing the soil to erosion and to the harsh rays of the sun, which creates barren, encrusted soils. When it does rain on these soils, the water washes away instead of percolating down.

Also at Ukulima, we're supporting researchers from Pennsylvania State University who are looking at root architecture. Some plants have deep root systems that are good at finding water in the subsoil, making them more drought resistant. Others have shallow root systems that allow them to take up nutrients such as phosphorous and nitrogen more efficiently in the topsoil. The Penn State team is trying to breed varieties of corn and other crops that combine these architectures to give smallholder farmers seeds that can improve their yields in the stressed conditions they face, where both water and fertility are low.

We need to focus on Africa's poor soils to get at the root of Africa's agricultural challenges. Soil is something that the poorest farmer in Africa can make richer, as these conservation techniques show. And if Africa's leaders need to be convinced that a Brown Revolution can lift up a country, they can find an excellent example in Brazil, as you'll discover in part 5.

Story 21½
Owners Make Better Farmers

On a recent visit to California's San Joaquin Valley, I had dinner with an innovative farmer who owns a significant operation there. He uses drip irrigation extensively, has progressive labor policies, and contributes a large amount of fresh food to a local food bank. We were having a great conversation trading stories about technology and other ideas, but then he said something that surprised me about farming in the Midwest.

"Around here, we're used to sharing information on what works, how to do it better. But we own our own land. I was talking to a friend who farms in the Midwest, and he was saying how contract farmers there are becoming so competitive, they are secretive. They are trying to show better yields than their neighbors so they can get the lease rights from the farm management companies."

Contract farmers? That's not a term you often hear in my part of the country. I have many friends who farm land that is a combination of land they own and land they rent, and it would never occur to me to call them "contract farmers." But the more I thought about it, I had to admit that my California friend was onto something. As farm consolidation has accelerated in farms across the Midwest, more and more farmland is leased to farmers from absentee owners, including large farm management companies. The leases may be for only a few years; then they are put up to competitive bids, and so there is a more aggressive, short-term focus as a result.

Farm operations have grown in size because more land is rented to fewer operators. The challenge of this changing dynamic is keeping resource management a priority for farmers who mine the soil to make a profit. *Photo: Howard G. Buffett*

The idea of secretive, competitive farmers bothers me. It goes against everything I like about farming, and it goes against the reason a bulldozer-driving kid like me who didn't know a disk from a disco was able to learn the business from some generous guys. But, I had to admit, not only is this trend changing the social dynamics somewhat; it has serious consequences for the soil. To win contracts to secure the land they want to farm, farmers need to prove only their ability to maximize short-term production. They don't need to demonstrate an intention to take care of the soil. Your attitude toward the long-term health of the soil is influenced by whether or not you own your land.

One irony of this conversation is that for years I have been talking about the importance of farmers owning their own land in the developing world. Talk about easier said than done. Land is a legal construction, and the right to control a particular section of the Earth has been the cause of wars, jealousy, and bitter wrangling since humans stopped hunting and gathering and put down roots. But everywhere in the world, farmers who own their own land take better care of the soil than those who do not. In any place where we are asked to invest resources these days, one of the first questions we ask is, "What is the land tenure situation? Are farmers connected to and incented to work and improve their land, or do they feel vulnerable and subject to being booted off their land?" One of Ethiopia's challenges, for example, is that the government owns all the land.

I wrote earlier about the frustration of Angola's farmers with the uncertain and uneven treatment of land titling in their country, but that country is not unusual. This comes up over and over all across Africa and Central America. You can make the case that the development of America's incredibly productive agricultural system came about in part because of our rules of private landownership. It began early in our country's history. Farmers here could always see a clear, long-term benefit for themselves and their offspring from taking care of their land and investing in and supporting the agricultural infrastructure of their communities: roads, electricity, storage capacity, equipment.

We have tried to support a variety of land tenure programs around the world, with the most successful efforts so far in Nicaragua. That's a satisfying example of progress we'll talk about in part 5. The land tenure situation in most African countries is less than ideal, and tribal customs and practices, which can hold even more sway in land management than national laws do, complicate matters.

One major challenge with land reform is that unwinding traditional practices or customs—or trying to return land to those who have been dispossessed of it by internal or external conflict—is not only difficult but also dangerous at times. Territorial disputes have led to violence and wars throughout history. And reform is complicated. Mexico has been struggling with land reform issues since the Mexican Revolution of the early twentieth century; for example, there are legal avenues for communal land parcels for agriculture to be distributed to individual farmers so they can hold title, buy or sell land, and use it as collateral for credit. Yet what should be a useful tool has hit barriers within the communities themselves. It can be difficult to figure out how to divide lands of uneven quality into individual parcels. But if individuals don't hold title, they don't have collateral for loans that could help them invest in equipment and inputs to help them farm more productively. Instead, the community rents out the land. But here we go again: farmers who rent land don't make long-term investments in soil.

A growing issue in Africa is that governments are auctioning off rights to foreign interests to farm large tracts of what good agricultural land there is, often through ninety-nine-year leases. It is so troubling to me to see land in Ethiopia, Sierra Leone, and Liberia being promoted as a prime investment opportunity for hedge funds and investors, when I have been to those countries and seen their desperate poverty and hunger. Millions of people there remain dependent on food aid, yet their governments are offering cheap deals to foreign investors and countries to farm that land and ship the food back to their home countries or sell it on the global market. The local people rarely benefit. In fact, the local people can be hurt by market distortions created by these deals. The investors try to suggest that the jobs created by developing the land will lift the entire economy. I am among those skeptics who point out that these outside developers tell governments they will employ thousands of people, but the prospectuses brag to investors that they intend to bring in high-tech farming that is much *less* labor dependent than other methods. Which is it?

Proponents of these land deals, investors and government officials alike, sometimes suggest that they are mainly leasing off "unused" land. Give me a break: investors buy or invest in the best assets, not the worst. Africa has been a net importer of agricultural products for decades.[1] I feel these countries should focus on helping their own people become better, more productive farmers. They should use that land themselves and increase yields in a sustainable way to feed their own people. What's more, in some cases, the land grabs are aimed at land currently used by pastoralists who raise cattle or other livestock and who need the corridors to remain open and producing natural grasses.

Anyone who believes that savvy investors are going to accept the worst land and stand behind others in line for critical water resources is naïve or delusional. When you have starving people, there is no "good" land that goes unused. Government leaders must come to value connecting their own country's agriculture to their own farmers' ownership of their own land. These decisions will shape the future of hunger in these countries.

There is a creative young Midwest farmer HWB will tell you about later who has an angle on trying to inspire more sustainable farming practices, even among farmers who rent or lease their land. But it's a little ironic that going to California reminded me not to ignore a trend happening in my own part of the country. Wherever they live and no matter how big or small they are, farmers take better care of land if they own it.

Story 22
Disconnects

When our foundation was focused on habitat and species preservation in the late 1990s, I had the idea to build a facility in South Africa to create a protected habitat for research on cheetahs. The long-legged, spotted cats have always fascinated me. *Acinonyx jubatus* is the Latin name for the African cheetah, the fastest land animal on earth. Cheetahs can go from zero to over sixty miles per hour in three seconds and can top seventy-five miles per hour in short bursts. They are considered a vulnerable species by the International Union for Conservation of Nature (IUCN), in part because in the wild, adult cheetahs are fast but not well equipped to fight off attacks from lions and hyenas, so their cubs are vulnerable. Poachers prey on cheetahs, and some ranchers will shoot cheetahs on sight. Meanwhile, the animals are difficult to breed in captivity. We wanted to better understand them in hopes of prolonging their survival.

We purchased fourteen pieces of property and assembled them into the Jubatus reserve, partnering with one of South Africa's most eminent cheetah experts, Ann van Dyk. We hired all local staff. And from almost the moment we arrived, and right up to our decision to sell the facility a decade later, it was the most intense crash course in cultural disconnects I have ever experienced. The lessons were invaluable. But I grew to hate the taste of humble pie.

Our early investments in cheetah conservation led me to understanding important cultural issues for our later investments. *Photo: Howard G. Buffett*

The culture shock began early in our work there. While we were negotiating to buy Jubatus, we realized that four families had been living on the land. They were essentially squatters. Under South African law, they could live there, but they had no rights to the land. Since our cheetahs were going to be free-ranging, even if we put a fence around their existing homes, we were concerned that having people that close to the animals could be dangerous. We wanted to be generous, so we asked our attorney to go through all the official channels to find these families new land parcels equal to or better than what they had. We took on the cost of moving them and compensating them for the disruption. We worked with both the government and the tribal chief. The families were willing—in fact, happy—to move.

Going the formal route took two years, and I was excited to attend a meeting where we planned to sign off on the deal. A staff member of our attorney's team, who spoke the language, was there to help us. Normally, he was very even-tempered, but he suddenly got a very angry look on his face. I started to ask what was going on, and he barked, "Not now, Howard!"

He got up and motioned for me to join him in leaving. As soon as we were beyond hearing range, he apologized for snapping but said he had wanted the group to realize that it had pushed us too far. Despite all the approvals and the considerable money we'd spent already, a local witch doctor had suddenly taken an interest in the move. He told the families they must not move. Our negotiator said he was sure this could be overcome with a few more months and more money—and that was exactly what happened. The insurmountable obstacles went away after the witch doctor got his cut.

The unpredictable intentions and involvement of figures such as witch doctors across Africa is a reality that even Africans call "TIA": "This is Africa." It is a common expression on the continent, often accompanied by a shrug or a wink. But there are many other variations of TIA that undermine development efforts by outside organizations. Finger-pointing is not my intention here; rather, my point is that parachuting into any foreign situation with the confidence that your way is the right way, or that your worldview is ideal, is doomed to fail. People in Africa (and everywhere else for that matter) have survived all manner of difficult situations for a long time, and many of their customs, habits, and outlooks are hardwired. I want to try to convey just how pervasive, as well as subtle, some of the TIAs can be.

The involvement of spirits, sorcery, and superstition in decisions about land or the timing of activities is not uncommon at all in Africa, and witch doctors can exert tremendous power to banish individuals or shape a tribal chief's decisions. A less obvious form of TIA can involve local people's sense of time and planning. At Jubatus, we had constant setbacks created by not planning ahead. Projects either took much longer to complete than they should have taken, or they just fell apart because different elements were executed out of order. I would upgrade or construct certain physical facilities, with the assumption that the research staff would be prepared to start using them immediately— and then I would learn they were not prepared. Despite having agreed on a plan, they would later admit they didn't think it would actually happen, so they waited before doing their part. We were trying to set up a research facility, which involved taking measurements and keeping track of different variables, such as changes in the animals' diets or movements. Often workers would not adjust the animals' diets at the right time or on the right day, or would be inconsistent in how they applied instruction. For a long time, I just could not understand this.

Witch doctors, like this one I photographed in Mozambique, can have a lot of influence over local decision making. *Photo: Howard G. Buffett*

One day I was driving down a local road called the Diepdrift. It's a decent road, and thanks to some private fenced game preserves, you can spot giraffe heads poking up among the acacia treetops or encounter a warthog family shooting across with their funny squat bodies and tails twitching. (African warthogs have never met a fence they can't dig under or bust through.) One day I saw that a Jubatus employee had a flat tire. I stopped to help and realized he did not have a spare. Now, this man was a hard worker and very competent. I told him I would drive him to the nearest store so he could buy a patch to fix the tire. He agreed. We got to the store about six miles up the road. He went in and found a patch kit. He then came out and asked if I could drive him back to his car so he could get his wallet and *then* come back to pay for the patch. I asked, mystified, "Why didn't you bring your wallet?" He replied, "I didn't need it when we left. Now I need it."

I think it is almost unthinkable to Americans not to plan ahead, or organize our days around some kind of schedule, or approach the future as a series of activities that flow logically from one to the next. Sometimes that is not the case in other cultures. In regions where development efforts are under way, many local people spend very little time coordinating their activities or complying with a shared schedule. I saw a hint of this disconnect in the 2006 documentary film *God Grew Tired of Us*, about the "Lost Boys of Sudan." During the Sudanese civil war from 1983 to 2005, an estimated twenty thousand Sudanese boys were orphaned or separated from their families by the conflict. They banded together in huge groups and walked hundreds of miles for years, looking for refuge in camps in Ethiopia and Kenya. Many died, and some are still in camps, but eventually more than three thousand of them were relocated to the United States.

In one scene in the film, a man charged with helping three young Sudanese men settle into an apartment in Pittsburgh shows them a clock radio and how it works. It is obvious that they are not familiar with clocks or the importance of being somewhere at a specific time. And why would they be? They had lived in a camp for displaced persons for years and lived meal to meal and moment to moment for much of their lives. "They have a saying in America that time is money," the man explains to the boys, who seem confused.

Our assumptions are often not valid in other parts of the world. In South Africa, where kids get a ride to school or employees come to work by donkey, people have a different perspective of time. *Photo: Howard G. Buffett*

"CREATING TIME"

A South African woman who has worked for me at our Ukulima farm for years has tried to explain to me the traditional view of time in Africa. "Africans don't see themselves as part of a larger flow of time," she said. "They see themselves almost creating time when they go off alone. They are very focused on the present moment; the future is very abstract. This is hard to understand for people who are not from Africa." That was true for me. I would get so frustrated when a project would stall or be undermined because employees did not anticipate or plan for the next job or activity. To them, "now" could be next week.

Over time I learned that in South Africa when you want something done right away, the correct term is "now-now!" You have to work with local managers who understand some of these possible disconnects, and they communicate the tasks to the workers in a style that uses a local sense of time and connections. Sometimes it is as easy as just finding a particular word in their language or a social convention that carries a nuance we lack. This is true in situations other than time and planning, such as in paying workers: we found that it caused serious upheaval to try to create incentive pay for the best work. Two workers with the same title had to be paid the same, or one would revolt. We finally learned that the answer was to give the higher performer a different job title, and the problem would go away.

We learned the hard way that we had to ask local people to help us set up management structures, but even more than that, we had to learn not to assume that our own lifestyle preferences applied to employees. We had some employees living at Jubatus, and we decided to build them a new house. Again, we wanted them to be comfortable. We purchased appliances for the home and figured that would make them happy. Not long after it was finished, and they moved in, I was driving by and noticed the brand-new stove sitting in the front yard. I figured it must have broken, so I stopped to see what had happened. I learned that the family had removed the stove and then created a fire pit in the middle of the kitchen floor. Nobody ever asked them if they wanted a stove. The women had always cooked in an open fire pit. They had no use for the stove.

My final TIA story took place on the Koevoet Road that runs along one side of our former Jubatus property, perpendicular to Diepdrift Road. A group of people referred to as the Koevoets were living across the road from us. Neighbors in the region told me that many of the men in this community were mercenaries in Angola and had also worked for the South African police as crowd controllers during apartheid. The South African government had established the settlement, but at the time we were there, the Koevoets were not popular with the locals.

The section of our fence that faced the Koevoet "camp," as many called it, was in an area with a lot of trees. The fence was high because it enclosed the preserve. We needed to keep people out, and cheetahs and other game in. Cheetahs are not great tree climbers because their claws are built for traction to give them speed on the ground. However, it is not good to have trees bridging both sides of the fence, as cheetahs will sometimes jump up onto low branches and could conceivably escape—or foolish people could easily climb in and be injured or killed. We also wanted some distance cleared for a firebreak, as lightning fires are common in the grasslands of southern Africa called the *veldt*.

Therefore, we began removing trees along the fence line following the road. We were paying attention to the spacing of the trees because we wanted to keep an enclosed feel to the fenced-in areas. We ended up removing dozens of trees, and so I had our property manager offer the cut-up wood from the trees to the Koevoet people, to use for cooking and heating. I thought it would help them, and we did not have a use for the wood. I felt it would demonstrate our intentions as a good neighbor.

The Koevoets, happy to receive the wood, carted it off and burned it. A few months later several men from the group approached our property manager and said they wanted more wood. Sorry, he told them, we've cut down all the trees we planned to. We need to keep the rest for the animal habitat. "But you have so many trees inside," the man from the delegation responded. "You have plenty of trees." We need them to stay up, our guy responded. We aren't going to give you any more wood right now.

Not long after, our property manager drove out to the road and found stumps all along the outside of the fence. The Koevoet men had gone away from the conversation peacefully enough— not happily but without obvious rancor. And then they just cut down the trees that they wanted on the outside of the fence. Our manager approached the representative and complained. "But you have plenty of trees inside the fence" was his answer. "You gave us trees before."

TIA. In many parts of Africa, the act of giving opens the door to expectations. If we had not offered the initial load of wood, the group probably would not have cut any trees. But once we did, an informal new relationship began, and the Koevoet members believed they had been given the sign that we wanted to continuously support them.

What I did not mention earlier about the man I had helped with the flat tire is that out of frustration and a lack of time, I did not drive him back to his car to retrieve his wallet. Instead, I gave him a few dollars in local currency to purchase the repair kit. When I told our work foreman about that, he frowned and said I'd made a mistake. A month later the water pump in that worker's car went out, and he asked me to replace it. He could not understand why I would help him with his tire but not continue to support his car's maintenance.

This attitude is sometimes mistakenly interpreted as people preferring handouts to working. I do not believe that. Once bags of food aid or other forms of assistance arrive, many African people in difficult situations adjust their views and believe it is the new way they will eat. It is a cultural response to new resources coming into their territory: "If you start feeding me, I will let you keep feeding me; and if you stop feeding me, I will demand to know why." If one NGO is giving out food and seed, and another is saying, "We will train you to farm in a way that will deliver higher yields next year," these farmers are likely to embrace the immediate resources. That's understandable.

In fact, the whole idea of charity and giving is not seen in many parts of the world the way that it is in the United States. Throughout our early years at Jubatus, I sensed a deep mistrust from many different people—including neighbors; professional, highly trained researchers; and local officials—regarding the idea that I was coming to Africa just to help cheetahs. This was its own form of TIA, in the sense that Africa has been exploited by foreigners for a very long time, and local people are wary of outsiders arriving with the stated reason of helping or contributing. In the United States, our tax code has so institutionalized the idea of giving that we generally treat it as common and desirable. In South Africa, for years we had trouble getting permits from local officials; we even sensed a lack of trust among our research staff regarding our intentions.

These experiences have convinced me that to create sustainable solutions, we need to get local people on board much earlier in any process that involves new ways of operating. We recently ended a project with an NGO that was teaching sustainable farming techniques in an area of Liberia where a previous organization had distributed seed and fertilizer. The point of the program we were supporting was to teach farmers to develop their soil with animal manures and other techniques that did not involve giving away anything. The farmers came at first, but over time they drifted away.

The problem was, the previous NGO group had set the expectation that foreign assistance consisted of dropping off bags of seed or fertilizer. Our partners did not take that into account in planning their program. Nor did they realize that the other organization had sort of poisoned the well in terms of a training package without aid attached. And so the money we spent did not change anything. In two years, nobody will remember that we were ever there. These discussions can make NGOs and others working in development nervous. But I am convinced that all the energy and good intentions in the world cannot trump cultural disconnects. To be effective, we have to ask questions of and listen to the people affected by what we want to do. Then we must engage them early in our planning and keep adjusting our approaches.

What Does Doing Better Look Like?

By Howard W. Buffett

My father had his epiphany about life's forty chances in a cold, drafty building filled with farm equipment at Sloan's in central Illinois. Mine came on a steaming hot morning while I was touring a small village in Thailand about fifteen months after the devastating 2004 tsunami that killed over two hundred thousand people.

I was twenty-two. I had finished my undergraduate work in political science and communications at Northwestern University, and I was pretty sure I wanted to go to law school. I also had traveled with my father in the developing world, and I wanted to focus my career on helping others. We had many conversations about development and aid projects that just did not seem to deliver on their promise. When I was in college, my father encouraged me to study the actual practices and structures of philanthropy and how it could be more effective, so I signed up for a yearlong program called the Philanthropy Workshop West, which taught the best practices of social change to individuals taking on new roles in philanthropy. For a dozen of us, the program included a trip to Thailand, where we focused on various environmental and humanitarian efforts.

The Indian Ocean tsunami (or Boxing Day tsunami, as many called it) followed a major earthquake in the Indian Ocean on December 26, 2004. It was one of the first major natural disasters to happen during the internet age. Because of the growing use of digital cameras and media sharing, people all over the world almost immediately witnessed the event secondhand through chilling photos and riveting amateur video. Thailand was a favorite winter vacation destination during the holidays, and many tourists were shooting footage from the balconies of beautiful resorts or other elevated spots that morning. They would be chattering about the weather or talking to their children about new Christmas toys while panning the pool area or the beach as unsuspecting tourists strolled or children played in shallow water. In so many videos, the first crush of high water hits the beach, followed by the massive wave that blasts through a scene that was orderly and calm just minutes prior. The water swallows people, screams erupt, and structures shatter into fragments of metal and wood. It happens so fast that many of those shooting video clearly are not even processing what is happening in their viewfinders.

Much of the actual cleanup of the 2004 tsunami had been completed by the time I arrived in Thailand. I spent most of the program's sessions in Phuket, where some dramatic wave footage had been shot, although the actual damage and loss of life there were nowhere near as severe as in many other regions. For example, in the province of Aceh, Sumatra, 170,000 people perished. In villages near Aceh, the tsunami had destroyed as much as four-fifths of some towns. The death toll across fourteen countries, including Thailand, India, and parts of East Africa reached 230,000.[1]

On my visit, I learned that countries committed billions of dollars to help the Thai people rebuild, and NGOs rushed in to help. In the immediate aftermath, tent cities sprang up, since thousands of homes had been leveled and their owners' possessions washed away or destroyed. There were fears of contamination from the dead bodies and difficult sanitary conditions, although thankfully widespread disease largely did not materialize. Huge shipments of food aid were sent to the region through disaster relief efforts that fed over a million people in Thailand alone.

The program in which I'd enrolled was trying to understand the lessons of the last fifteen months. We took a number of field visits to villages that had been rebuilt by NGOs. People were working diligently; the landscape was humming with activity. There I saw hardworking, sincere, devoted relief workers and NGO staffers still on the job. Their stated goal was a good one: to help the nation rebuild, and to protect the health and well-being of those who had survived that terrible disaster. There were some touching stories, and I heard about people who had showed great bravery during the crisis. I met a young woman from the United States who had been visiting Thailand with her fiancé over Christmas 2004. They were asleep in their hut when the waters hit. He was swept out to sea, and she never saw him again. She decided to stay in Thailand to help with the reconstruction; when I met her, she was serving as a counselor to those who lost loved ones, and I remain in awe of her courage and compassion.

And yet I also had some disheartening conversations with local experts about the use of the resources that came pouring into Thailand. To me, the most troubling signs, literally, were the actual signs erected all over the villages we visited that promoted the involvement of different NGOs. In some towns, there were twenty-five or thirty homes, each one bearing a large, billboard-style sign or shiny plaque promoting the NGO that had helped reconstruct that village. There were more signs on the road on the way in and in public areas. I couldn't help but think, "Really? They have so thoroughly restored this community that there are resources left over to *advertise* that? Couldn't the money and the effort to erect signs have funded more resources for a clinic, or vaccines, or some agricultural assistance that ensured enough food for those who had been wiped out?"

In Thailand, hundreds of signs like this advertising the sponsoring NGO went up even before construction of much-needed housing was complete. My aim isn't to point fingers at any one organization, so I have obscured the name on the sign in this instance. *Photo: Howard W. Buffett*

WINTER GARMENTS IN THE TROPICS?

I also learned during our conversations with NGO experts, academics, and other local leaders that there was extensive wasted effort and disorganization in the early phases of the crisis—mostly the result of poor coordination. Containers of donated clothing had been shipped to Aceh, but it was heavy winter clothing. Thailand's average daily temperature during its coolest season is 75 degrees. Other inappropriate or even damaged material was shipped to Thailand in the guise of aid as well. Earl Kessler, deputy executive director of the Asian Disaster Preparedness Center in Bangkok, stated in a report, "Response to this disaster was unprecedented. It has proven to be a blessing and a curse. It should never happen again that used winter garments, outdated medicines, and broken toys and other debris from donor countries be distributed to affected families as part of a 'job well done.'"[2]

One aggressive NGO came in, brought their plans from some other part of the world, and quickly began constructing two-story homes. The problem was: Thai people in the particular villages we visited don't live in two-story homes. They were uncomfortable with the idea of moving upstairs. So they would rarely use the second stories—wasting 50 percent of the materials, labor, and living space in the house. Foreign workers and project managers also installed toilets inside some homes, expensive add-ons that would never be used because by custom these villagers never placed those facilities so close to their living quarters. In many phases of the tsunami response there was a dramatic disconnect between what the local people were used to or desired, and what NGOs (or in some cases, government officials) from outside the region had imposed. Consultation was minimal—or nonexistent. Imagine if in an American city devastated by a hurricane, a foreign aid organization came in and rebuilt an entire community using 220 volt wiring instead of the standard 120 volt?

In a 2005 research paper from the Human Rights Center at the University of California, Berkeley, the lack of local community participation was seen as a key theme across the entire region. "Across all areas studied," said the paper, "survivors complained that decisions about relief, resettlement, and reconstruction aid were largely taking place without consultation with their communities, leading to frustration and despair."[3] Preexisting human rights problems, corruption, inequities in aid distribution, lack of coordination, and land development issues were among the other themes.

The agendas of aid organizations also explained some of the bizarre advertising I saw in the Thai villages. Clearly, the publicity about the tsunami and the global response meant that NGOs were trying to both raise money based on the publicity about the situation and also show their donors a quick response and tangible contribution. However, one of the local disaster coordinators shared with us that in a couple of villages, local officials realized that some NGOs had more resources than they could deploy but were under pressure to demonstrate prompt action. So the villages conducted unspoken "auctions" of sorts, requiring cash under the table for the exclusive right to work in a particular village. Yes, that's right: NGOs were bidding cash against one another for *permission* to be charitable.

In turn, NGOs would bring major donors to these villages to talk with local leaders, who would reinforce the "tremendous impact" their donations were having on the victims' lives. The donors felt good. The NGOs looked good. But the villagers? Well, I'm not sure exactly what the reality was beyond the "arrangement," but while NGOs were competing to work in some areas, other victims received little or no assistance because they were out of the way or their village was not as politically visible or well connected. Eventually an NGO called Disaster Tracking Recovery Assistance Center (D-TRAC) was established specifically for the purpose of coordinating the activities of other NGOs, to try to spread the resources more equitably and more efficiently.

As the Human Rights Center report noted, "While [NGOs] indicate that their primary responsibility is to those in need, in reality they answer to central officers far away who define the objectives and strategy." Here's a good example: a prominent NGO had promised to build homes, but a restriction in the organization's worldwide operating procedures specified that it had to use specially certified wood—which could not be obtained in Thailand, particularly after the tsunami. Apparently, although other wood was available, the NGO focused on importing only this special wood. When the plan to do that became cost prohibitive, it announced that it could not build the structures after all.

There were so many examples of interventions and intentions that seemed to miss the mark. In a journal I kept during the trip, I wrote, "I find it hard to understand how—if you're building a set of homes for a community that just lost everything—you don't get their approval for what you're building before you build it." It reminded me of a term I had heard my Uncle Peter use: "philanthropic colonialism."

After that visit, I was preoccupied with my frustration. I know that disaster response is by definition a reactive exercise. The benefits of sending in a variety of resources that you think you may need and that you can assemble quickly outweigh the risk of some waste or inefficient deployment. After a catastrophe, there is chaos and confusion, as communication structures and plans are formed. But this situation seemed to have gotten out of hand and stayed that way. People all over the world responded generously after the disaster, but then some organizations exploited that generosity by wasting resources. According to representatives from D-TRAC and other local groups, the corruption, inefficiencies, and posturing were still widespread even fifteen months later.

Thailand raised some other issues about the traditional NGO model for me as well. My father and I had talked many times in different settings about the inevitable challenge of large NGOs that hit a certain scale. Having to fundraise means that the organization must show tangible progress even when working in complicated, difficult situations where improvements may not occur for some time. Thus, the tendency is to pick activities that are doable but will likely have less long-term impact, rather than evaluate what is needed so that there is something to show for the efforts. Showcasing one town that received world-class support, while other communities got little or no help, seemed to be a clear example of that.

The more serious concern is that over time this approach tends to institutionalize narrow thinking. I focused on this thought: doing good does not excuse us from *doing better*.

I can only hope that bidding cash for the right to provide charitable aid and then advertising that fact to foreign donors is as unusual as it is shameful. I suspect it occurs mostly in the kind of media fishbowl that develops following some high-profile, heavily covered disaster. However, trampling on local customs and norms because of ignorance or a lack of planning is not uncommon in aid projects around the world. In northern Kenya during a drought in 2000, food agencies ignored the fact that pastoralists' diets consisted of meat, milk, and tea, and sent food aid in the form of maize. The result? The food was not eaten, and the immediate need remained unmet. In Mali, a friend of ours told us about one NGO that shipped in large numbers of sewing machines to try to help women who had been forced to prostitute themselves to survive. The NGO's intentions were good. Unfortunately, Mali is located in the middle of a desert where fine sand is absolutely everywhere, and it quickly jammed up the mechanisms. Not only did the machines stop working but the women also became terrified that they would be blamed for breaking them.

In the years since my experience in Thailand, I have become far more preoccupied with the second element of my reaction to the postdisaster response. I had seen what disorganization and lack of a culturally appropriate plan looked like. That single experience affected my way of approaching any project, place, or partner in the future, and forced me to ask the following: What would *doing better* look like?

HOW DO WE STRENGTHEN THE ACTUAL DESIGN OF PROJECTS?

Philanthropists, NGOs, and government agencies tasked with helping those living in conditions of hunger and extreme poverty have made great strides in identifying global needs. However, every approach requires refreshing over time. One area of practice due for a makeover is the structure and framework of the relationships among NGOs, donors, and the communities they serve. Keeping the donations flowing to large NGOs with significant overhead to support makes it necessary to convince donors that their money is being put to good use. That goal has a tendency to result in narrow-focused, quick-turnaround projects that have highly visible results: such as digging a well, for example, or delivering agricultural inputs including seed and fertilizer to help local farmers increase yields. There is nothing wrong with these projects' goals, but both my father and I have come to believe that there often *is* something wrong with the process used to design them and the lack of sustainable impact.

This issue goes well beyond the emergency aid world. It is even more frustrating to see these design flaws in projects intended to address chronic hunger or limited access to clean water, or where NGOs have plenty of time to plan and the experience to get things right. Many aid development projects break too easily. They may be dependent on technology that has to be taught, or products and services delivered over uncertain roads or through territory plagued by thieves and guerrillas. They may require training and the expertise of team leaders, but when the people who brought the project to the region leave, it becomes unclear who will carry on the efforts. Later we will highlight some initiatives that take a more sustainable, market-oriented approach, but it's fair to say that short-term, project-oriented interventions are still the norm. The failing norm.

Rather than just throw stones—because development is hard work, and I know these are difficult problems to solve—let me say that I'm truly hopeful about some of the new models that are being developed, including some supported by our foundation. All of us involved, in whatever capacity we have to take on poverty and hunger, need to rethink old structures and abandon those that no longer work. And we must do a better job of investing in the social value of communities and their committed leaders so that we can produce comprehensive results for the people we're trying to help. Even if we are doing good where we can, I'm also convinced that each of us must do better. Otherwise when the aid stops, everything will go back to the way it was before, like the tides taking back an abandoned sand castle.

Story 24
"Who Came Up with This Crazy Idea?"

In December 2005 a 7.6-magnitude earthquake killed at least seventy-five thousand people in Pakistan and injured twice that many, according to the World Health Organization. It also left at least two and a half million people, many in remote mountain villages, homeless just as the brutal Himalayan winter was approaching.

A few weeks later, I went to Pakistan to see if our foundation could be of assistance, and, at the suggestion of Allen Greenberg, who runs my late mother's foundation, I made sure to visit a WFP operation at a Pakistan military base in Abbottabad.

When I arrived, workers were shuttling thousands of bags of food nonstop—primarily basic staples such as flour, cooking oil, and peas—from trucks to storage facilities and onto helicopters. The region is so mountainous and the population so spread out that helicopters were the only realistic option to get the supplies to people who needed them. Yet that option came with some risk. The weather was freezing cold, windy, and foggy. I saw WFP personnel loading up Russian-manufactured Mi-8 helicopters, and I managed to get permission to go on several of the delivery missions.

When I saw how precisely the World Food Programme executed this complex food aid drop in Pakistan, it helped refine my thinking about the proper use of food aid and led to one of our foundation's most significant partnerships. *Photo: Howard G. Buffett*

The situation for survivors was dire, and the landscape was alternately beautiful and bleak. We flew over craggy mountains with evergreen forests dusted in snow, but also over villages that had been crumpled, even flattened, by the quake. We could see tent camps made of hastily arranged tarps flapping in the strong winds; they seemed barely adequate to protect supplies, much less people. Settlements in this region are so isolated, with few roads, and between the quake and the wet weather, mud slides had left many existing roads impassable.

We flew an hour to Chattar Plain (elevation, five thousand feet), where we picked up more bags of flour and some other supplies. Chattar Plain was a staging area for the next leg up into the truly thin air. The helicopters had to be loaded carefully—not exceeding weight limits, as the high elevation depleted fuel much faster. As we traveled to Kandol (elevation, seven thousand feet), we were well bundled in parkas and gloves. When we landed, it was painful to see people waiting for deliveries dressed in the traditional thin-fabric *shalwar kameez*—long tunics and baggy trousers—they wear year-round, with just an extra sweater or two and a scarf or a blanket around their shoulders. Some children were waiting by the makeshift landing pad. Many had no gloves. One girl appeared to have little more than striped socks around her lower legs despite the freezing cold. Another group of men had hiked down the snow powder of a nearby hill to collect supplies. We saw the deep trough created by a trek that we knew would be even more difficult for the men going back, carrying heavy bags of flour and other vital supplies.

As we came in tight between the mountains at eight thousand feet, through the window I could see men wrapped in loose clothing waiting to help unload lifesaving food. *Photo: Howard G. Buffett*

However, the WFP operation was as precise as a finely crafted watch. The plan was ten relief flights per day per helicopter, for a total of forty-five tons of food assistance. We had to be in and out quickly. We could not waste time on the ground, and the personnel on board were poised and ready to hand off the supplies to the locals the minute we touched down. The coordination was extensive, and from what I observed firsthand, it was lifesaving for thousands of people who easily could have starved or died of exposure in these remote, snowy mountains.

Food aid is vital in emergency situations. But making sure that food aid is available on an emergency basis is a more complicated challenge than many people realize. It takes preparation, storage, and a transportation plan that can be activated in short order. To be prepared to offer food aid quickly, US farmers need policies and incentives to support production at full levels. With close to a billion food-insecure people in the world, there are plenty of emergency food aid situations where that capacity will be needed, but we can't wait for an emergency to reauthorize an investment. Emergencies happen when they happen.

My former boss at Archer Daniels Midland, Dwayne Andreas, was a friend and supporter of Senator Hubert Humphrey of Minnesota when he fought for a permanent food aid program that became the Public Law 480 Food for Peace program, initially signed into law in 1954. Officially the Agricultural Trade Development Assistance Act, managed by the USDA and USAID, the program was to use American grain surpluses to fight world hunger and help our farmers find markets for their crops—and support our shipping industry as well, as Congress eventually called for at least 75 percent of the aid to be transported on US-flagged vessels. The PL 480s were designed as a win-win-win for American farmers, shippers, and the world's hungry. And as the name suggests, "food for peace" food aid can perform an important diplomatic function, too.

But in August 2006, just a few months after I was so impressed with WFP's emergency food aid operation in Pakistan, I went to Mozambique to review several agricultural projects that had a conservation-agriculture component and also some water initiatives.

I was in Nampula City in the offices of CARE. I asked if I could borrow the fax machine to trade some documents back and forth with my team in Decatur. I was standing at the fax when I overheard two CARE officials talking about completing a commodity trade in the local market. This struck me as completely bizarre. What was CARE doing trading commodities?

The local administrator explained to me, somewhat sheepishly, that they were planning to take food aid sent from the United States and "monetize" it: in other words, take the in-kind aid of grain, sell it locally, and then use the proceeds to help fund other development programs.

I knew that Mozambican farmers grew corn and sold into the same market. My first thought was "Who came up with this crazy idea?" Selling imported commodities turned NGOs into quasi grain traders. It would add supply to the local market that was bound to undermine prices for local farmers. I could imagine how US farmers would feel if an American charity talked Brazil into sending it container ships of surplus soybeans for the charity to sell on US grain markets—raising money to do good works but also creating a surplus and lowering prices. More specifically to the developing world, this market distortion would devastate local prices while also having an unintended consequence of discouraging farmers from growing that crop in the future. What was the point of wrecking the price that poor local farmers could get for crops, making them more food insecure, and then turning around to use the cash from that to provide farm training services to the same people or overhead for an NGO? It was worse than just being wasteful; it was wrongheaded and even harmful. If the idea of aid is to get people back on their feet so they can better help themselves, why would we possibly weaken the local market?

This conversation was my introduction to the concept of monetization. I had no idea that it began in the 1980s, when the US government was struggling to get rid of a large surplus of subsidized grain. In the 1990s, cuts at USAID meant that NGOs had to find a way to offset direct cuts in cash funding they had been receiving, and so they became even more active traders in foreign markets. It has become a big business—and it can be an inefficient one if your goal is to fight hunger. We take food grown in the United States, ship it to remote areas at great cost, and then when it gets there, NGOs don't distribute it to hungry people—they sell it so they can take the cash and use it for other program and budget expenses. A June 2011 report by the US Government Accountability Office (GAO) found that the $722 million in cash used by the government over three years to buy US commodities for monetization resulted in only $503 million in cash at the other end of the pipeline.[1]

According to existing PL 480 regulations, the bulk of US food aid must be moved on US-flagged vessels. Therefore it is no surprise that the US shipping industry has been lobbying to keep this program intact, joining forces with US agriculture interests and NGOs in what is sometimes called the "iron triangle" that has kept monetization going for years—even though the practice hurts many of the people it is designed to help. In some cases, it works out that the cost of shipping a particular food aid commodity for monetization is more than the commodity is worth. The GAO reported one 2008 case in which it cost $4.5 million in shipping charges to send Malawi ten thousand metric tons of wheat worth $3.9 million. We could have had much more impact if we had just used the total $8.4 million to support local purchase programs.

US shippers and some food processing and agricultural interests have vowed to fight for the existing regulations to stay in place. Some shippers have resented my speaking publicly about this issue, but I continue to do so. The program's provisions generate significant shipping costs that should be going to help feed people. It was a small step in the right direction in 2012 when Congress lowered the minimum requirements for using US ships to transport aid from 75 percent to 50 percent. However, it is hard for me to imagine any dramatic changes happening soon enough, and it is likely that the new minimum threshold requirement will have little real-world impact. I think our food aid programs need to be reevaluated to ensure that they are first and foremost about feeding people. That means shipping food aid at competitive rates when that is the best option, and buying food locally if that maximizes the value of the aid dollars.[2]

FOOD AID BECOMES A BUSINESSMAN'S MORNING CROISSANT

It concerns me that NGOs know the negative impact of monetization in the communities they serve, and yet a number of them continue to use monetization. Put simply, it is about self-preservation. According to the GAO, nongovernmental organizations traded 1.3 million tons of US-grown food for cash in thirty-four countries from 2008 to 2010. I should point out that the CARE official I spoke to in Mozambique in 2006 was not proud of the organization's history of monetizing commodities. But one of the reasons I mention CARE by name is that it was already in the process of adopting the brave and principled position not to use the monetization process any longer.

To understand the sacrifice that CARE made, you need to realize that it had the closest ties to the US government of any NGO. The charity was formed by Americans at the end of World War II to send to survivors in Europe packages of food recovered from army surplus. Washington's support of CARE grew as the group expanded its work to fighting poverty in eighty-four countries.

By 2006, CARE was generating $45 million annually from monetizing US commodities. That money was paying for poverty-fighting programs that formed the nucleus of many of CARE's country offices, several of which depended on monetizing US food aid for half their budget. The money paid for about twenty development programs in Africa, which did everything from teaching farmers how to make more money by growing alternative crops, such as sunflowers, to teaching them about soil conservation and agroforestry.

But here's what happened: CARE's leadership developed the position that it needed to get poor people more involved in making decisions about programs that are intended to help them. A central tenet of this "rights-based" philosophy is that CARE officials should consider whether their poverty-fighting programs have unintended consequences. Monetizing US commodities became a moral issue because they realized it was harming farmers in places where CARE was acting as a grain trader. What's more, CARE officials realized that the basic proposition that food aid from America was supposed to be consumed by poor people was being distorted; when monetized, it was ending up in the hands of middle-class and upper-class consumers *in developing countries*. For instance, in Uganda, some US food aid ended up at a bakery across the street from the US embassy. In Ethiopia, some cooking oil monetized by CARE ended up at a Sheraton hotel in Addis Ababa.

Daniel Maxwell, a senior CARE official based in Nairobi, told us that the revenues raised through monetization had been important to the organization, but he and others became increasingly uncomfortable with it. Dan's concerns about monetization grew as he worked on a book, *Food Aid After Fifty Years: Recasting Its Role,* with a friend from graduate school, Cornell University economist Christopher Barrett. They concluded that the primary objective of food aid had devolved to where it was less about helping food-insecure people than it was "heavily oriented toward domestic concerns in donor countries."

What's more, the extent to which NGOs were dependent on monetizing food aid for project funding made them leery of lobbying for reforms that would stretch the food aid budget. Eliminating the PL 480 cargo preference mandate, for example, risks angering shipping companies that might withdraw support of food aid in general. Similarly, agricultural interests like the safety net that the program offers for the government to buy surplus crops.

Dan and Chris presented their findings to a gathering of senior CARE executives in 2004, and by 2006, the organization moved to stop the practice.*

The decision to stop monetizing commodities blew a hole in CARE's budget. The value of support in all forms from the US government sank 18 percent in the charity's fiscal year that ended June 30, 2007: to $243 million from $298 million in FY 2006. By 2011, US government support to CARE had dropped further to $176.1 million. The organization gave its country offices until 2009 to wean themselves from monetization, hoping that would be enough time to find alternative funds to keep the programs alive. But many of the monetization-backed CARE projects have disappeared.

CARE is still paying the price for its stand in 2006. Five years later the organization raised $589.7 million, 10 percent less than it had to work with when it was selling US food aid to generate cash. "It is an understatement to say we weren't truly prepared for the practical implications," says Helene D. Gayle, president and chief executive officer of CARE USA. "That said, I think it has also hastened our adaptation to a new development paradigm and made us more prepared to embrace new (and we think better) ways of doing development."

I admire the people at CARE for doing the right thing. This decision took guts, and it cost them. CARE had to lay off hundreds of employees across several countries and shrink its number of projects. From what I understand, CARE asked other NGOs to follow its example, hoping that a unified front would prod Washington to shift the monetization budget to other programs that they could all use for development work. Instead, the other NGOs quit the Washington food aid lobbying group to which CARE belonged and started their own. The money CARE no longer collects flows to

---

* CARE does continue to sell commodities in one instance: the government of Bangladesh buys CARE-brokered food aid for a school program because no other local supplier can handle the logistics, and CARE is certain where the food goes.

other NGOs, which apparently justify the practice as a necessary evil. I find this development troubling, given the mission of these organizations.

Once I learned more about monetization, I realized that farmers in different parts of the world had been complaining about it to me for some time. I just didn't realize what they were talking about. Probably a dozen times, farmers had asked me why "the US" was depressing their prices by dumping our commodities into their markets. In Ethiopia, a grain trader once showed me a warehouse of bagged commodities that he said he was unable to sell because of US commodities flooding the local market. At the time, I thought that some independent grain trader with ties to the United States or some expatriate businessman was behind it. I didn't realize—and maybe the farmers didn't either—that it was actually NGOs supplying the commodities for these trades. European countries had once allowed monetization as well, but in the mid-1990s both Europe and later Canada moved to change their aid policies; ever since, they've sent cash for purchasing and distributing food locally.

Monetization of food aid should be stopped, as should the requirement of moving US food aid commodities mainly on US-flagged vessels. Shippers contend that the guaranteed business helps keep a fleet of ships ready in case of war or disaster, and that maintaining a large maritime fleet is essential to national security and jobs. However, according to the GAO, the shipping preferences don't contribute to that preparation, at least in part because the ships used are not militarily useful.[3] Plus, many of the American vessels ultimately are owned by subsidiaries of foreign countries. Food aid commitments will still support considerable business for US shippers, but the companies should charge competitive rates.

Many parts of the world need our in-kind food aid, as in the case of Pakistan. But rather than allow NGOs to monetize our commodities and allow such a large portion of those revenues to get diverted to shipping costs, we should move to a model that involves sending cash to regions where there is enough local agriculture that we can purchase food aid locally. In part 5, I will tell you about a pilot WFP program called Purchase for Progress, or P4P, which gives food aid administrators more flexibility to buy commodities from smallholder farmers. This practice lifts a region's economic base while at the same time getting food to people who need it. Using this model, WFP can not only provide food aid but also offer smallholder farmers opportunities to become competitive players in agricultural markets and thus improve their lives—and even exit poverty, permanently.

TOO RIGID

I also think the US government is too rigid about the amount of money it spends on food aid. Rather than peg food aid to a hard budget, Washington should commit to keeping the volume of commodities it sends abroad at a more constant level. In the 2010 US federal fiscal year, the $2.3 billion food aid budget generated 2.5 metric tons of food aid. A decade earlier, before the grain-price shocks of recent years, our government was able to send 6 million tons of food aid with a budget of $1.7 billion. The trouble is, emergency hunger levels do not adjust to market prices.

US-grown commodities will always play an important role in food aid, in part because we can mobilize large amounts of grain relatively quickly and because there are times when food shipped from across the ocean is the best alternative. As startling as this seems, I have seen data showing that it costs twice as much to move grain from Yambio, South Sudan, to Darfur than to ship grain from a US port all the way to Darfur. The roads are at times impassable due to weather and other conditions, and the security needed to accompany the shipment is so expensive that it renders this route impractical. And moving it by air can double the price.

Ideally, agencies such as USDA and USAID should focus on the right mix of aid or cash to respond to a need, whether with a high-wire, effective operation like the one I saw in Pakistan, or with a well-organized process of supporting local farmers by buying food aid from them when possible.

A Six-Beer Insight

I don't drink alcohol.

When I was a little kid growing up in Omaha, my maternal grandfather, William Oxley Thompson, lived two blocks from us. Beginning when I was five or six, I used to walk to his house from time to time. He would lift me up and sit me on his lap, and talk to me about life and give me advice. One of his warnings was, "Howie, every time you drink alcohol, you kill brain cells." Then he would pause and add with a smile, "And you don't have any to waste." That gives you some idea of his sense of humor. He was a wonderful, fun person, and I always appreciated his advice. I just was never interested in drinking, and I'm sure that has been a good thing. Since most things that I enjoy I tend to do to excess, I'm glad I never developed a taste for or a curiosity about drinking.

Naturally, the rest of the world was not in on my grandfather's wisdom. In many cultures, drinking is a sign of goodwill, of friendship, of respect. I appreciate the importance of showing respect to local culture and customs. Being invited to have a drink is a gesture that one does not just brush off. In some parts of the world, it is traditional to conduct certain kinds of business over alcohol. I usually find some way to get out of drinking, but it hasn't always been easy.

In 1991 I visited Moscow in February. Mikhail Gorbachev, president of the USSR and general secretary of the Communist Party, was grappling with factions in his government that wanted to realign Russia's entire agricultural system. I traveled there as both a farmer and a Nebraska county commissioner, along with former congressman John Cavanaugh of the agricultural consulting firm Summit Ltd.

We had a series of interesting meetings with farmers and local officials several hours outside Moscow, close to the city of Tula. I remember the frustration of farmers I spoke to who were motivated to improve their methods and grow more food but were battling government bureaucrats who were not anxious to give up any power or authority.

It was still the USSR then (although the Soviet system would be disbanded by December), and travel around the country was restricted. As we were leaving Tula, a military vehicle appeared with lights flashing and pulled us over. The military officers ordered us all out of the car. I got a sick feeling that something bad was going to happen. Our driver and guide motioned us to climb out, as military officers jumped out of the truck, huffing and stamping their feet, their breath creating ominous clouds in the cold air. The temperature was probably at least twenty degrees below zero. Another car pulled up, and some officers got out. One set up a whole chorus line of vodka bottles on the hood of the military truck, while another brought trays of hors d'oeuvres. And another guy passed around shot glasses. "They are here," our guide confided, "to thank you for your visit and to drink a toast to your safe travels."

It was so cold that having a drink "on the rocks" would have been redundant. But the men seemed in a jovial mood, already smiling and laughing and looking forward to the liquor. I grabbed a bottle and made a big show of taking a (fake) swig right from it. "Hah hah, here we go, drink up, everybody!" I called out. I walked from officer to officer splashing vodka into their shot glasses. "Here, enjoy, this is great." I'd take a step or two away with my back turned and appear to take another sloppy swig, and then turn around. "Who wants more?" We continued like this for an hour or so, them getting drunker and me getting louder and more exaggerated in my performance. Soon the bottle and maybe one more was empty, and I wiped my mouth on my sleeve. "Okay, hate to break this up, but thank you for this fantastic send-off." I was so relieved when the car started and we were off again.

SOBERING INSIGHTS

My abstaining has produced an odd benefit over the years. I've learned a secret that journalists and spies know well: being the only sober person in a roomful of drinkers can be useful.

In 2007 I traveled to South Sudan for an agricultural meeting involving an NGO. There was a "dinner party" in a run-down shack. It happened that I was feeling very discouraged—almost angry—about how little the projects we were supporting seemed to be accomplishing. And the chatter among development critics and experts was getting louder: "With all the corruption in Africa, shouldn't there come a point where we just stop sending aid? Won't that send a message to thugs and corrupt rulers that until they clean up their act, we're not going to reward them for it?"

Unquestionably, the situation all around us was grim. South Sudan later achieved independence in 2011. Today it is Africa's newest and youngest nation, a landlocked country in northeastern Africa bordered by Ethiopia, Kenya, Uganda, DRC, CAR, and, of course, Sudan. These neighbors star all too frequently in news stories and documentaries about the worst nightmares in Africa: cruelty, famine, child soldiers, desperate refugees. You name the challenge, and it's swirling around this region. Sudan's president, Omar Hassan al-Bashir, is wanted by the International Criminal Court on charges of genocide and war crimes in the Darfur region.[1]

Until the mid-1950s, Sudan was called Anglo-Egyptian Sudan, but it gained its independence from Egypt and the United Kingdom in 1956.[2] Two prolonged civil wars followed, with upwards of two million lives lost, splitting off the southern part of Sudan into an autonomous region. When I visited, the central Sudan government in Khartoum had been fighting in both South Sudan and the country's western region, Darfur.

One of the surprising theories I heard on the trip was the quietly expressed view that the United States had set the stage for South Sudan's independence when President George W. Bush invaded Iraq. According to some of my dinner companions, Iraqi president Saddam Hussein had been sending not only arms to Sudan but also fighter pilots to train the local air force, which probably would have beaten back the southern forces battling Khartoum. After Iraq became focused on the US invasion, however, that support disappeared, and eventually Khartoum had to choose which conflict to fight, and it picked Darfur. I had never heard this expressed anywhere else.

South Sudan has been a troubled region for a very long time. Today, it has a population of eight million. The economy is predominantly rural and relies on subsistence farming and raising cattle, but the country is littered with the residue of conflict: horrible roads, lack of infrastructure, and many farmers forced off their land, which is now fallow.*

At that 2007 dinner, I was seated next to a man who had been a general in the Sudan People's Liberation Army (SPLA), which had originally fought in the second civil war but subsequently made up the military of South Sudan. He was a dignified man, and he had lost a leg in the conflict. Initially, he was circumspect, reserved, and polite. He did not speak much. We began by eating and talking in general terms about general topics. But from the minute we sat down, he was drinking beer. I was drinking Coke.

In my experience, the most interesting comments seem to occur

---

* It's hard to exaggerate the difficulty of life in Sudan. Many thousands of young people have spent their entire childhood in camps for displaced persons, such as the Kakuma camp in Kenya, which I have visited twice. While getting a tour of the facilities, we opened the door to a medical storage room and bats came streaming out. As I write, another uprising has created yet another generation of "lost" children fleeing violence in the Nuba Mountains.

once my dinner companions have passed the six-beer mark. After the former general entered that stage, he leaned toward me and said he would normally never tell anyone what he was about to tell me.

He had me at *"never."*

Earlier, I had asked him if food aid was making things worse in countries where corruption was so rampant. He wanted to get back to that. He narrowed his eyes—a little annoyed, perhaps, at my simplistic assessment.

I did not take notes, but this is the gist of what he said: A few of the armed groups in South Sudan had developed a technique to get their hands on foreign aid. They surround a village and prevent any entrance or exit, and no food aid deliveries. Since for so many villages a jug of fresh water can mean a mile walk, this blockade becomes life threatening, particularly in an area where people are weakened from hunger. Next, the rebels get word to a local NGO: send food aid, or the villagers will die. The hard-line position would seem to be a classic "never negotiate with terrorists" scenario. The African countryside is peppered with tiny villages, and if you start cooperating and sending food, would this extortion ever stop?

But while the thugs are heartless and cruel, they are sophisticated, the general explained. They take only 30 percent or so of the food aid because they know that if they take it all, the NGO will no longer send any. So they take enough to eat or sell but allow just enough to get through so that the people don't starve to death.

"What do you do?" he asked me grimly. Is it so simple to say, "No more food aid; we're teaching [the rebels] a lesson"? This scenario is one of those unimaginable elements of the conflict-corruption-starvation ecosystem.

Responding to the extortionists unquestionably perpetuates the practice. But NGOs are neither governments nor arms of the military. They are there to help the poorest and most vulnerable people who have no other recourse. If you send aid, you can keep an entire village of men, women, and children alive, and the thugs will move on, and your response will engender some small amount of protection for the innocents. If your organization is in Africa for humanitarian or religious reasons, that is your mission. So, when they can, the general confided, the NGOs do it. They don't like to talk about it or publicize it. I have mentioned this story to others, and sometimes I receive blank stares.

It is estimated that in South Sudan an AK-47 costs around $10. In rural areas of this pastoral country they seemed to me to be nearly as common as cows. *Photo: Howard G. Buffett*

Whenever I hear people who have not been to Africa and not seen hunger up close talk about banning all food aid, I think back to this beer-fueled insight. When the status quo is chronic poverty and low-yield agriculture, it doesn't make sense to keep responding with crisis intervention-style aid. Those financial resources are better spent, and ultimately will save many more lives, if you can figure out how to change the fundamentals. But when the issue is conflict or natural disaster, the "fundamentals" are irrelevant until you restore order. Often you are talking about the most helpless people on the planet, and I've come to believe that you can't always decide to help on the basis of whether what you do is "sustainable" or not. There is no safety net, there is no government program to take care of meaningful numbers of people, and there is no mercy from the forces battling for power that surround them. In these situations, which at some level are temporary, withholding the aid does not teach anyone a lesson or motivate better behavior. These are the sobering trade-offs of the real world. Can we keep a village of innocent people under siege alive long enough to later teach them to feed themselves so that they are less vulnerable in the long run? When we give aid in conflict, postconflict, and humanitarian situations, that is what we're trying to do.

On the same trip to South Sudan I met a boy whose parents had named him "World Food Programme" because WFP aid kept his family alive under the most dire circumstances. I keep that boy in mind whenever I feel frustrated and am tempted to give up trying to make a difference in difficult places such as his country. I like to think that boy will become a man motivated to live up to such a powerful, important, peace-seeking name.

When I stopped to photograph this child, I learned his name was "World Food Programme." He caught my attention because of the camo army uniform he was wearing, right down to the shoulder lapel emblems. His father was a general in the SPLA. *Photo: Howard G. Buffett*

Story 26
Less Than Sparkling

It's dangerous to drive on rural roads after dark in Africa. It's hard to see the deep potholes and animals that can cause a wreck. And it's hard to see the people who walk in or near the road at all hours. In 2007 I was on a trip to Togo, a small country in West Africa where four-fifths of the population depend on agriculture for survival. We were heading back to our hotel after a long day in the field, and I remember how bright the stars were out in the countryside, which meant it was very dark on the ground.

The headlights of our SUV caught a young girl walking all alone by the edge of the road with a water jug balanced on her head. She was inches from the vehicle in front of us. The dust from the first SUV and then our headlight beam moving on made her disappear as quickly as she had materialized. Thankfully, we did not hit her, but it was close.

The next day, CARE workers took me to a town called Dapaong to see a new water depot where local residents could buy clean water. The depot looked like a concrete tollbooth painted blue and khaki, built by the side of a dirt road. I noticed that one of the spigots was placed at least seven feet off the ground with chest-high controls—so that women and girls could stand underneath it with containers on their heads. That way they didn't have to hoist the heavy buckets or jugs back up after filling them.

Girls often begin carrying water at the age of five. The responsibility frequently prevents them from attending school. *Photo: Howard G. Buffett*

I borrowed a bucket and went over and stood by a lower faucet and filled it up. At the point where it was nearly full, it felt heavy and awkward. A girl who could not have been more than six, with her own bucket and a flat rock, had been watching me. I poured my water into her bucket. She placed a flat rock in the middle of her headscarf to create an even surface, lifted the bucket to the top of her head, and then she headed home.

In so many poor areas of the world, limited water access goes hand in hand with food insecurity. Women and girls pay an enormous price for that. Water is so scarce in parts of rural Africa that women and girls walk miles to fetch enough for the family's needs, and the water they do obtain may contain pathogens or other contaminants. In India, which also battles shortages, water distribution is uneven, as government workers manually open and close valves to distribute it. Water duty, waiting by a spigot with a container, hoping that it begins to flow, may take many hours a day and keep girls from attending school. As you drive around the country, you'll sometimes see a crowd of women and girls gathered around a pipe that has sprung a leak.

A girl in India spends hours of her day waiting as water drips through a leak in a pipe so that she can provide water for her family's needs. *Photo: Howard G. Buffett*

THE MOST BASIC NEED OF ALL

Because it was so important to my parents that my sister, my brother, and I pick important, not easy, problems to work on, I constantly ask myself how our foundation can have the biggest impact possible.

Clearly, expanding and protecting people's access to clean water is one of the planet's biggest challenges. Only 2.5 percent of all the water on Earth can be classified as an accessible freshwater resource. The average person needs to drink less than one gallon of water each day to stay alive, but it takes about eight hundred gallons of water to produce just one person's daily food needs, according to the FAO.[1] Water is so important to life that families will put a child on a dangerous road night after night with a burden that a grown man would struggle to carry.

Not long after I visited Togo, I had the idea that just as my parents had given me the funding in a dream scenario of sorts—here is a billion dollars to make the world better, so get busy—what if I could gather experienced people already working on water issues and urge them to "think big" about water? If we could represent a new source of funding that did not involve raising money project by project, what would their ideas look like?

We gathered some leading NGOs for a meeting in Omaha. I figured that between the group they had about 250 years' experience. To prime the pump, so to speak, I asked, "What if we put our support for wells on steroids; say, commit to funding ten thousand boreholes?" We had done some limited funding of well-drilling projects, and it was satisfying to see a community get that resource. If we drilled thousands of wells for disenfranchised, fragile populations, how many kids could now go to school? Could we reduce the incidence of waterborne illnesses? Could we raise the quality of life and conserve the energy from all those millions of trips back and forth for water? Is that the Big Idea we could fund?

The NGOs were reserved and thoughtful in their responses. One reason well drilling had become so popular, they explained, was that it is fairly easy to raise money for that. Many donors are drawn to what seem like dramatic, simple ways to help a struggling community, and there are NGOs that do nothing but drill wells. But wells are not the answer to every community's water challenges. It may be for a technical reason, such as that the water table is too deep, or one of several other more complex factors.

Access to water is not just about having a source of water. Priorities can be very contentious within a community. Should water for drinking be the top priority? Should one farmer closer to a water source be forced to conserve so that others downstream can have more? How do you measure who is using what? Does it make sense to drill a well when, if you could just keep livestock away from a pond or river, you could have a ready, clean source? In other words, the NGOs said, to improve a water access challenge, you have to study it first. You must understand who the important parties are, what their existing sources of water are, and how any given community upstream or downstream might be linked to another. Just deciding where to locate a well is often so tied up in local power structures, rivalries, customs, and geographic idiosyncrasies that it can create bitter resentments and conflict.

My idea—ten thousand boreholes—clearly was not the Big Idea; the NGOs made a good case that water planning and management is a messy, people- and time-intensive process far more complicated than drilling wells.

Okay, if not wells, then what?

The NGOs all agreed that the short-term budget cycles and time horizons of donors posed obstacles to Big Ideas, which often cannot be executed in a two- or three-year time frame. Thus, the incentive was to look for small, manageable projects with quick but not necessarily sustainable impact, so they could point to success. They said if they had longer time-frame support, they could plan and execute more comprehensive and long-lasting solutions for vulnerable communities.

That made sense to me.

Second, they felt restricted because donors typically are not interested in spending money on governance or long-term planning. Many philanthropists and foundations do not have the patience to put in place the people and processes needed for long-term solution management, or what we often call "capacity building." I understand their hesitation. It's easy for an NGO to tell me how many people gained access to an improved water source, but it is difficult to show me the impact of setting up a local water committee so that communities can determine the best and most affordable solution for their need. But if you don't create a local management structure, the NGO will be in business with that community for a long time. It will never equip the local people with the tools they need. What happens when the well is damaged or a part breaks? What kind of resources are there to get it fixed? In the regions we're trying to help, there is no Ace Hardware or Rural King handy, and no money to buy the parts anyway.*

I agreed that we should support these "soft" activities and the NGO partners could leverage resources for equipment and technology from other donors. In other words, our dollars could improve the outcomes for the funding that the NGOs said was much easier to secure.

Third, you can't escape geography and politics. Whether you are in California or Cameroon, water issues almost always pit those upstream against those downstream, and rivers and lakes that cross or share borders are common. I'll never forget going to northern Angola to inspect an area of extensive springs where an NGO was trying to raise funds to create a diversion system in order to irrigate more Angolan crops. It seemed to me there was a lot of water that could go a long way to alleviating food insecurity locally in Angola. But Annette Lanjouw, a veteran of conservation initiatives in Africa who worked with me at the time and was on that trip, pulled me aside.

"Do you realize where we are?" she asked quietly. "These are the headwaters of what becomes the Okavango Delta. These waters flow

---

* There are thousands of broken wells all over Africa, and there is growing frustration because too many organizations measure whether a new water source has been created as "improved access" but do not measure if water is flowing from it five years later.

through to Botswana. Diverting water here could have big ramifications downstream to one of the most important ecosystems in the world and the people who live there as well." I made doing a thorough environmental impact report a precondition of funding. This study never happened, so we never funded the project.

The NGOs convinced me that in order to make a difference, you have to work locally, within a region of a country, nationally, and also between nations. Advocacy is a way to leverage investments on the ground to achieve impact on a bigger scale. In many areas of the world, it's about figuring out how to make governments accountable for taking care of their own people. We added advocacy and transboundary work to the plan.

The scope of all this was much broader than I first envisioned. My original suggestion of wells on steroids was turning into everything from sanitation education, to community coordinating, to technology assessments, to dam studies. I didn't realize it at the time, but we were assembling a Big Idea around water-related projects nobody else wanted to fund.

I had some concerns, but I knew that to make a big impact, we had to make a big bet. I agreed the foundation would ask for proposals with a ten-year time horizon and welcome a broad array of activities. This breadth made me nervous, but I liked that our funding was going to what was needed but not as readily available.

What I wanted was for our NGO partners to unleash some innovation and creativity. I wanted them to think like a team on this, not compete for our support. I wanted them to share information and be open to learning from one another. I wanted to make sure the programs targeted the rural poor, the most vulnerable people in the most difficult situations. We agreed to focus efforts in four countries in Central America, five countries in West Africa, and four countries in East Africa. We established regional coordinating committees to oversee efforts. These reported to a global steering committee that included representation from the foundation. To provide some leadership, we designated one multinational NGO as the project lead in each region.

I did not want to micromanage this, nor did our foundation have the staff to do so. Our partners brought us the first round of proposals, and we generally funded what was put in front of us with few changes and little feedback on their proposals. I knew an alternative approach would be for the foundation to hire staff and consultants who would systematically analyze and organize the opportunities and bring on staff with the technical expertise to monitor and evaluate what we were calling the Global Water Initiative (GWI). But that would take a long time and resemble existing approaches. I don't like building up a lot of bureaucracy inside our foundation because it triggers exactly what frustrates me about the larger NGO world: activities designed to perpetuate overhead and staff. I'd rather empower people with rolled-up sleeves in Nicaragua or Mozambique than hire consultants to think big thoughts in Decatur. I am impatient. I would rather learn the lessons faster, even if more painfully, by setting doers in motion to see what happens.

We started writing checks—some of the largest the foundation had ever written for a single initiative. What happened?

The short answer: given what we spent, not enough.

REVERTING TO OLD THINKING

Within a year or so of the launch, I realized that GWI wasn't working the way we had discussed or planned. I wasn't hearing enough interesting or creative ideas. Over the next three years, I realized we needed more help and brought in several consultants to provide more management advice and guidance from the foundation's perspective. We even commissioned an independent external review, which came back more positive than I expected but which revealed an initiative that did not resemble what I thought I was launching. After five years and about $70 million invested, I was frustrated and disappointed.

So, what went wrong? We saw few programs I would call innovative. We did not even inspire creativity in proposal writing, as the annual funding requests we required with each passing year started to look more and more like a typical one-year project proposal. Every year, the organizations complained that they had to renew their funding with us, when they thought they were going to have a ten-year commitment. My response was, you *do* have a ten-year commitment, so present a ten-year vision with milestones, and we will hold you accountable every year to your progress against this plan. But their internal bureaucracy and accounting systems worked against that idea. Our contacts within the NGO would say that their organizations were preparing to release staff assigned to GWI every year, pending our approving their budgets. It took awhile for us to realize a basic disconnect: the NGOs wanted a ten-year time frame with guaranteed funding for the duration, whereas we thought we'd made it clear that we wanted a ten-year plan and evidence they were creating sustainable progress on the ground.

It also became clear as time passed that the "global" in GWI was in name only. The NGOs had failed to create a mechanism to share information or practices across regions. The three regions created incompatible systems to monitor and evaluate their own activities, so as a foundation we could not even communicate or compare what GWI was doing on a global basis. Regionally, some of our partners seemed to practice "don't rock the boat" management. Instead of funding the best ideas and holding each other accountable, the committee politely made sure that every country and every partner got an equal share so that nobody would be offended. The structure was so complicated that way too much money went to trying to hire enough staff to make the cross-collaboration work. And with each passing year, more and more of our funding went to hardware and water systems as the other supposedly "easy to raise" donor dollars never materialized.

All was not entirely bleak. There were some individual successes, and it is fair to say that thousands of people now had access to clean water resources thanks to GWI, particularly in East Africa. In Central America, our GWI partners created a process for helping communities and local governments map out their resource options, manage watersheds more sustainably, and implement simple tools such as user fees and metering to take over the challenge of better water access for the long term, which was somewhat encouraging.

For example, in Nicaragua, the municipality of La Trinidad was a GWI success story. Thanks to GWI, La Trinidad had joined forces with two other municipalities to establish a watershed committee to save the local river, which had been decreasing year by year due to low rainfall and losing water quality due to deforestation and contamination by surrounding communities. The committee launched an environmental and sanitation education campaign supported by the minister of education and worked to reforest critical areas. It created an office for conflict management to handle water disputes, so that for the first time, the population had somewhere to bring issues. Even though Nicaragua had a national water act in place, GWI helped the municipality establish local ordinances to regulate water use, ban the burning of trees, and encourage the adoption of drip irrigation, which helped lower water use during farming.

Also in Nicaragua, in the community of La Pacaya, we met with an eight-member water committee also established with the help of GWI. One of its first acts was to provide each household with a water meter, which allowed the committee to charge a small fee per connection per family, so it could build a fund for water system repairs. The water committee was appointed by the population at large, and it was impressive the way it took ownership of the water management issues across the board, from reading meters and keeping a water use log, to simple projects such as building natural rock filters to treat wastewater so that it could be used on plants after twenty days.

These projects impressed me. The trouble was, these successes could have been achieved with a lot less money and bureaucratic complexity. GWI seemed to illustrate a frustration I have with large, multinational NGOs: even an almost blank check, a long-term commitment, and a willing donor could not overcome institutional issues that I believe hold these organizations back. Their size and bureaucracy stifle their ability to solve problems on a large scale where it seems they should be able to operate. They focus on projects and activities, not enough on outcomes, and not enough on learning to work together instead of competing for the same dollars in the same way.

In fairness to NGOs, a lot of these behaviors are donor driven. Donors want to see and understand where their money went, and it's easier to explain activities and outputs in stories about improvement in one village or another. But sustainable outcomes demand bringing partners to the table and figuring out new ways of working together, making sure that the best people take on aspects of the challenge suited to their strengths, and building a plan meant to eventually end an NGO's involvement, not sustain or grow it. Fortunately, we do have projects where we are seeing some of this innovation, so I know it can happen, and we'll talk more about those in the next two chapters. But it has not happened with our GWI yet.

That's a pretty harsh critique, I know. These organizations are working in difficult conditions in some of the world's most challenging and unstable regions. We also played a large role in GWI's not living up to my hopes for it, and it's a lesson that informs decisions we make today. We let too many projects start up in too many places simultaneously; later we could work backward from where each ended up and see what went wrong, but in real time it was too much to oversee. Given how broad GWI's scope was, we probably would have needed three or more full-time people to actively manage the grantees in a way that kept them on track and accountable to the original vision. At one point, we even realized that one of the NGOs had accumulated $1.5 million in its bank account but never spent it, even as it continued to submit new funding requests that we continued to consider. (The bank account is now applied to ideas we approved.)

In 2010 I decided I wanted our annual report to acknowledge our failures, highlighting the lessons we had learned that year from investments we had made. In the Central America region, the GWI team became aware of a community in Samulali, Nicaragua—made up of six hundred families and three thousand people—whose water systems were failing on several fronts. The water source was contaminated from pesticide usage and coffee production, and sanitation conditions were poor. People were drinking the same water that farmers were using for livestock. A GWI partner came in and held meetings to try to organize a community-based response but did not consult families most likely to benefit or key community representatives. Nonetheless, the partner appointed a water committee to manage some of the sanitation and water metering elements. Unbeknownst to that partner, friction within the community led to a rival committee forming. GWI tried to work with both to compromise on a plan for shared costs, but the situation became so volatile that actual threats were made to GWI staff. The project had to be abandoned.

In East Africa, the GWI team wanted to introduce drip irrigation technology in Kenya. GWI funded a plan to set up three demonstration gardens attached to three primary schools. The idea was that local farmers could come see the demo plots, while the food grown could supplement school feeding programs, and students could actually learn the techniques and eventually introduce the technology to their families' farming. Those were admirable ideas, but here the main problem was that the technology plan just did not fit the program. Pipes to storage tanks did not have adequate pressure, so students had to transport water manually. Silt in the water supply from the river and open-water sources clogged the drip lines. The technical issues in Kenya could have been predicted if someone familiar with drip irrigation systems had been consulted.

In both cases, I'm much less disappointed by the failure than by what those failures represent: lack of community consultation; designs not informed by prior experience or technical background; and, even if they had both "succeeded," the reach of these ideas was merely local. Out of the three geographic regions and thirteen countries we were funding, we had only one major Big Idea success story, in my view: our funding allowed our West Africa team to get a seat at the table and inform the planning and implementation of large-scale dam projects. Dam construction is going to increase in coming years, and planning these projects with some sensitivity for and attention to the tens of thousands of poor people who will feel the impact is vital.

A GOOD DAM PROJECT

The Akosombo Dam was built in Ghana in 1965, flooding the lands and homes of eighty thousand people. It created the largest man-made lake in the world and secured Ghana's electricity supply. Since then, West African countries have built more than 150 large dams. With GWI's backing, a nonprofit organization called the International Institute for Environment and Development (IIED) spearheaded a study examining the social impact of several dams and turned that data into something it used in an advocacy effort in West Africa, in close partnership with the International Union for Conservation of Nature (IUCN), which is made up of hundreds of conservation-oriented NGOs around the world.

Dam projects are on the upswing again as countries grapple with food insecurity, climate change, and other pressures to create additional energy sources. The people in the region most affected typically do not have a voice in the process, and there is considerable debate over how much these massive infrastructure projects benefit the vast numbers of people who are displaced. At regional planning meetings, IIED and IUCN provided impact studies that had hard evidence of elements that planners needed to keep in mind to ensure equitable treatment of the people affected and that the project's objectives are actually met.

For example, after a major dam was completed in Mali in 1981, displaced farmers were theoretically given improved land resources and irrigation technology when they were resettled. However, they were not trained how to farm rice instead of the wheat they had previously grown under a rain-fed system. The result was that they did not know how to produce this crop, and so they failed. In some cases, they just abandoned their plots or had them taken away.

This work is not a "typical" NGO project. It's not about building anything concrete or installing equipment. It's about the soft resources that can mean the difference between success and failure for tens of thousands of people who have few advocates. It's about working with the policy makers who can effect real change that outlives the activities. Because of this research, IIED and IUCN can show governments and dam project planners that a training component for this kind of shift is essential. Also, thanks to work that GWI helped support, the Niger Basin Authority adopted some principles to assess and manage social and environmental impacts of future plans to manage a river system that runs through nine countries: Benin, Burkina Faso, Cameroon, Chad, Ivory Coast, Guinea, Mali, Niger, and Nigeria. This is the kind of big-impact thinking we'd hoped to achieve. This is what we think of as transformational change at scale: Big, positive, sustainable progress for large numbers of people.

The problem is, the money allocated to dam-related work made up just 2 percent of our entire investment in GWI so far. That's not even close to a passing grade.

We have subsequently relaunched GWI. We challenged all the participants to reimagine the next five years as informed by what they have learned to date. We asked them to come back with new proposals centered around the one or two Big Ideas in their regions. We eliminated the bulky committee oversight. We asked the lead NGO in each region to define who they thought were the best partners to achieve the strategy, while requiring each to allocate funds to coordinate learning and advocacy on a global scale. Since our primary mission as a foundation is food security, we pulled back the scope to focus on water for agriculture.

In all cases, we required the new plans to use our funding to knit together the best ideas and experiences from across the sector, while also identifying critical research and information gaps. Our partners are shifting to focus on policy-related initiatives so that governments will focus more on rain-fed agricultural systems that could improve food security for huge numbers of smallholder farmers across several countries. We hope to build networks of experts who can inform and use the evidence base we build to advocate for solutions to better manage water use for agriculture and meet the water needs of small farmers.

In rain-fed areas, collecting water for small-scale irrigation systems can be backbreaking work. *Photo: Howard G. Buffett*

The good news is that we learned our lessons faster than we would have in a more traditional, bureaucratic, consultant-heavy approach, so I'm optimistic that we can make progress going forward. But we have to be willing to identify and admit to what did not work. We are packaging the first five years' worth of lessons learned, to help inform everybody trying to make a difference in improving access to water. If we come back to the conclusion that today's NGOs largely cannot break out of the boxes they've created for themselves without a lot more direction and management, well, we'll have some decisions to make. Do we see a path where it makes sense for us to create that management support and infrastructure? Or do we need entirely new models we haven't seen or tried yet?

Time will tell if GWI's new structure and focus will unleash the Big Idea change that originally inspired us.

PART 4

Challenges We Need to Figure Out

You've just read about some lessons we've learned through trial and error or by witnessing or experiencing good intentions that did not deliver. In this section, the stories involve challenges where we are going in eyes wide open to the difficulty, but we're experimenting and trying some new approaches to creating a more sustainable future for struggling populations. Some stories are about questions that will demand research; others involve new ideas for challenging a failing status quo.

Elephants and Experts

In 2012 I was drawn to visit the Okavango Delta in Botswana by a startling statistic. I had to understand it for myself.

I had visited the region before and was excited to go back to the Okavango, a 6,500-square-mile oasis created by the annual flooding of the Okavango River. It is so vast, so undeveloped, and so biologically diverse that it is a wildlife photographer's dream. More significantly, it is one of the planet's most important ecosystems, and the region is home to considerable food insecurity and thousands of smallholder farmers.

It was August, the winter dry season, and much of our helicopter journey from Maun Airport was over a bland, grayish combination of savanna and floodplain crisscrossed with animal migration tracks. As we neared the delta, more wildlife appeared: there were giraffes ambling across open stretches, zebras grazing near isolated water holes, small groups of elephants with their young camped under the few shade trees, and a herd of African buffalo at least one thousand strong. All on an enormous expanse of land.

However, once we reached the delta itself, the wetlands exploded with bright, colorful life. Lush green weed beds and other vegetation lined both blue- and brown-tinted waterways in the flooded area. Hippos splashed in marshy pools, flocks of cranes and other birds soared over the wetlands, and a giant crocodile with a silvery, log-like back swam up what could have been a channel of strong coffee. Many pools were choked with lilies and sported algae blooms of the more exotic colors from the Crayola 64 box, such as raw sienna and goldenrod. Concentrations of salt formed from annual flooding and evaporation dotted the landscape with white patches. Gray termite mounds were everywhere.

I was headed to a remote camp where researchers our foundation is helping support are working on a complex and unusual conflict related to food security. As we descended on an open field by the researchers' camp on a small island, I saw something peculiar along the perimeter: a clothesline of what looked like baby-sized black pants swinging in the breeze. I would soon learn those lines had nothing to do with laundry—and everything to do with that statistic and the tense standoffs we were there to investigate.

Anthropologist Amanda Stronza from Texas A&M University's Department of Recreation, Park, and Tourism Sciences and her two colleagues from the Healthy Ecosystems and Livelihoods (HEAL) Initiative met us and steered us to a small table they'd set up with drinks and fruit. Dr. Stronza is collaborating with two other scientists: Dr. Anna Songhurst, a conservation biologist who studied at the Coulson Lab at Imperial College, University of London, and her husband, conservation ecologist Dr. Graham McCulloch. Dr. Songhurst directs the Okavango Elephants and People Research Project.

Indeed, the main topic of our visit and that incredible statistic involved elephants. Botswana has the largest free-ranging elephant population in Africa, with the highest densities occurring in this northern region of the country. There are roughly 130,000 elephants in all of Botswana, but Dr. Stronza pulled out a map and pointed to our location: a triangular area, roughly the size of Yellowstone

National Park, called the Okavango Panhandle. She explained that it is in a section that abuts the Namibian border and is not far from Angola. The local elephant population, swollen from the years of civil war in Angola that drove many elephants south, is exploding. Meanwhile, the human population is growing rapidly too, at more than 1 percent per year. According to Dr. Stronza, in this study region, right now there are approximately fifteen thousand elephants and fifteen thousand people.

Botswana has the largest free-ranging elephant population in Africa. The area we visited had roughly one elephant for every human. *Photo: Howard G. Buffett*

Given the expanses of land, that might not seem like such a huge problem. But it is. Each day during the dry season, water becomes increasingly scarce out in the remote bush, and many of the animals migrate to the delta on paths that take them right past farmers' fields and settlements and across the area's few roads. It can create situations that remind me of the TV sci-fi series from the 1970s *Land of the Lost,* where a family tries to co-exist with dinosaurs. Conservationists call the resulting issues "human-wildlife conflict," or HWC. "You have people and elephants trying to stay out of each other's way, but they are competing for basic resources," Dr. Stronza explained.

HWCs are not unique to Botswana. In Africa, wherever agriculture encroaches on or abuts animal habitats, farmers battle crop raiding by all kinds of animals, from monkeys to porcupines. But in one sense, the elephant conflicts erupting in the Okavango are different from many HWCs I've heard about and investigated elsewhere in the world. In many situations, numbers of cheetahs or gorillas have plummeted to near-extinct levels because local people are deforesting habitats or poaching the animals. In 2012 the widespread poaching of African elephants to fuel a skyrocketing market for ivory in Asia was a widely covered story, and in some areas, elephant herds were dwindling rapidly. In Cameroon in early 2012, poachers slaughtered more than three hundred elephants in just one month, and a few months later rangers at Garamba National Park in the DRC discovered twenty-two dead elephants they believed had been shot from helicopters.[1] The continent as a whole may be losing tens of thousands of elephants to poachers annually now.

However, the scientists we visited explained that while there is some illegal poaching in the Panhandle area, that has not been a significant factor in terms of the elephant-related issues. Botswana is considered one of the most conservation minded of African countries, with a thriving ecotourism industry. Its government promotes photographic safaris as opposed to trophy hunting. (Not long after we left, the government announced it was going to outlaw all trophy hunting by 2014.)

The particular conflict we were trying to understand in the Okavango Panhandle is mostly about there being too many elephants raiding the crops of subsistence farmers, and confrontations have turned deadly for both.

One of the reasons we traveled here was to see a dramatic, usually daily phenomenon at this time of year. The elephants spend much of their day in the bush, miles away from the people and their crop fields. But during the dry season, the bush "pans," or watering holes, evaporate away to muddy puddles and, eventually, to dry, hard dirt. Late in the day, the elephants begin to move. Scores, even hundreds, of elephants at a time walk to well-trod paths and begin their trek to the Okavango River to drink. You can see their migration paths from the air: they walk by crop fields and homes, they cross roads, they trudge—even swim—through canals. They pluck tasty branches from mopane and other local trees as they go, leaving behind a path of destruction and broken vegetation. And when corn and other crops are ready for harvest, they sometimes go into the fields and consume and trample a subsistence farmer's livelihood.

I have seen many different road signs in my life, but I have seen a sign warning of elephant crossings in only one place—Botswana. *Photo: Howard G. Buffett*

"THEY SEEM TO KNOW"

Elephant experts sometimes joke that these animals are like "six-ton squirrels." They are intelligent, perceptive, and determined, and can be aggressive in pursuit of food or to protect their herds. They can be crafty in evaluating their surroundings and outfoxing attempts to thwart them. And some researchers have even reported what they call "spite" crop raiding, where elephants will trample and wreck a planted field without even eating any of the food grown on it.[2] Crop raiding occurs throughout Africa and Asia wherever elephant habitats are near agriculture, but the concentration of elephants and humans here, and the increase in both populations, is cause for concern. And what the researchers at our meeting explained next was sobering.

We had scheduled our visit to include a drive at dusk along a common elephant pathway near a local village. I had seen photographs of these massive migrations, with the elephants passing by cars and structures. Schoolchildren coming home sometimes even play a potentially lethal version of the game Red Rover, dodging their way through the thundering line of gray tree-trunk-sized legs.

"I have some sad news," Dr. Stronza said. "Sad in a number of ways, but I think it means we are not going to be able to show you the elephant crossing."

Dr. Songhurst then continued: "Last week a female elephant got into a farmer's grain storage area, and she was shot and killed by the farmer. That was on Monday. On Thursday a woman was walking near the area where the elephant was shot. They don't know exactly what happened, but they think the woman somehow surprised a female elephant, possibly from the herd of the dead elephant; it chased her down and mortally wounded her. The woman was alive when they found her, but it took hours for an ambulance from the nearest town with a hospital to get here, and she died by the time she got to the hospital. So the Department of Wildlife went out and found the elephant. They identified her by the blood on her tusks, and she was part of a larger breeding group. They killed the whole group. Six elephants.

"This woman was the sixth person killed by an elephant since 2006. The effect right now is that the elephants have stopped coming down during the day."

"Wait a minute," I asked. "All the elephants 'know' about this incident? All these thousands of elephants, many of whom were miles away when the woman was killed or the group of six elephants was

killed, have communicated to each other that it is now dangerous to
come down as a group for water?"

"They seem to know," Dr. Stronza replied with a nod. "The villages know, the elephants know. It's a tense time."

When elephants kill people, people kill elephants. As human/elephant conflict
increases, it will result in casualties for both groups. *Photo: Howard G. Buffett*

We talked at some length about the region and its issues, which are
far more complicated than just too many elephants. In some ways, the
backgrounds of the researchers we met with reflected this complexity.
The elephant expert Dr. Songhurst said that she had been captivated
by elephants since she was a little girl. One irony of her work here
is that she doesn't spend much time with elephants but, rather, she
spends time with the farmers, trying to help them protect their crops
without resorting to harming the animals. Dr. McCulloch's original
research was on birds and broader issues of ecosystems and habitats.

Dr. Stronza, however, is a social scientist; she works on the people side of the equation, and has spent two decades in the Amazon
and other research sites studying how and whether ecotourism and
wildlife management can be done with an appreciation for the issues

and the well-being of local communities in a region. She is trying to understand the issues and customs we often lump under "culture clashes" that need to be factored into helping a community take ownership of solving these complex problems. A wildlife management model sometimes called "fines and fences" or the "Yellowstone model"—revolving around fencing off protected areas—can seem like a good idea to preserve endangered species and wild places. But it can have negative consequences for local people, and even for the animals.

One of Dr. Stronza's initial research efforts in Botswana was to study trophy hunting and evaluate whether a professional, regulated trophy hunting industry might support animal conservation. "It seems counterintuitive to talk about killing for sport as a solution for conservation," she acknowledged, "but it's not so simple." There is an argument to be made, she continued, that a well-organized, limited trophy hunting operation can be run in a sustainable fashion with practices such as quick, humane killing and not shooting mother elephants with young offspring. In some situations, it is an economy that employs local people whose families have been trackers and skinners for generations. "These people are not criminals," Dr. Stronza emphasized. Allowing the revenues from the licenses for limited numbers of trophy hunters to flow back to the communities (by charging expensive fees that are shared with local villages) makes the community feel invested in protecting the resource. It can even discourage poachers. However, there are trophy hunters who do not follow ethical policies, and their misdeeds rightfully enrage local people and conservationists alike, Dr. Stronza pointed out.

It's always critical to look at the livelihoods of the people in situations where animal habitats are stressed. Although at least half the population in this region lives in villages with fewer than five hundred people, the land is controlled by a board that determines where people can expand and plant crops. Dr. Stronza offered data from a recent national agricultural survey showing that over three years

(2003–2006), the area of land planted for traditional agriculture increased by 46 percent, alongside a significant increase in the number of subsistence farmers. There is some floodplain farming that takes advantage of the Okavango River and its seasonal flooding, but many of the farmers even quite close to the delta are at a higher elevation. Their farms are rain fed, and they have no way of transporting the water from the river to their fields. The soils here are sandy and low in nutrients, and many crop fields are exhausted and produce low harvests. When rainfall is low, yields fall even further. Farmers apply for permission to plant new crops on better soils, and the land board keeps awarding these plots not only near existing fields but also closer and closer to traditional elephant pathways. Naturally, this incursion results in trouble when elephants find themselves no longer walking through sparse bushland but near fields full of sorghum or maize.

Botswana farmers are permitted to shoot elephants that are menacing their animals or stealing or damaging crops, and the government pays a small amount of compensation when there is crop raiding. However, the payments lag well behind what the government pays cattle ranchers when wild animals kill a cow, for example. This discrepancy leads to even more conflict between ranchers and farmers, as well as the bitter description that some local farmers have for elephants: "the government's cattle." They believe the government's policies protect the elephants at the expense of its own poor, hungry citizens.

Many different human, animal, and environmental factors are colliding here. And community attitudes about the elephants are not uniform, Dr. Songhurst has observed. A local man helping the scientists told us that many local people hate the elephants and are in favor of culling these herds to a less threatening size, as the government has considered. But at least one local tribal group believes that elephants embody the souls of its ancestors. They not only honor elephants but also would never kill them or eat their meat. Other tribes have no such taboos and will dry elephant meat to preserve it as backup food. Still others in Botswana are being employed by photographic safari camps where visitors come to view and photograph wildlife. They support the proconservation policies that attract tourists.

All that said, Dr. Songhurst and HEAL are working hard on practical solutions. She has introduced some mitigation strategies to try to keep the elephants out of crop fields and other areas. Some farmers string cans together on wires around their fields to create a noisy racket when an elephant pushes against the line. They have rigged up battery-powered electric fences designed to throw off repelling shocks if the elephants come in contact with them. Most crop raiding occurs at night, so blinking lights charged during the day by solar panels also discourage the animals from approaching. Some farmers carry solar-powered flashlights and sleep at night in watch huts, running into the field if an elephant invades, and banging drums and shining lights to ward it off.

However, the black cloths on the line at regular intervals are one element of the area's most widespread mitigation tools. Elephants, it turns out, hate chilies; the chemical in the seeds, capsicum, irritates the lining of their trunks. Throughout Africa, farmers in areas where elephant encroachment is an issue have been experimenting with how to disperse chili capsicum in the air to get elephants to back off. Some farmers create "cakes" of dung mixed with chili seeds. Then they build small, rectangular troughs along the perimeter of their fields and set the cakes on fire when the crop is at a vulnerable stage right before harvest. They're designed to burn for hours and throw off the chili scent.

The black cloths flapping here in the Okavango have been soaked in oil and ground-up chili seeds and hung about five feet above ground. According to Dr. Songhurst, elephant footprints around her camp (the researchers have a large garden plot behind their tents) show that the large mammals lumber straight up to the fence, but then wheel around and leave once they encounter the chili-soaked cloths. It's cheap, it's nonviolent, and it works without putting people or elephants in jeopardy.

To protect themselves and their crops, villagers in rural Botswana build fences draped with chili pepper–soaked cloths to repel the elephants. *Photo: Howard G. Buffett*

Mitigation tools like this will be vital for the foreseeable future. Dr. Songhurst is also attempting to teach local farmers to improve their yields and techniques so that they produce more food without having to take over more land. This prompted me to think that the region could be an excellent laboratory to further demonstrate our conviction that conservation agriculture is important whether you're farming one thousand acres of soybeans in Illinois or two acres of sorghum in Botswana.

Dr. Songhurst and Dr. McCulloch believe that if yields can be improved economically, the size of agricultural land needed by farmers can be reduced. Farmers will protect and enhance their existing soil quality instead of wearing it out and needing to move on. Higher yields can mean smaller fields, which are easier to protect from raiding animals. I went into one of the local fields and came away optimistic: although the soil was sandy, there was organic matter in the top inches. Planting cover crops, leaving plant residues in place, and applying some fertilizer to the soil would be likely to have a pretty dramatic effect on yield at the field I visited.

SHOULD FARMERS LET THE DOGS OUT?

Unfortunately, Dr. Songhurst has found the local Botswana farmers reluctant to use new methods. They still plow, and traditionally they plant by tossing, or "broadcasting," seed by hand, which is an inefficient method. I asked the researchers to arrange a meeting with a local chief and some farmers so that we could talk about this when I was there. We met in an open-air concrete structure in Gunotsoga, a local village that survived mostly through subsistence farming. (Funny aside: in this remote place, where many adults and children did not even have shoes, quite a few people attending the meeting periodically would answer their cell phones and duck outside for a quick conversation. It reminded me of meetings at companies in the United States—except for the bare feet.)

The farmers appreciate the work Dr. Songhurst has done teaching them mitigation techniques such as using chilies. I offered to send several farmers to a training program at our Ukulima Farm in South Africa so that they could bring back information on more sustainable soil and farming techniques to teach their peers (this happened in February 2013). We also discussed whether obtaining a seed variety that has a shorter growing season might help these farmers by allowing them to harvest their fields before the most intense elephant migrations take place during the dry season.

As I was leaving, a man came up to me and offered his own idea: training dogs to chase elephants out of the crop fields. I've seen trained dogs used in some creative ways in Africa, including scaring off cheetahs from menacing cattle. "I think you may have something there. That's an interesting idea!" I told him.

There are other ideas to resolve this situation that might stand a better chance of changing the fundamentals, but they would demand regional and even cross-border cooperation. If there was a way to create transborder corridors for the elephants so they could migrate beyond the Okavango Panhandle back into Angola and Namibia, the issue of their density here could be relieved. But so-called veterinary fences block their reentry along stretches of those borders. These fences were erected in the latter half of the twentieth century to separate local cattle from water buffalo and other species that transmit disease. Unfortunately, they also bisect certain migration routes. Their impact has devastated migrating herds such as wildebeest and zebra, which are sometimes trapped during periods of drought—and the fences have bottled up thousands of elephants. "Some from the communities want to reinforce the fences, others want to remove them," noted Dr. Stronza.

I explained in the story of our water initiative that I once had the opportunity to explore an irrigation project in Angola designed to capture more water from the lush springs that serve as the headwaters of the Okavango Delta system. I passed on the plan when I realized that those involved had not invested in any kind of research or analysis of what the downstream impact of diverting the water might have on the Okavango. However, there is growing pressure in Angola to revive these plans today. That decision will have important consequences here to the south. Realizing how connected all these issues are, I reached out to Dr. Ed Price to see if we can get an assessment through Texas A&M to understand the dynamics of the irrigation projects in Angola and determine what the effects could be for Botswana.

Dr. Songhurst's work is focused not just on mitigation and conservation farming development. She also is trying to sort out some of the fundamental ecosystem elements. How fast are the elephants reproducing? Getting accurate data on this question is not easy. Despite this density of elephants, they do not generally live in giant herds that can be tracked easily. Even from the air, you rarely see more than twenty or thirty at a time, and usually you see fewer than that. Making headway on this may involve purchasing radio tracking collars for a select group of elephants.

Another challenge is to sort out fact from fiction. Human-animal conflicts can stir intense but also primitive emotions. I have observed on our own property in South Africa that farmers sometimes perceive a threat from wild animals to be greater than it is. One of our neighbors at Ukulima who raises livestock called our farm one day to say that one of our cheetahs had gotten out and onto his land, where he had trapped it. We were skeptical because our cheetahs have radio collars, and we track them, and we knew they were both inside our fence. When we investigated, it was not a cheetah at all: it was a serval, a spotted cat less than half the size of a cheetah. After a tragic event such as the incident involving the woman who was killed by an elephant shortly before our visit, exaggerated stories of rampaging elephant herds can begin to spread.

Our hope is that studying a system this complicated can help the people affected right now and also help us develop better models for untangling complex conflict situations elsewhere. I went to the Okavango in search of a mental image for that startling statistic of one elephant for every person. I returned with my mind and camera bursting with images of life in this diverse, priceless ecosystem. Now the question is: What is the right combination of experts to bring together to work on this complicated problem?

Story 28
Can Smarter
Carrots Save Soil?

If you are an American who paid federal taxes in the last two decades, I can tell you where some of the money went. Since 1995, I have received $306,274 in US Department of Agriculture subsidies. I opted out of the program in 2009.[1]

Farming subsidies are a touchy subject in America, and US subsidies are a touchy subject around the world. Depending on where you stand, subsidies can trigger a heated and emotional response from farmers, from groups battling for federal funding for other important sectors such as health or education, and from agricultural interests abroad that feel the subsidies depress international commodity prices.

There is no question that subsidies began as a way to shore up a depressed and struggling sector of the US economy during a period when most farmers were poor. Today many of these payments end up in the mailboxes of absentee landowners. The USDA calculates that the top 12.4 percent of US farms in terms of gross receipts received 62.2 percent of the government payments in 2009.[2] This exists despite the fact that Congress imposes payment limits on high-income farmers.

My dad made headlines in 2012 when he remarked that his assistant pays a higher income tax rate than he does. Financially, he benefited from that situation, but the discrepancy began to concern him. Some people thought he was a hero for stating this openly. Others suggested that he mischaracterized the situation for political reasons and that his motives could not be as simple as pointing out a basic inequity. I can tell you that my father does not like to overpay for anything. He was speaking from his core beliefs.

Farming has helped support my family for thirty years, and I'm not at all ashamed that I used every technology and legal opportunity I had available to maximize my return. But my thinking about the larger consequences of our subsidy policy has evolved as well. Like my dad, I realize this change in my thinking means I may make new friends and lose old ones, or solidify old friendships and scare off potential partners or allies.

SUBSIDY DESIGN NEEDS TO EVOLVE

Subsidies were essential to building a thriving agricultural system in the United States. There is a vital role for them at home and in the developing world in the future. A government's most basic duties are to protect its people and ensure that they are fed. Subsidies, agricultural extension, and other forms of farm support keep governments engaged in the capacity and flexibility of the food system—as they must be to ensure the long-term viability of the food supply and respond to emergencies. One of the most disastrous contributions the World Bank made to Africa in the 1980s was to outlaw agricultural subsidies—indeed, to deemphasize agriculture—and try to shove fragile economies into a "free market" mode too early and without the ability to compete.

In the United States, we have subsidized crop insurance, a program that goes back to the 1930s and helps protect farmers against natural perils or dramatic price drops for commodities. Because farming is both vital and uniquely risky, subsidized crop insurance has remained critical for the sector. As I write, the US agricultural sector is still recovering from a dramatic drought in 2012. On my Illinois farm, we harvested 23 bushels per acre of corn on ground that has averaged 175 bushels per acre over the past five years. It was the first time in my farming life that I cut soybeans that outyielded my corn. Without crop insurance, a year like that could have pushed many farmers out of business.

Despite the positives of these programs, I believe Washington must learn to use subsidies in a more practical and rational way. We should end nearly eight decades of subsidizing crop production and instead figure out how to subsidize and incentivize highly productive farming practices that conserve limited natural resources—namely, soil and water. If you haven't slammed this book shut yet, let me tell you how I got here.

INCENTIVES FOR EXPANSION

A pivotal moment in US history was the Homestead Act of 1862. At the time, land to the west seemed limitless, but US leaders debated how they should manage that expansion. The South wanted large land parcels to go to plantation owners, who wanted to use slave labor to farm them. But the North prevailed, and the federal government instead invited small farmers to go west for the promise of getting title to their own land. A US citizen could gain title to 160 acres of public land for free in exchange for farming it. Homesteaders eventually claimed 270 million acres of land, including nearly half the entire state of Nebraska.

The politics of the day were complicated, but the upshot was good for American agriculture: With that land title came pride and a long-term, multigenerational perspective. It gave farmers collateral to obtain credit. It helped them put down roots. To be sure, a lot of homesteaders weren't successful, but the program created the right conditions to establish a new class of independent farmers in America.

Around the same period, Washington also established the US Department of Agriculture to fund research, regulate markets, and provide economic information to growers. The federal government's involvement in agriculture expanded into subsidies during the Great Depression, when Congress decided that the nation's food security was a vital asset. Because of low commodity prices and drought in Dust Bowl states such as Oklahoma and Kansas, farmers were abandoning their land. About a quarter of the nation's population lived on farms then, and as a group, they formed one of the poorest segments of society.[3]

There are many important sectors of the economy, but the food supply is so essential that the government's support during these difficult times was appropriate. Aside from the obvious importance of food itself, farming is a uniquely risky enterprise: farmers are at the mercy of the weather, interest rates, currency prices, government policies, and fluctuations in the commodity markets. High prices aren't much good to farmers when a crop disaster has left them with nothing to sell. Big crops tend to depress prices received by farmers, and they can't quickly adjust what they plant and produce in time to recover from plunging prices in a given season. Farmers depend on commodity markets in which they have no leverage. As my dad says, "When a farmer pulls his truck into an ADM elevator, no one asks, 'Is that Howie Buffett's corn?'"

To stabilize the farm economy, early on Congress established a target price for certain crops such as wheat, corn, and cotton. By 1940, federal spending on agriculture and rural development represented 16 percent of the budget, more than defense and second only to spending on commerce and transportation.[4]

Ever since the Depression, when market prices for a bushel of these crops fell below price-support levels (these have been adjusted by Congress over time), farmers received federal money for the difference. The more bushels a farmer produced, the bigger the federal check. Farmers could afford to operate at full production even when prices were low. That gave us surpluses to sell on international markets and to provide to countries in great need. And it meant that in the case of a natural disaster or a food shock of some kind, US farmers were ready, willing, and able to support unexpected needs.

This strategy has generally been a good thing, I would argue. We are not talking about subsidies for exotic financial instruments or the luxury car industry; we are talking about food. Ensuring the safety and productivity of our food supply is the right role for government, and these programs have helped do that.

However, the food situation in the United States has changed. Although we do have significant food insecurity, Americans generally have access to sufficient quantities of affordable food. According to the US Department of Agriculture, US families devote a smaller percentage of their household spending to groceries than do families in any other country it surveys. Americans spent less than 10 percent of their disposable income on food in 2010, down from 25 percent in 1933. In nations such as Nigeria, Kenya, and Pakistan, about 40 percent of household expenditures are for food. For the poorest people in Chad or Cambodia, the number can top 80 percent.

The financial situation on the US farm has changed a lot too. USDA farm subsidies rarely end up in the pockets of the poor anymore. Farmers now represent less than 2 percent of the population and farmers today operate on a larger scale.[5] Thanks in part to labor-saving technologies, the size of the average US farm has more than doubled since 1950 to 420 acres. That figure doesn't do justice to how US food production has become dominated by larger and more sophisticated farming operations. Farms that generate at least $1 million in annual revenue now control more than half of industry-wide sales compared to about a quarter of that market in 1982, according to the USDA.[6]

In 1933, Americans spent 25 percent of their disposable income on food. Today it's less than 10 percent. American farmers like my Illinois neighbor pictured here can feed eight times as many people as they did in 1940; one US farmer now produces enough to feed 155 people. *Photo: Howard G. Buffett*

THE NEW CHALLENGE

I am concerned that Washington's decades-old way of encouraging farmers to produce food is hurting our long-term food security. Our farm subsidy programs are still entrenched in the Great Depression era, but the threats to our food security as a nation have changed. Primarily output-based subsidies are encouraging short-term thinking by farmers, in the same way that "contract" farming motivates farmers who do not own their land to maximize their yield for a single year. Sometimes farmers are rewarded for pushing their land as hard as possible, which makes it easy for them to put off investing in readily available and well-understood technology to conserve soil and water. I believe the critical issue today is not whether US farmers can produce enough food for our current needs, but whether the way we are producing our food is mortgaging our ability to produce food tomorrow.

While US farmers reduced the amount of soil erosion by 43 percent between 1982 and 2007, that isn't nearly enough to protect America's long-term agricultural capacity, considering that experts believe it takes five hundred years or more for nature to form one inch of topsoil. It's also possible we are not even measuring that impact accurately. The adoption rate of soil-saving, no-till farming techniques has slowed in the United States in recent years even as more and more research shows its benefits. We lost 1.73 billion tons of soil from US cropland in 2007 due to water and wind erosion.[7]

The impact of losing fertile soil is bad enough for the farmer, but the soil washing away from the farm belt carries fertilizer and pesticide into Midwestern rivers. This is a big factor in the hypoxic zone in the Gulf of Mexico near the mouth of the Mississippi River. In an area roughly the size of Rhode Island or Delaware, the excessive nitrogen and phosphorus fuel explosive growth in the algae population, which monopolizes so much life-giving oxygen that marine life can't survive. In 2011, when widespread flooding across the Midwestern farm belt pushed a large amount of nutrients into the Mississippi River, the dead zone grew to an area the size of New Jersey, or about 6,770 square miles, according to the National Oceanic and Atmospheric Administration (NOAA).

The amounts of nitrogen, phosphorus, and sediment running off farms into the Mississippi River have attracted the attention of environmental groups, and it is only a matter of time before the Environmental Protection Agency will propose daily load limits similar to what the EPA is already doing to a half dozen states in the watershed of Chesapeake Bay. If that happens to the Mississippi River, farmers in states such as Iowa and Illinois would have to cut back on their use of fertilizer so sharply that their yields could be affected. Yet if we can limit the soil loss with cover crops, as well as no-till and strip-till farming, this contamination can be limited. Right now, shifting to more soil-sustaining farming techniques is the smart and right choice. We need to motivate farmers to make that choice before conditions get so bad that the transition is forced on farmers.

Also the modern farming methods being used across the country are consuming water more quickly than it is replaced. Agriculture is using water from the Ogallala Aquifer for irrigation faster than the massive underground reservoir can possibly replenish (in fact, as a so-called "fossil" aquifer, it holds water trapped eons ago, not constantly refreshed by rainwater or snow melt). When I drive across Nebraska, I still see fields flood irrigated, which is extraordinarily wasteful, and twenty-five-year-old center pivots that aren't nearly as efficient as today's technology.

A farmer can cut water use in half by converting from flood irrigation to modern and efficient center-pivot equipment or drip irrigation. If we realign subsidy payments around conservation-based efforts, including incentives for improved irrigation methods, we could trigger a modernization push and significant water conservation across the country. By further expanding the Environmental Quality Incentives Program (or EQIP), in which the USDA shares part of the cost with farmers who voluntarily make environmental improvements to their land, our government can encourage better and smarter use of our water.

I am impressed with the strides that California farmers have made in implementing drip irrigation over thousands of farm acres in the state's rich Central Valley growing region. They had to: California has been battling droughts for decades, and urban development is laying more and more claims on water. California's water battles are going to be repeated around the country. State and federal laws have mostly protected farming's claim on resources such as water. But I would bet that the presumption of agriculture being the owner of these rights will be challenged during the next twenty to thirty years, as America becomes more and more urban, and water becomes more scarce.

GREENER FARMING FOR THE LONG HAUL

Government subsidies should be a long-term investment in society, not an incentive for producers to maximize short-term profits. Everything we do in agriculture consumes finite resources. Soil is finite.

Water is finite. Phosphate is finite. If we don't farm in a thoughtful and planned way, we will end up where many African countries are today: unable to feed their own people, let alone export food to the ever-growing world.

The USDA does have voluntary conservation programs, but they are underfunded and often first to get cut during any budget crisis. In 2011 the USDA spent about $5.9 billion on programs for such things as paying farmers to idle land for up to ten years and sharing costs of conservation-related improvements. That amount can't compete with the $15 billion the USDA spent in 2011 on programs that encourage growing crops through subsidies on farm income, production, and crop insurance.

Washington needs to shift money from production-oriented crop subsidies and put it behind "green payments," which I think can be done relatively quickly. We don't have to build a green payment system from scratch. The USDA already has plans that pay farmers for conservation performance. Created as part of the 2008 Farm Bill, also known as the Food, Conservation, and Energy Act of 2008, the Conservation Stewardship Program has many elements that could be used to build an incentive system that would extend the life of our farm belt. Unfortunately, it has been underfunded and must turn away participants due to a lack of resources.

HWB signed up our Nebraska farm for the Conservation Stewardship Program in 2011. It pays a farmer up to $40,000 annually to start new conservation practices and to maintain existing ones. As he explains, "CSP is a contract program, so the federal government contracts me to improve the general environment through my conservation practices. That contract makes it possible to take on new conservation practices that a farmer might not otherwise be able to afford." The plans vary from state to state, but farmers can choose from dozens of practices, from installing drift-reducing nozzles on spray equipment, to planting a cover crop that scavenges excess fertilizer from a field so that it doesn't end up in the river.

Part of what has held back conservation practices is that the financial benefits are slow to materialize compared to the quick money that can come from farming the land aggressively. If a farmer had a way to compute the dollar value of the topsoil scoured from a cultivated field by a single thunderstorm, conservation practices would be a much easier sell. What's exciting about this program is that the USDA is putting a monetary value on specific soil-saving or water-saving practices for farmers to see for the first time.

HWB joined the Conservation Stewardship Program by signing a five-year contract with the government that obligates him to plant up to four hundred acres of cover crops, such as radishes, and to upgrade monitoring equipment to increase the efficiency of his center pivots. The cover crops help replenish nutrients in the soil, and the changes to his pivots help him gauge more precisely how much water his crops need, preventing water waste and allowing for resource conservation.

Because the United States plays such a vital role in world agriculture, it is essential that we figure out how to get more farmers on board with plans that conserve our resources. In the process, we can set an example that could even help African governments leapfrog straight to smart subsidies the way they leapfrogged telephone landlines to a vast cell phone network. If African governments begin subsidy programs by connecting them to the goal of long-term food security, they won't have to figure out how to change farming behavior designed to maximize short-term yields at all costs. Societies have been focused on how to get the most food out of the ground today. Now we have to think about how the world can produce enough food in the future.

Chains That Unlock Potential

By Howard W. Buffett

I can vouch for the expression "strong as an ox." Oxen can also be stubborn as mules, especially when pulling a plow.

In 2010 I was in Afghanistan's Bamiyan Valley breathing thin air above eight thousand feet in elevation. The temperature was in the low forties, but I was dripping with sweat. I had been steering a plow pulled by two oxen for only a few minutes, and twice they had dragged me onto my knees on the brown, hard-clumped soil. Despite the handmade plow's guidance system and accelerator (respectively, a stick broken off a nearby tree and an occasional swat to the ox), the furrow I left behind in the hard soil looked like the trail of a drunken stagger.

The local farmer who let me try to plow was laughing his head off, as were my father and other members of the US agricultural delegation I had brought to visit the region. That is, they were laughing until some of them tried it too.

I think about this day quite often. The physical setting was stunning. The Bamiyan Valley has a rich history, falling along ancient trade routes of the Silk Road. We had flown here from

Kabul by Blackhawk helicopters, and the snow-covered mountain ranges were spectacular from the air. However, there was no snow on the valley floor, and the day was clear, opening up the view of the golden brown limestone mountains speckled with caves on both sides.

The landscape was extraordinary, but the truly inspiring aspect of meeting these hardworking farmers in Bamiyan was their desire to improve their families' livelihoods. *Photo: Howard G. Buffett*

On the valley walls a few miles behind the potato farmer's field, we could see the reconstruction efforts under way on the famous Buddhas of Bamiyan, huge statues that had been built by Asian Buddhists who lived in the valley in the sixth century. These statues, some standing nearly two hundred feet high, have been vandalized several times in their history. Most notably, in 2001, Taliban leaders dynamited them for being "un-Islamic," to the dismay of most Afghans and historians and archaeologists around the world.[1]

We had just emerged from inspecting a dark, cold potato storage facility when we stumbled by accident upon the farmer plowing his potato field. The Afghan potato farmer was typical of so many subsistence farmers all over the world. Day after day, he performed backbreaking, difficult labor to coax a crop out of nutrient-poor soil to feed his family. If he was lucky, he harvested enough to eat and perhaps some small surplus to sell or trade locally.

Yet unlike many parts of the world where our foundation is involved in development efforts, Afghanistan had once played a significant role in global agricultural markets. It had a tradition of growing and exporting a wide array of crops, from pistachios to raisins. Decades of conflict and chaotic political control, however, had taken a terrible toll. Many farmers had been displaced, and their markets and transportation options were limited. In addition, as the consequences of war plunged the country into poverty, many farmers had switched from food crops to poppies, the raw material of heroin. The Taliban banned poppy production but were known to be using it selectively to raise funds. Since the early 1990s, opium poppies had become the nation's premier crop, and in 2010, Afghanistan supplied more than 90 percent of the world's heroin.[2] Much of the agriculture infrastructure needed to grow food crops, such as irrigation, had been destroyed over the years, and production of legal crops suffered as a result.

I was in Afghanistan working as part of a special task force established by the Secretary of Defense. We were trying to restore Afghanistan's agricultural infrastructure and develop innovative ways to modernize it as quickly as possible. We were there to help the people rebuild, reduce widespread food insecurity, and thrive again. Among other priorities, it was important to me to make sure we did not repeat the kinds of mistakes I had seen in post-tsunami Thailand. That meant getting out in the field and talking to farmers in order to learn what they were up against—and what mattered to them.

It was hard to judge the Bamiyan farmer's age from his weathered skin and few remaining teeth. If he hadn't been working so hard he would have been freezing out here, I thought, as he wore just a thin V-neck sweater over a single layer of clothing. His brother was breaking up sod clumps with a pickax as the farmer drove his oxen in their crude wooden yoke up and down the field. This plowing is hard on the farmer, and it's not a good way to protect the topsoil, of which there was precious little on this field. His grit and resiliency were typical of the Afghans I met. What they lacked, however, was the infrastructure and what we call the "value chain" support that begins well before planting and continues long after harvest.

Value chain development may sound abstract, but it can be the difference between success and failure when you are trying to help poor farmers participate in a viable economy. When my father writes about his disillusionment with one-off projects, the lack of a value chain is a big component of what he is talking about. If you just provide bags of seed or fertilizer, you can increase yields and feed more people for a short time, but when you leave, the situation will slip right back to where it was when you arrived. Value chains are about creating an agricultural ecosystem that is sustainable and where individuals and businesses have an incentive to work together to create a strong economic sector.

DRUG WARLORDS UNDERSTAND VALUE CHAINS

The irony of the poppy trade is that drug warlords and traffickers understand value chains all too well. They realize that to succeed, they have to surround the actual production of opium (or coca or marijuana, depending on where you are in the world) with the necessary resources: ranging from fertilizer to sufficient water to the downstream processing facilities and transportation assets needed to prepare and ship the product. They are also aided, of course, by bribing police or government officials and employing violence to make sure their form of the chain holds together. In Afghanistan, the drug chain is further reinforced by strong incentives put in place for the farmer. Farmers are paid for their crops up front, which provides financial security and opportunities such as education for their children. Poppy seeds and fertilizer are delivered directly to the farmer, and the harvest is picked up when he's done. That means he has no capital outlay, no crop risks, and no loans. These kinds of guarantees and incentives can make it nearly impossible for a farmer to find a more advantageous alternative.

Building legitimate agricultural value chains requires a much different approach. The ideal value chain is a voluntary, cooperative structure where everyone benefits by working together. It reflects local culture and people's actual desires, it often involves community leaders, and it tends to inspire entrepreneurs who fill gaps in the chain with services or resources that make it work better and more profitably for everyone.

My road to Bamiyan began in 2010, when I joined a Department of Defense task force focused on economic development in Iraq and Afghanistan. I had worked in the Department of Agriculture and then in the White House, but I was eager to make a difference in these challenging conditions. Our goal was to bring private enterprise, foreign investment, and philanthropy into Afghanistan to help reactivate agriculture, stabilize communities, and support a more secure environment for agribusiness. DoD called the task force "an expeditionary group of business specialists," and we had a unique authority to request direct help from the military to move throughout the countryside. That helped us avoid the bureaucracy and the stricter security protocols that many other US agency personnel had to grapple with every day. This form of economic development was seen as critical, and the top of the military command urged us to take the risks required to get results.

I worked mostly out of the Pentagon near Washington, but commuted to Afghanistan for extended posts. During these visits, the spirit and tenacity of Afghans impressed me on a daily basis. A large part of my work was characterized by pursuing answers to a deceptively simple question: What would permanently improve the lives of struggling farmers? Clearly, a top priority was increasing the yields of farmers' crops, so that in addition to food to eat, they would have food to sell. But the larger challenge was to work not only on the supply of food itself but also on the elements that enable the food to enter regional and global markets in an efficient, productive way.

One reason I put the delegation together to go to Bamiyan was to meet the local governor of the province, Dr. Habiba Sarobi. She— yes, *she*—was the first female provincial governor in the country, and she was well known for promoting women's rights and equality. We met to express our support for her accomplishments in the province and to confirm her support for our general goals and efforts. We also went to inspect a new cool storage facility for local potato farmers, which we hoped to replicate throughout the province as a successful model for reducing postharvest loss. This model is a good example of an essential value chain component: potatoes are hardy, but they have to be kept in cold and—importantly—dry storage before they are shipped or processed. Otherwise they will begin to sprout.

An agricultural value chain begins with high-quality seeds and fertilizer and tools and technology, whether it is crude hoes or high-tech tractors. But after crops are harvested, critical "downstream" links in the chain include the logistics of storing, packaging, perhaps processing, and shipping crops safely. The chain also requires business infrastructure elements such as access to markets, and getting buyers, contracts, and fair prices.

In Afghanistan, the processing of certain kinds of crops into value-added by-products was of particular interest to us. Processing raisins involves drying and deseeding and turns more fragile grapes into a commodity with a long shelf life that is easier to ship. In this part of the world, there also is a big demand for processed tomato sauce made from tomatoes that otherwise would have a short shelf life. Processed tomatoes are highly valued throughout the Middle East. In some communities in Afghanistan, they are produced mostly by small groups of women whipping up big potfuls in their kitchens and ladling the resulting stewed mixture into mason jars by hand. Sometimes in clean conditions—sometimes not so much.

Just as a chain is only as strong as its weakest link, you have to address the entire value chain comprehensively. On a separate trip, I visited a large-scale tomato processing plant. At first glance, its operations looked to be modern and clean—until I happened to look up and realized that ventilation holes in the roof acted as large nesting places for swarms of birds. At times, these birds would fly above the processing bins and tanks, making their own contributions to the production process. Outside the facility stood hundreds of empty blue and yellow containers. These were left open and exposed to the elements, with layers of old tomato paste caked inside the bins. The containers received no more than a rinsing out with water from a hose before reentering the facility and being used to store the paste temporarily until it was canned. At the time, the facility's tin can sterilization machine was broken, so the sauce was poured directly from the containers into the cans and then shipped off to local markets around town.

I'm sorry to share these appetite-wrecking observations, but they were an obvious concern for the health of locals eating the product and the absence of sterile processing would prevent these products from reaching broader markets. Whether the product was tomato paste, saffron, or flour, to sell commodities on regulated international markets, farmers and processors needed an advanced commodity testing laboratory to certify both raw and processed food quality. Lacking such a laboratory, along with the necessary training, was a critical gap in the value chain. Having basic regulations is one way to motivate a processor to clean up a facility and install safeguards such as mesh over ventilation holes. If a processor knows he can't sell into a market unless his product meets specific standards, he will respond or otherwise go out of business. But without the laboratory facilities to test and reassure that he can meet these requirements, standards cannot be established, let alone enforced.

As my time on the team progressed, I learned a considerable

amount about the challenges of working in such a difficult, at times dangerous, and certainly infrastructure-poor environment. Earlier, I mentioned that our task force was unique. When I led the delegation of agriculture experts to Bamiyan, for example, we had the transportation flexibility and security to cover a lot of ground in a short period of time. Literally hundreds of other US development and foreign affairs officers were stationed at the US embassy and could be required to wait for weeks to travel "outside the wire," or move in unfortified territory. I recall thinking that it was no wonder that some critics back home complained about the waste of resources in Afghanistan, since it is impossible to figure out what farmers need and to rebuild an economy from behind the wire. To make progress, you had to go talk to farmers and visit the locations that needed help.*

Our task force had access to its own operating funds, expedited hiring, creativity in contracting, and congressionally appropriated investment capital. Freedom of movement outside normal government travel and living structures meant the team could go places and build the local relationships necessary for focusing on a wide variety of development needs. One team looked at transportation issues and how to try building roads and a commercial airport in Bamiyan: critical value chain components. Other teams worked with mining industry partners to help develop Afghanistan's mineral resources in a way that would avoid circumstances found in some diamond and gold mines, such as child labor in horrendous conditions and wealth that never returns to the community. The thinking was that the more we helped make development and prosperity the result of organized, lawful, market-based activities, the less appealing it would be to young people to join forces with extremists or drug growers and traders.

During a different part of our delegation's trip to Herat, we had

---

* These restrictions were not just bureaucracy in action: Afghanistan was still an active war zone, and many of our task force projects demanded significant security support. There was at least one instance I can recall when the security needed to protect a construction team cost more than four times the costs of labor and materials.

some conversations with Afghan farmers who had grown poppies but were now growing saffron. Saffron is the world's most expensive spice, and it grows well in the dry regions of Afghanistan. At the time, the price of saffron on world markets was high. "We are farmers, we are poor. We will plant whatever gives us more income," one farmer explained. Catholic Relief Services had started a program to distribute what are called corms, or the swollen part of the saffron stem beneath the soil surface that is used to propagate them. At least according to one farmer, that was the key primer for that particular value chain—and one with significant downstream social benefits. "If free corms are given one time, that is enough, and we can harvest future corms from our own land. The most important effect of no poppy production is that we will not addict young kids," he said.

Farmers showed us the saffron they had planted in the fields once used to grow poppies.
Photo: Howard G. Buffett

Dire circumstances push individuals onto paths they would rather avoid. This was a reality of the upheaval in Afghanistan in recent decades, and we ultimately focused on several programs aimed at restoring and supporting legitimate agriculture.

The results in rural western Afghanistan particularly pleased us, given the challenges it faces. Nearly a million people in Herat Province are unemployed, and small-scale agriculture is the primary way of life. Herat is the breadbasket of Afghanistan, yet farmers there lacked both production and processing resources that would have brought significant income to the community. Despite these challenges, we predicted that investing in Herat's value chains would bring a high rate of success.

Initially, we worked on establishing farmer-owned cooperative councils, which are organizations that brought together more than 1,400 farmers across the province into producer associations. These associations provided local communities with increased food security, stability, and the benefit of economies of scale. As with the cooperative structure in the United States, farmers can save money by organizing business coalitions and buying seed or fertilizer in bulk. This council also provided training so that farmers could improve their production and understand and execute contracts.

LISTENING TO THE PEOPLE WHO WILL MAKE IT HAPPEN

Next, we worked with *shuras*, or village councils, and organized farmers around a center-pivot irrigation project focused on wheat and alfalfa. That was an important technology investment. Relying on a long-term commitment from the governor of the province, this project offered the possibility of not only improving an individual crop but also enabling the farmers to plant two crops a year back-to-back, because one could now be irrigated during the dry season—increasing both income and food security. And we did not just show up with technology, install it, and leave, expecting them to figure it out on their own.

In our very first meeting with the *shura* in a tiny village in the Guzara district, about fifteen of us gathered in a small room in one farmer's mud-brick house. Shoes off, we all sat around a beautiful crimson rug while discussing irrigation options. One concern was managing the technology once it was installed: US farmers typically use a pivot that can irrigate a single 160-acre field. Here in Afghanistan, the smaller pivot we hoped to introduce would irrigate 68 acres, but it would simultaneously cover thirty or more small plots owned by different farmers. However, the group's immediate enthusiasm and energy convinced us that we would all figure it out together. The farmers' desire to boost their productivity was inspiring, and we got to work.

We sat with members of the local *shura* in a village in the Guzara district to discuss options to replace poppy production. The discussion led to the construction of center pivots, allowing replacement crops and a second growing season. *Photo: Howard G. Buffett*

At this and subsequent meetings, the farmers guided the process. We worked through how we would proceed together, making some early assessments of what size pivot and infrastructure would be needed. Originally we were going to use diesel pumps to operate the pivots, because we determined that the local electricity infrastructure would not supply enough energy. Local administrators, all the way up to the provincial governor, understood the value this could bring to their community: higher-yielding crops and even the prospect of harvesting crops twice in one year thanks to water provided during the dry months. They decided to build out their own electricity infrastructure so that the pumps were not subject to the uncertainty of obtaining diesel fuel to operate them. The result from just the initial pilot was that thirty-two farmers increased their production and family income, and the plan was for larger-scale expansion throughout the province.

We also supported nearby villages in designing and building rural food processing centers, relying on their preferences and needs to guide project design. We identified a group of local women prepared to run a center and connected them with a local architect. He proposed a facility that these women said they thought was too big, as they did not feel they could manage so many people at one time, and we followed their guidance to get it right. Eventually the completed centers provided 120 new full-time jobs and the ability to process eighteen different commodity types, including pastes, sun-dried fruits, jams, and jellies. These centers created an immediate increase in value-added processing capacity, and they are owned and operated by local women's associations. They now provide consistent availability of nutritious food and income throughout the year. These centers also promote stable village-level markets for vegetables and fruits, and they created jobs for many of the women in these rural communities for the first time in their lives. Visiting these women after the centers were constructed provided one of the most lasting impressions of my experience on the task force, as I think back to their huge smiles and the tight grip of their embraces.

Finally, we focused on long-term capacity building for Herat. We put in programs that strengthened agriculture education, development, and technical capacity. These programs ensured that local farmers could be properly trained well into the future, and also allowed for important research and featured a commodity testing laboratory. As I mentioned before, this kind of lab is critical to help local farmers and processors prove that the safety and quality of their products meet standards to sell on global markets. Not only were these programs locally designed and built, but they stand to support a stable, agrarian economy that can last for generations to come.

Too often one-off development projects and foreign contracts dominate the landscape. But my work in Herat convinced me that the more a community owns an outcome, and the more comprehensive the strategy, the more likely it is to succeed in improving livelihoods. My father and I have woven this notion into the work of our foundation, and our approach has evolved over the past decade. Now, we are more focused on comprehensive strategies to revitalize multiple aspects of a region and create lasting changes for its population.

There are many situations around the world where focusing on only limited elements of a value chain has created terrible outcomes. In Ethiopia, in the early part of this century, farmers experienced two years of record harvests, and yet by 2003, starvation returned. Development efforts, led largely by the government, had focused on encouraging farmers to use fertilizer to increase yields. The country had also experienced above-average rainfall, which led to bumper crops, and the farmers enthusiastically increased their planting. The problem was, other elements of the chain had not been expanded or developed to handle a surplus. Terrible roads and weak shipping options meant it was difficult and expensive to move surpluses of grain in one part of the country to another region that needed them. The bumper crops depressed local prices, and the farmers had no way to store the crop; nor were there resources to access wider markets where they might get higher prices. As a result, huge amounts of grain spoiled. By the second season, some farmers even left their crop in the field to rot because it was not worth the effort to harvest. There were no financial infrastructure investments in safeguards such as subsidies for when prices dropped, or crop insurance to hedge against weather disasters, and no financing programs to help the farmers increase their productivity—let alone investment in the physical infrastructure needed to store and transport the crops.

Designing and then nurturing a value chain means creating incentives and support for different components, but this work must be done carefully. Joe DeVries points out that countries will never develop their own seed industries if governments or aid organizations keep buying and distributing seed that cannot be reused by poor farmers. The governments may need to subsidize seed purchases while both the farmers and the seed companies are trying to gain traction, but at some point, the system must anticipate how the private sector will sustain all the elements of the chain. The companies need to sell high-quality seed, and the farmers need to learn to increase their yields using it so that they can afford to buy more.

TRYING TO GO "OUT OF BUSINESS"

Many organizations still use a template that is decades old: gather aid, deliver aid, leave a few years later. Instead, we need coalitions and portfolios of partners who are experts in vital areas that close gaps in the chains. Too often NGOs with the same capability compete for the same dollars, targeting the same traditional activities for the same populations. And donors need to consider the particular core competencies of their major partners and also fund specific links in larger value chains. Ideally, aid programs would be viewed more as "investments" and less as "charity" if we gave more thought to what happens after we leave a particular intervention. Through my grandfather's philosophy of value investing, an investor looks for opportunities that are undervalued in the marketplace today, but that with the right support and development will increase in value over time. On its face, that might not seem like a realistic model for philanthropy, but I have watched my father apply this approach to our foundation and I think it is: the same way an unskilled investor might buy stocks that are priced too high or flip stocks to make a marginal profit, donors and NGOs should resist short-term impulses by avoiding projects that only give quick and visible "wins." They must think about how to put themselves *out* of business by putting their beneficiaries *into* business. True success over time—either making money in the market or making a difference in a community—is about a long-term orientation. In business, we call the approach value investing, which means creating new value for economic gain by taking a long-term approach; in philanthropy, it is about social value investing, which means creating new value for society by taking a long-term approach.

The Defense Department was looking to maximize the social value return on its investment in Afghanistan by unlocking the local community's potential to create a stable, prosperous society that would discourage terrorism, drug trafficking, and extremism. And in this case, the threat of risk was outweighed by the significant need. From the farmer councils to the pivots to the processing centers, each link in our value chain strategy was built, managed, and owned by the community receiving the benefit. But most importantly, we found that this approach transformed those who would be beneficiaries into shareholders. The work ethic and the determination of the people I met in Afghanistan were extraordinary. And it was exciting to work on developing and creating an environment to benefit farmers across the country. But when times got challenging, I thought about my friend in Bamiyan, and how I hoped someday he would represent one link in a thriving value chain, helping to raise the entire community's standard of living.

Women May Be Key,
but Don't Ignore Men

My father never told me that I would someday find that many—maybe most—of my wisest and most insightful friends, colleagues, and advisors would be women. He didn't have to tell me that. I saw the deep respect he had for my mother and also for so many other brilliant and accomplished women.

My mother gave me a dramatic lesson about the *lack* of respect many women live with, although, as usual, she was crafty about it. She didn't give me a speech. She asked if I'd like to go on a trip to Mexico with her.

I was still in high school. My trip to Prague had been my first adventure outside the United States, and this would be my second. I don't know what I was expecting, but I'm sure it was nothing like what we ended up doing.

My mother had become active in a number of projects designed to help poor women in the developing world and wanted to visit an area she was supporting. We flew to San Diego and then drove south across the border to Tijuana. There was no sightseeing, although I recall that I had a startling sense of being in a foreign country. People dressed differently, they spoke differently, they even seemed to move around on the streets differently: gathering to talk and sit outside in groups. It was one thing to fly for many hours and land somewhere foreign; I remember it seemed odd to be able to drive from a place like San Diego and change cultures so fast.

Tijuana was obviously poor, and we drove to an area away from the shops and cantinas. There were lots of people on the streets, and we went into a house in a long row of many homes. My mother explained that we were going to speak with individual women about their situations, but we needed to be low key about it.

There was someone from the organization translating, but I sat apart from her, and I don't remember the individual women or what they said. My mother said little. She listened intently and asked a few questions. She'd hug the women as they left. But my sharpest memory was how scared they seemed. They came and went individually, and I remember that they did not stand together outside or join their friends afterward. Some were upset when they spoke to my mom. This behavior confused me. If we were here to help, why were these women so afraid to be seen talking with us?

My mom explained that many of these women lived with husbands who might hurt them if they were even aware of the meeting. Many of them had five or six children they were having trouble feeding, but in this culture, the men considered it a sign of machismo to father a lot of children. The women were turning to this organization for advice about family planning, to try to limit their future pregnancies, but this topic was a great taboo to talk about in public.

This trip was only the second time I was aware of seeing real fear on a number of adults' faces. In Prague, I'd seen the protesters beaten by the police, and I had observed the nervous looks of people on the street when soldiers stopped them. But in Mexico, I saw a different kind of fear. The violence these Mexican women suffered wasn't the result of an invasion, it was a fact of life, embedded in this culture—as it is to some degree in most cultures. Including ours, I would later learn. These women lived with the constant threat of violence from within their own family, a danger they had to navigate around every day.

I have never witnessed or experienced violence in my own family or in friends' families. This experience with my mother and my later travels have taught me, however, that domestic violence often plays a role in situations where food security is an issue. When resources are scarce, food is power. Interfere in the balance and exchange of any kind of power in a community—even within a family—and you can unleash conflict and violence.

AIMING TO EMPOWER WOMEN IS NOT ENOUGH

Stories about women's empowerment in the developing world have become a lot more common in recent years. This is an area where my brother's NoVo Foundation and ours overlap, particularly in postconflict areas. We share the belief that to create lasting positive change we have to help women and girls develop lifelong skills and attain assets. This also means contributing to their communities' needs so that the community supports their efforts. We are committed to working on preventing violence against girls and women, and partners such as CARE have been involved in a global effort to specifically promote engaging women in development. There are many examples of microcredit programs that can help improve a family's standard of living by loaning money to women to create small businesses or buy new seeds in order for them to be able to sell some of their surplus and send their children to school. Ritu Sharma, cofounder and president of Women Thrive Worldwide, has coined an addendum to the old adage "If you give a man a fish, he eats for a day. If you teach a man to fish, he eats for a lifetime." Ritu points out: "If you teach a woman to fish, everybody eats."

I get it. I agree. As former secretary of state Hillary Clinton said often, "Women eat last and eat least." Women are powerful targets for many kinds of development programs because they tend to focus on an entire community's needs—food, health, and education—not just their own. I have seen this tendency over and over. I have seen mothers in refugee camps forgo food in order to feed their children. When our foundation has sponsored training focused on improving agriculture, I know it always is more successful when women are part of the process. Whenever I meet with farmers and propose to help fund special training, I always say right away that I want to make sure the community sends both a man and a woman. We have found that is the best way to ensure that the training is most effective in reaching every farmer in a village or community.

In many areas I have visited, village savings programs work well. Women control the savings, make loans, and can respond to emergencies. *Photo: Howard G. Buffett*

For many years, agricultural assistance resources were aimed at men, even though women represent at least half the farmers in the developing world. So I am pleased that there is more equity these days. But if you think I'm leading up to a "however," you are right. Often what you won't find are organizations admitting that it is not so simple as saying that if you target women, these programs will work. There are a lot of breakdowns here as well. There are many examples of training programs, microcredit projects, savings associations, cell phone–based credit plans, and other ideas aimed *solely* at women that have failed or even had disastrous consequences.

It's not politically correct to talk about this failure, but while acknowledging the potential of women is good, it's not the same as improving conditions for women. Women still face inequality and little or no legal protection in many areas of the world. I am convinced that domestic violence represents an overlooked and toxic undertow in many areas struggling with food insecurity. One-third of all women around the world experience domestic violence, and many experts believe the number is even higher in Africa. I've had the sickening experience of asking a man translating my conversation with some women farmers in an East African village why so many of them were missing their front teeth. He made a fist, feigned a punch, and laughed, as if to say, "What a silly, obvious question!"

Those of us working in development need to pay attention to this attitude. Slogans aside, when you teach a woman to fish, she may go home and feed everybody—and then get beaten up because her husband is resentful and feels threatened by her newfound knowledge. Or he's angry or jealous about her new access to money or her plan to pay school fees with it instead of letting him get his hands on it. At other times resources are wasted designing a program in which the women would love to be involved, but, fearing a violent reaction from their husbands, they don't want to risk showing up.

NGOs around the world know that improving conditions for women is more complicated than it's sometimes portrayed, but often they don't want to talk about those details. Those downcast eyes and embarrassed reactions I've seen in the field extend to the corner office. Organizations admit that they don't want to be seen as promoting "women's rights" or interfering in local customs and culture. They figure that if they focus on measurable impacts such as crop yields and microloan repayments, they will be welcomed by the (often largely male) leadership of a community as economic enablers, not as meddling do-gooders. Gender issues scare people. NGOs go into communities in the developing world where, frankly, just like here in the United States, it seems impolite to talk about domestic violence.

As with a lot of problems, if it stays hidden and unspoken, it will remain unresolved. And, in an odd way, it is disrespectful to men if we degrade their roles in their community. I once had a conversation with some men in Afghanistan, in which they talked about how after their wives were trained in food processing and began bringing home more money, their marriages and relationships improved. Our exchange was a little stiff because of the need for an interpreter, but they were very up front about this when I probed. One man said he had begun to better appreciate his wife's contributions and realized that he should show her more respect.

When Women Thrive's Ritu Sharma travels, she forces herself to live on the local equivalent of one US dollar a day. That might mean that she has to choose between buying pain reliever for a headache or eating dinner, or between buying phone minutes or some clean water. I like that Ritu is willing to be frank about her experiences, and what some people find surprising is that she is a strident advocate for organizations addressing *gender* issues in development, not just focusing on women.

"We can't ignore men. Women's empowerment targeted at women only without helping men too can backfire on the women," Ritu explains. "We need NGOs to get on board with empowerment of everybody in the community. So many development projects fail because of this. They can't figure out why the women aren't coming, or why they are dropping out, or why the program is not reaching its goals. But talking about this is taboo. They say, 'We can't do this. We can't force women's rights on men.' It's not about that. We think most of the men are good people, but you have to help them get on board.

"One common mistake is when NGOs go in with a plan and don't ask the women in advance what they need or how to design the program. They can tell you. Women understand their communities and how they work. We have our own cultural mindset and projections, and too often we don't take the time to ask them what is appropriate in their village. Corporations call this market research, but if the development community doesn't take the time to do it, then the project fails, and they don't want to talk about why."

DON'T ASSUME, ASK

I agree with Ritu. Sometimes the mismatch is the result of donor demands or a program design that is well intentioned but ignorant of local customs and lifestyle. For example, a microcredit program to finance a business where women make and sell crafts may bring a big jump in a family's income and seem like a great idea. And in many places it is. However, in some situations and cultures the participant's husband takes that money and buys another wife! You can imagine how after that has happened once or twice, there might be a sudden drop in enthusiasm from local women.

It is important for development organizations to tell the truth in case studies so that we don't keep following one another over cliffs like lemmings and then scratch our heads wondering why what worked in Pakistan failed in Togo, or why a savings association that began with great energy and enthusiasm lost its main organizer and members gave up on it. We can't just fall back on terms such as "poor communication" or "lack of engagement of community leaders," we have to speak more honestly. If a woman in a savings association got beaten up because she kept money on account instead of bringing home the cash, we need to figure out how to deal with that head-on. To make the program work, perhaps we need to educate men about savings associations and give them a role in the plan. We need to find a way to make them see that this approach can help the entire family.

What puts a damper on more honest assessments by development organizations is the possible fallout for fundraising or the threat to other forms of support if a program is seen as having been poorly designed. Ritu appreciates the larger dynamic that keeps these stories covered up. "It's risky to talk about failing," she reflects. "There are always people out there who want to kill aid. Publishing details about a failed project can give them ammunition to do that. There are organizations working on being more transparent about their failures, even though it makes them nervous."

There are many variations on gender inequality around the world. It's just in this century that some countries have begun to address domestic violence and women's rights in their legal systems. Prior to 2007, for example, domestic abuse in Sierra Leone was not even against the law. Women had no control over what happened to them in their own homes. Only in 2010, with the approval of its new constitution, did Kenya begin allowing women to own land and extending other rights, including the power to leave abusive marriages.

I had the pleasure of taking my mother to Ghana in 2002. The trip was organized by World Vision, and we were visiting a village where, in preparation for our visit, the chief had ordered Ghanaian clothing made for my mother and me so that we could join in a traditional dance. One of my fondest memories is watching my mother mix and dance so happily with the people in this village; she had a gift for instantly making other people feel comfortable and important no matter where she went. But on the trip we also heard stories of how difficult life could be for older women and widows in some villages, and that affected her. My mother was concerned about that and urged me to pay attention to people of every age and both sexes when I was figuring out what kinds of programs to work on.

One of the few opportunities I had to return the enormous amount my mother had given me was to take her to Ghana. *Photo: Howard G. Buffett*

DON'T DUCK THE TRUTH—OR EXCLUDE MEN

There is progress for women in the developing world on many fronts, but there needs to be much more. It's a good sign that more and more women are holding political office in Africa. More countries are beginning to codify legal protections for women, including land rights. In the meantime, however, if our food-security initiatives are going to have the desired effects we seek, we have to ask men *and* women to help us design and implement these programs.

I don't believe that any woman values violence as a revered cultural tradition. Violence is a human rights violation. The degree to which some women believe they must tolerate it, or teach their daughters to tolerate or manage it, is a product of circumstances, not preference. Given the enormous potential women have to improve their own communities, these inequities limit the whole community's potential. Educating and enfranchising *everyone* has to be part of a good plan. Ritu explains: "You may have a good credit program available, but a woman's husband won't allow her to borrow money because he does not understand it. Nobody taught him how it works. That's why we talk about empowering men *and* women, understanding the different gender roles in a given culture so we can work with everyone effectively."

I attended an event taking aim at domestic abuse in Burundi, a landlocked country situated between Rwanda, DRC, and Tanzania. An NGO was conducting a role-playing exercise attempting to educate local men that women deserved respect and that everyone's life —men's and women's—would be better if men stopped abusing their wives. The approach made sense to me. The organizers said that taking the abuse out of the shadows and having men experience a performance together created a different attitude among them. Instead of being singled out, this format created a shared learning experience and made domestic violence less socially accepted. It exposed the suffering of women without identifying specific men as weak. It made them feel stronger for showing respect. I was impressed, and I went out in the field where the demonstration was under way and helped out. I acted out a drunk man talking about how it was still important to respect my wife, and it didn't make me more of a man to hit her.

This approach is aimed at the unique elements of a culture without giving up on the more universal value that no woman should have to resign herself to domestic abuse as a condition of where she lives. As Ritu explains, "Sometimes the narrative around women today is, 'Let's invest in women and girls because we get a better return on that—we improve child survival rates, raise the age of first pregnancies, and get higher economic productivity.' That's all true, but what sometimes gets lost in that is that the women's advancement is a goal in and of itself." We have to ask questions and address domestic violence and gender roles in communities. Ignoring those factors can sabotage otherwise promising development ideas.

Story 31
Souped-Up Yields
from Stripped-Down Tools

We have an open-air shed on our Ukulima Farm in South Africa where we park the agricultural equivalent of muscle cars: tractors, bulldozers, and other big iron. We shipped most of this equipment to Ukulima when we were trying to determine what farming methods would be most helpful in trying to coax higher yields out of food crops on the African continent, as well as figure out what constraints commercial farmers there face. With 9,200 acres and twenty-one center-pivot irrigation systems, we built a sophisticated farming operation. We also sent over some agronomists and experienced farmhands to oversee it.

Unfortunately, one lesson we learned was that the maintenance and operating demands of mechanized farming aren't always practical in this region. South Africa is much more developed than most other African countries, yet we had so much trouble getting simple replacement parts for equipment, that when I heard about friends or business colleagues traveling to South Africa, I sometimes asked if they would mind packing tractor parts in their suitcases. Clearly, that was not a sustainable supply chain!

We have had some important successes at Ukulima, particularly in developing improved seed varieties suited to different African climates and soils, as well as other conservation-based practices. But we are further expanding some of this research, and have shipped some of the agricultural equipment back to the US to our new research farm in Arizona.

In South Africa, there were times when our mechanical equipment for fertilizing or picking corn would break, and we had to finish the job with human labor before we could get replacement parts. *Photo: Howard G. Buffett*

However, there is a smaller, sturdy, low-tech implement also parked in the Ukulima shed that we are starting to believe may have more potential, pound for pound, to help poor, fragile farmers feed their families than big tractors and planters can. It's not fancy or shiny, and our guys welded modifications to the original design themselves. You will not find it on a farm equipment dealer's lot. I suspect many US corn or soybean farmers would not even know what it is.

It's called a roller crimper, and it looks like an oversized kitchen rolling pin with a raised-pattern surface. If this research plays out as I hope it will, it's a chance for us to show global agricultural companies that it can be worthwhile to create products for the millions of smallholder farmers in addition to expensive, high-powered systems used on large industrial farms.

The roller crimper at Ukulima is a heavy metal tube about two feet in diameter and five feet long, with distinct ridges that run along its entire surface length in an elongated chevron pattern. It has a frame welded to each end of the axle that meets back at a bar connected to a pair of tires, and then a metal shaft extends forward about six feet. We hitch a yoked ox team on either side of that shaft. The animals walk forward, and the tube rolls on its axle. If you stand behind the team as it walks over sandy dirt, you'll see the chevron pattern on the ground an inch or two deep.

The roller crimper we are working with at Ukulima is one of the simplest yet most effective tools for conservation systems because it kills cover crops without chemicals. *Photo: Tim LaSalle*

As the oxen walk forward into an area of a field with grasses or weeds a foot or more high, the plant stalks get flattened. If you looked closely at the individual stalks, you would discover that many have broken every seven or eight inches, where the blade edge of the ridges hit them. That breakage will disrupt the stalk's ability to transport water, keep it flattened, and kill the plant.

What is the value of killing a plant like this?

The answer is that we don't use the device on the food crop, but on cover crops. Cover crops are a vital element of good soil conservation practices. Many, such as hairy vetch, clover, or rye grass, fix nitrogen in the soil, increase organic matter, and hold the soil in place even in rain and wind. However, what do you do with these plants when it's time to plant your actual crop? You don't want tall cover crop plants shading the new crop seedlings or competing for scarce water and fertilizer.

So, the first benefit of the roller crimper is that it flattens and kills those cover crops. That process creates a natural mulch that decays and adds organic matter to the soil. The other benefit involves weeds. Weeds are never your friend in farming. They compete with young plants for nutrients, sunlight, and water. If you plow soil, you bury some weeds, but you also germinate new ones, and a plowed field exposes those young weeds to the sunlight that makes them grow. The matted mulch the roller crimper creates retards weed growth by not allowing sunlight to reach the weed seeds. Meanwhile, when you plant your crop seeds using a no-till approach, you don't plow: instead, you slice through the mat and drop the seed in it. The opening created is just large enough to encourage the crop's germination and early growth, without also encouraging weed growth. And in the intense heat of much of Africa, the mulch helps the soil retain moisture and stay cooler, which also helps the planted crop.

THE CHALLENGES AND OPPORTUNITIES OF "ORGANIC" FARMING

I first saw a roller crimper in 2009 when I visited an organic-farming research farm in Pennsylvania called the Rodale Institute. I read in a magazine that Rodale had achieved 220 bushels of corn per acre using entirely organic methods, and I had to see that for myself. While I consider myself a conservation-oriented farmer, I am not an "organic" farmer. I've mentioned that I don't agree that farmers should abandon synthetic chemicals and genetically modified seeds. I'm not opposed to organic farming for philosophical or political reasons, but, for practical and technical reasons, I don't think the world can reasonably embrace it to feed billions of people. Organic farming is more labor intensive and complex, and, on a large scale, less efficient for staple food crops such as corn, wheat, and soybeans. I believe we will make a meaningful impact on global hunger only if we continue to improve yields of those staples at every level of farming, from the largest mechanized farms to the small plots of subsistence farmers.

In my opinion, the most critical technical problem that no one has solved yet is that natural manure fertilizers are less efficient at providing nitrogen by volume, and there is a geographic challenge in having sufficient amounts of the fertilizer where it is needed. Technology advances are making herbicide and fertilizer applications more efficient with less excess in the environment, but it is currently impossible to produce with organic systems the yields the world needs. I also feel that the advantages of genetically modified seeds and appropriate herbicide use enable no-till soil conservation farming to succeed, which far outweigh their drawbacks. Soil conservation advantages of no-till are so paramount to me that this is where I focus my attention. No one has been successful making continuous, no-till organic farming work at a commercial scale.

But I am open to any idea that makes no-till farming more productive. And that's how I ended up at Rodale. I called the then-CEO, a scientist named Tim LaSalle, and asked if I could visit the institute and see how it managed to get such good yields in an organic system. He showed me a number of innovations, but the one that caught my eye was a fifteen-foot roller crimper they had tested, which they had mounted on the front of a tractor that pulled a four-row planter behind it. Creating a mulch mat from a cover crop was innovative. The method also saved some steps by knocking down the cover crop, creating the mulch, and planting in one pass, and eliminating the need for synthetic fertilizer and herbicide. I could see that this implement had something to offer both environmentally and economically.

My first thought: "I wonder if we could make one much bigger that could work on large-scale farms." Tim connected me with a man named Jake, who made Rodale's roller crimper. I asked him to build me one twice as long. Months went by, and I heard very little; I kept calling and emailing, and Jake stopped responding. When we finally reached him, he said, "There was no point in answering your emails; we can build it, but it won't work." But Jake connected me with a farmer for whom he had tried to build a similar device a few years earlier. I called him, and he listed problem after problem he had run up against trying to make such a wide, heavy implement that could be mounted on the front of a tractor. So I asked Jake to make me a version that we could pull *behind* the tractor instead. We bought one for South Africa and another for our Illinois farms.

This larger roller crimper, also at work in South Africa, is pulled by a tractor. We are exploring how this technology might be implemented in large-scale conservation farming systems in both Africa and the US. *Photo: Tim LaSalle*

One challenge in the original Rodale design was that the planter had to be the same width and be pulled directly behind the roller crimper to make sure the seeds were going into the proper row alignment with the matted cover crop. However, as GPS-based steering became the norm, we realized we did not have to roll, crimp, and plant in the same pass. By setting the GPS, we could pull the roller crimper behind the tractor, and then just come behind that with the planter and be sure we were in the precise alignment we wanted. We tested this technique on the thirty-foot roller crimper, and it worked perfectly, smashing down the black-oats cover crop and creating a mulch we could slice through to plant. I then convinced John Deere to adapt a twenty-four-row tool bar to handle a sixty-foot roller crimper, which Jake has modified. We used it for the first time in the spring of 2013. If we get the results we are hoping for, our research and development could provide more efficient and sustainable conservation-based approaches for large-scale farmers anywhere in the world.

But back to the five-footer at Ukulima, because no-till on smallholder farms is the real game-changer. Tim LaSalle was excited about the idea of using what he learned at Rodale to help subsistence farmers. We discussed my aversion to the term *organic*, in part because even though they may qualify, poor farmers in distant places cannot afford the costs of the certifications needed to be designated "organic." Here at home, the term puts off a lot of mainstream farmers who would otherwise be receptive to some of the techniques that enable better soil conservation.

However, it is true that, as Tim explains, "By financial capacity and input availability in many African regions, smallholder farmers will need an organic system by necessity." In many regions, the farmers are so poor and the resources so limited that they have no choice but to use what I prefer to call biological methods. Manures, composts, hand hoeing of weeds, and hand harvesting are the only tools available. So I hired Tim to come to South Africa and figure out how he could use what he had learned at Rodale to help these farmers. He says, "We are focused on a regenerative and sustainable system for soils that, of course, will be using no-till."

Tim and I figured we could develop a much smaller roller crimper that could be pulled by oxen. The weed suppression is particularly important, Tim explains: "My experience and travel over the years have educated me to the fact that much of the challenge in organic farming systems is weeds. Coming from a farming background from the Central Valley of California, I learned early about weeds, and our approach was usually cultivating or, with hoe in hand, addressing our cotton, peaches, or walnut groves early in the season and keeping the fields and orchards clean. Unfortunately, we did not know of the advantages of no-till."

The beauty of the small roller crimper is that it is a solid piece of equipment that does not need expensive fuel. It does not have fragile electronics or lots of moving parts; it can be drawn by oxen and shared by many farmers; it can create that same weed-suppressing mat that the farmer can then slice into or poke holes in to plant by hand. Our team at Ukulima is also testing a small two-row planter from Brazil that we have modified to be drawn either by oxen or by a small tractor.

AN OPPORTUNITY TO WOO EMERGING FARMERS?

We have interested John Deere in creating some prototypes for further testing, and we're launching another research project using a roller crimper in Ghana, also designed to be pulled either by oxen or by a small tractor. Small tractors are an interesting new trend: big US agricultural companies are concerned these days about the growing influence of Chinese and other global companies expanding into Africa. Companies from China and also India, for example, are designing and building small, relatively inexpensive tractors and other equipment that farmers in some of the more advanced developing countries are beginning to be able to afford. But in terms of the larger population of true subsistence farmers, it will be a long time before many farmers in the developing world can afford modern mechanization. In the meantime, there may be money to be made by selling equipment that is simpler and easier to operate, requires fewer inputs—including fuel and fertilizers—and still helps farmers improve their yields. As the farmers become more prosperous, they will trade up. It's value chain development, and it's early. But I've been trying to tell US companies they may make big money by thinking smaller.

As for us, I like the idea that philanthropic organizations or even governments might be able to provide an ox-drawn roller crimper or other similar tools with some confidence that their value does not vanish when we leave. One roller crimper can be shared for a long time by a whole village, which also can share in the task of feeding and managing the oxen.

And one final benefit: an ox-based system even generates its own fertilizer.

Story 32

Does Aid Plant
Seeds of Violence?

By Howard W. Buffett

The terms "faculty meeting" and "war zone" don't ordinarily go together, but as I discovered east of Jalalabad near the Afghanistan-
Pakistan border, disruption and improvisation are what war is all
about. The question of the day was: Could our foundation work with
a committed and energetic group of improvising educators anxious
to bring hope to young farmers operating in this unusual and dangerous setting?

In 2010 my father and I attended a lunch hosted by Afghan farmers
and the faculty at Nangarhar University College of Agriculture.[1] The
day's activities were varied and, frankly, stressful. On the ground, we
traveled by large armored vehicles with V-shaped bottoms, designed
to deflect blasts from the ground underneath. Improvised explosive
devices, or IEDs, were common in this area. The troops escorting us
tensed up as we approached the border. Another part of our journey
was through a mountainous region where Taliban factions were hiding, and the US armed forces were trying to root them out.

The lunch itself felt completely different than the journey. We received a warm welcome from the group of agriculture faculty, farm-

ers, and other community members, and we were invited to sit down inside a large shed at picnic tables set up with fruit and bread. We arrived with a mission to learn about local agriculture but left with an appreciation of the struggles these farmers faced every day.

Nothing can replace a face-to-face meeting, even in a war zone. We would never have fully understood the Afghan farmers' needs or challenges without visiting them, despite the extreme travel requirements such as this Mine Resistant Ambush Protected (MRAP) vehicle. *Photo: Howard G. Buffett*

The farmers and instructors both said that what they needed was a physical building where they could retrain their country's young people in the science and practice of farming. Years of war had disrupted activities, and there was no adequate place to conduct classes or extension in an area critical to food production. My dad was intrigued. One of the principles we always talk about at the foundation is that US agriculture became great in part because our government invested so significantly in our national extension system. It made perfect sense to us that investing in capacity and training here could have positive, long-term consequences.

But here was the problem: For the past several days, we had come to appreciate the complexities of life in a war zone, including seeing the abandoned shells of buildings and homes decimated by bombs. My dad wanted to help, and I thought the facility was a good idea. But we had never funded a construction project in the middle of a war before. Would the Taliban or their sympathizers hide and watch, waiting until we finished the project to triumphantly destroy it in order to mock our investment or the West's involvement? In this kind of environment, I wondered, might development aid spark violence rather than quell it?

When you are working in conflict areas, you must look past the current destruction to envision the future. *Photo: Howard G. Buffett*

We promised to think it over, and during the next couple of weeks we talked about this dilemma, the risks, and the potential rewards. Would doing what the farmers needed be the equivalent of throwing away a million dollars? Would our help lessen the regional strife, or incite greater hostilities? We didn't know the answers. And we decided that we *couldn't* know the answers in time to help us with the decision. So we pursued two courses: we funded the project in Afghanistan; but back in the United States, we also financed the pursuit of answers to those questions, so that we or others could make more-informed decisions in the future.

Promoting peace and stability is a big reason why developed nations and donors like the US provide aid. But we know frustratingly little about whether development aid is doing the job. I'm referring not only to specific daily activities such as feeding refugees, helping farmers increase their yields, and rebuilding destroyed homes, but also to this larger job of promoting peace and stability.

When Norman Borlaug was awarded his Nobel Prize in Oslo, Norway, in December 1970, it wasn't for a breakthrough in agricultural science. While Dr. Borlaug had revolutionized crop breeding, he was being recognized for advancing peace by fighting hunger. The Nobel committee understood how hunger and conflict are knotted together. Not only does war often cause hunger and famine, but hunger itself can spawn violence by making people miserable, desperate, and angry. By helping smallholder farmers in Asia grow more food, Dr. Borlaug helped defuse what was then called the "population bomb." As he explained in his Nobel lecture: "If you desire peace, cultivate justice. But at the same time, cultivate the fields to produce more bread; otherwise there will be no peace."

My father and I called Texas A&M's Dr. Ed Price, who had been with us in Nangarhar, and we told him that we would support the farmers' education. But we also wanted to help his researchers investigate conflict and development in a rigorous manner. Dr. Price had already been thinking about how to set up a center at Texas A&M to study the interplay between conflict and development aid. Finding money had been difficult, though, in large part because Dr. Price wanted to look at conflicts *caused* by aid as well as conflicts resolved by aid. He explained that "peace and development" would have been an easier sell to donors, few of whom look to pick fights.

DOES FOREIGN AID ACTUALLY FOMENT VIOLENCE?

Subsequently, Dr. Price has put together a talented team of young researchers to build a unique database that shows what has happened to conflict—both internal and international—in more than two hundred countries that have received foreign aid. They have plugged in sixty years of data on international conflict alongside foreign aid data from the World Bank and the Organisation for Economic Co-operation and Development (OECD). Data on a laundry list of socioeconomic indicators, such as poverty, mortality, literacy, and GDP growth, are going in as well.

The preliminary results are fascinating. They suggest that foreign aid in general isn't effective at thwarting violence in developing countries. Indeed, the data show that violence has the upper hand in the relationship. There is some evidence that violence attracts foreign aid, and that those who perpetrate violence may do so to get hold of aid resources, whether food or building supplies or other assets.

The researchers are drilling down into the data to study different types of foreign aid, such as building schools, immunizing children, and anticorruption training. They are trying to better understand the differences in the type and impact of aid to see precisely what their relationship is to conflict.

Not surprisingly, this work is difficult. It involves juggling a lot of variables, and the OECD's country-level data on different types of aid go back only to 2002, which is too short a period for drawing concrete conclusions. Still, the data that Dr. Price's team has been able to evaluate so far suggest something we have long suspected. "When all forms and sources of foreign assistance are considered, agricultural development and food aid actually do reduce international conflict as well as intracountry violence," says Dr. Price. At the same time, other types of foreign aid—such as projects for building infrastructure, certain health services, and improving government administration—can increase the risk of further conflict.

How is this possible? Dr. Price suspects that the issue is in how the aid is distributed. Foreign aid that flows into the pockets of the privileged people in any poor society will increase income inequity, which itself is a good predictor of conflict. A lot of foreign aid, such as for hospitals, roads, and building government institutions, tends to gravitate toward urban centers, which can benefit the elite.

Shahriar Kibriya, the associate director of the Center on Conflict and Development at Texas A&M, estimates that only 5 percent to 10 percent of the resources allocated in a typical government-funded foreign assistance project directly reach the lives of the impoverished. He adds that studies have shown that most foreign aid money ends up in bank accounts in the West, either because it passes through the hands of a society's elites or due to multiple levels of administrative overhead and inefficiency in development aid organizations and NGOs.

Agriculture development aid—be it teaching better farming techniques or creating breeding centers for improving seeds—is especially potent at reducing income inequity because the benefits can't help but flow to a large group of poor people: namely, farmers. "It is hard to administer agricultural development aid unfairly," observes Dr. Price. Assistance in the form of training, irrigation infrastructure, or improved seed development, for example, is of little use to thieves or corrupt officials.

To get clearer answers, the researchers at Texas A&M are using an analytical method developed by a man whose own background offers a poignant irony on this kind of research. Noted UCLA computer scientist Judea Pearl, who won the computing field's equivalent of the Nobel Prize, the 2012 Turing Award, is the father of the late *Wall Street Journal* reporter Daniel Pearl, who, while on assignment, was kidnapped and then killed by a militant Pakistani group in 2002.

Judea Pearl's contributions have been in the field of artificial intelligence using "Bayesian networks" to illustrate causal dependencies.

The idea is to use computers to think more like humans by helping them reason through data with uncertainties and limitations. Dr.
Pearl's work is also giving scientists a new way to better determine
causal relationships when many variables are at play, which is essential for analyzing the field of conflict and development. Texas A&M
economists are weighing relationships between everything from terrorism and commodity prices to child survival rates. "Dr. Pearl's work
is making it possible for us to see connections we couldn't see before,"
says Dr. Kibriya.

In one exercise, Dr. Price's team exposed a major problem with
food aid shipments to Sudan, where 40 percent of the population is
undernourished, according to the FAO. Alarmed by the conflict in
Sudan, some international agencies were sending wheat there, not
realizing that wheat is eaten mostly by privileged people living in
urban areas. According to Texas A&M's analysis, the wheat shipments expanded domestic supplies, which lowered bread prices, and
primarily benefited the rich. Thus, the aid gave no direct help to the
poor, who produce, eat, and sell mostly sorghum and millet. And
more perversely, the analysis shows that violence increased because
of the disparities. This disconnect reminds me of the frequent mis-
matches that occur with monetizing food aid shipments: food grown
and shipped for the purpose of feeding the poorest people can end up
making breakfast muffins in fancy urban hotels.

According to Dr. Price, it will probably be a few more years before his team has enough detailed data on the different types of foreign aid to use Dr. Pearl's methods to their full potential. I anticipate
that the results, when we get them, will help us advocate for smarter
ways to provide aid, whether it is more money for agricultural development in postconflict countries or determining how to distribute
aid so that it reaches the poor more efficiently. USAID is funding
the center with a grant that we are matching, bringing together
seven universities to work collaboratively on combining research and
in-field development. Then-Secretary of State Hillary Clinton rec-

ognized the work as "harnessing science and technology to save and improve millions of lives around the world."[2]

Some forty years after Borlaug's Nobel Peace Prize, we know the ties between conflict and hunger have grown only tighter. According to the World Bank, people who live in fragile and conflicted nations are more than twice as likely to be hungry as people living in peaceful, developing countries.[3] Today's armed conflicts are more likely to cause hunger emergencies than they did during the Cold War, in part because they are displacing more people for longer periods of time. Likewise, we're seeing more and more examples of food insecurity generating instability. Since 2008, street protests fueled in part by food-price shocks have helped to upend governments in countries all over the world, from Haiti to Madagascar to Tunisia.

Unless we take this reality more seriously, we face a future with more of the same. One person in eight in the developing world is chronically undernourished, and most population growth in the coming decades is expected to come from the developing world. By most assessments, food prices will likely stay high and primed for the sorts of spikes that fuel rioting by the urban poor and competition for land.

The world's developed nations are as worried as ever about poor nations spawning conflict, and they are as convinced as ever that one cure is development. Their combined annual spending on foreign aid has climbed by nearly two-thirds to roughly $130 billion since the terrorist attacks on the World Trade Center and the Pentagon in September 2001. Many of the countries on the receiving end of foreign aid are agrarian societies battered by hunger and conflict.

Yet foreign aid for agricultural development—helping smallholder farmers in poor nations grow more food—is still small compared to the amount of foreign aid going into the developing world for other institutions such as governance, education, health, and physical infrastructure for transportation and communications. According to the World Bank, the share of development assistance devoted to agriculture dropped from 17 percent in the 1980s to just 5 percent by the eve of the food crisis that began in 2007.

IMPERFECT ACCESS TO RESOURCES A COMMON TRIGGER

Ed Price has been in Afghanistan helping to rebuild the extension service for an agriculture sector so devastated by several decades of war and Taliban rule that the country now depends on foreign food aid. This turn is tragic for a country that used to be a net exporter of food and was once a leading exporter of raisins.[4] The war was particularly hard on three million pastoralists known as the Kuchi, whose migration routes for forage were blocked by fighting. They're struggling to rebuild their herds of sheep and goats.

"I believe that agricultural scientists have an obligation to reduce the causes of conflict. The roots of so many problems are about the imperfect access to resources," says Dr. Price.

Our foundation also launched the Institute for Economic Stability (IES), in Maryland, to explore in more detail those development approaches that had been successful in Iraq and Afghanistan. Through this new institute, IES will develop practical case studies and explore lessons learned, which will inform the military and the development community at large.

I don't know that this research will ever help answer the toughest questions, such as when it makes the most sense to construct a building in a war zone. For our part, we accepted the risks and built the facility; photographs we have received show that it is equipped and operational as of this writing. Based on reports we have received, it is already a source of pride for the community. Nangarhar University is one of the most important agricultural resources in Afghanistan, and the new facility boasts plenty of room for growth, offering new courses in agronomy, soil science, animal science, horticulture, and extension. We believe it is essential to study the impact of aid and the dynamics of conflict so that we can make better decisions across the broad landscape of development. But it's also a good feeling to know that those courageous farmers and educators we broke bread with in the midst of a war feel more empowered as they work toward a time when their children will have greater opportunities—hopefully in the midst of peace.

PART 5

Reasons to Hope

My wife, Devon, often calls me the most pessimistic optimist she knows. Sometimes I get discouraged and it is frustrating, sometimes heartbreaking, to travel to different areas of the world and meet people in distress and realize I cannot figure out how to help them. However, the grim mood usually doesn't last long. I am an optimist at heart and I am constantly inspired by people, organizations, and ideas that are improving the food security outlook in creative ways. In this final section, I've chosen some powerful reasons for hope, from an entire country's systematic progress in turbocharging its agricultural sector, to exciting new entrepreneurial models and internet-enabled tools, to some inspirational individuals who are charting new and innovative paths. More and more, I'm excited to see innovators craft ways to address food insecurity and poverty that are based not so much on pegging success or progress to purely monetary terms, but rather on whether the people of a community or a nation possess the freedom and resources to make choices to improve their own circumstances.

Opening What
Once Was Cerrado

The corn growing on Ricardo Gomes de Araujo's fields was so thick that I waded rather than walked between rows to watch his combine harvesting the eight-foot-tall stalks. Ricardo's farm, Bull's Leather, sits on more than two thousand acres of land about fifteen miles from the city of Londrina in the state of Parana, Brazil. As a farmer, I was impressed.

It was the spring of 2012. Rolling hills of soybeans, wheat, and citrus groves surrounded us. Another field nearby featured green corn plants just inches tall. Where I farm in Illinois, the more distinct seasons mean that there is time for just one corn crop each year. Ricardo will harvest twice.

Ricardo speaks Portuguese, but he talks and looks like any tech-savvy farmer from the American Midwest. He drove out to meet me in a pickup truck. He wore blue jeans and a knit shirt, and he was toting a laptop holding years of his crop data. His operation is comparable in size to mine. We both plant genetically modified seed, and we both use high-horsepower mechanical implements.

The difference between us is that I farm some of the best soil on the planet, and he started with some of the worst. What Ricardo has accomplished in terms of the variety and volume of food grown is impressive, particularly given the serious technical challenges of growing cereal grains in this climate and on acidic, tacky, and heavy clay soils. This soil quality holds true for Brazil in general. I'm always looking for good development models, and for a number of reasons, Brazil represents what a country committed to agricultural development can accomplish.

Brazilian farmers have shown they can build a significant, productive agricultural system and reduce hunger in their country despite farming some of the most difficult soils in the world. *Photo: Howard G. Buffett*

In the last three decades, Brazil's leaders have put together smart and motivated agricultural research that is paying off. What's more, the government has developed an entire ecosystem of supports and policies for large-scale, sustainable agricultural development. Leaders of countries grappling with food insecurity in some of the most difficult farming regions in the world, such as sub-Saharan Africa, should find reason to hope in what has worked in Brazil.

The Portuguese name for the tropical savanna that covers one-fifth of Brazil is *cerrado*, which means "closed." That's how intimidating this vast savanna region of reddish acidic soil was to early settlers. They didn't even bother with it. Later, in the 1950s and 1960s, European immigrants came to southern Brazil and tried to open it to farming, but their reliance on traditional plowing methods was a disaster. Unlike the deeper, more structured loams of Europe, Brazil's soils were fragile, low in organic matter, high in aluminum (which is toxic to some plants), and subject to intense rainstorms that would liquefy plowed and planted soil and send it flowing into the rivers.

The northern fertility belt in which the US is located produces nearly 60 percent of the world's corn and 45 percent of the world's wheat,[1] but Brazil is well south of that. The fertile zones can span dry desert areas to a few high-altitude polar zones, but mostly they have a temperate or continental climate with defined seasons, adequate rainfall and aquifers, annual freezes that wipe out many pests, and soils that still have a relatively deep layer of mineral-rich topsoil with a healthy component of organic matter. As we move toward the equator, however, those conditions change. The higher year-round temperatures mean that organic matter decays so quickly on the surface that it doesn't easily nourish the soil structure, which tends to be either sandy or high in clay content. There are many more bugs and fungi that thrive in a more humid climate without freezes. And as the Europeans discovered in Brazil, the torrential tropical rains can wreak havoc on planted fields.

To understand the magnitude of what has happened in Brazil, realize that it was not about following a recipe that worked elsewhere. Farmers cannot just transplant an agricultural system designed for a fertility belt environment to the tropics or to a savanna with weathered soils. One of the reasons I object when people talk about addressing hunger in a place such as Africa by "exporting" American high-yield agricultural practices is that farming doesn't work like that. We've had several hundred years to develop seeds, techniques, knowledge, equipment, and planting strategies that work for our climate and geography. Other regions of the world need techniques and inputs optimized for their own conditions, and then communicated and taught to farmers through agricultural extension agencies. This is a long-term undertaking that demands commitment.

THE WILL TO TAME THE SOIL

Brazil's rise as a farming power was a deliberate strategy of its government, starting in the 1970s. For Brazil to have space to grow, it had to move inland from the coasts and from its long-settled southern region into its vast interior. But with that migration had to come a way to grow food to support the population moving there. Brazil set up a government corporation in 1973 to pump money into agricultural research. This corporation is called Empresa Brasileira de Pesquisa Agropecuária, which is Portuguese for Brazilian Corporation for Agricultural Research. EMBRAPA's original mission was to figure out how to farm the cerrado region. Soon Brazil was employing thousands of agricultural researchers and spending more on agricultural research and development (R & D) than even developed countries such as the United Kingdom and Canada. It now has an annual budget of about $1 billion.[2]

EMBRAPA researchers figured out that applying large amounts of lime would tame the acidity of the soil, making the cerrado more hospitable to crops. EMBRAPA also modified Africa's species of the perennial grass *Brachiaria* to grow in Brazil; it serves mainly as forage for feeding cattle but it has unique properties that help it raise nitrogen levels in poor soil. And to conserve the improving topsoil, EMBRAPA promoted no-till practices, which are now used on 80 percent of the cerrado cropland, and can reduce soil erosion by 75 percent. Ricardo, for example, plants cover crops in between harvests to replenish organic matter, improve the structure of the soil, and prevent erosion. These crops also help keep the heavy clay soil from becoming impossibly dense. Traditional farmers often plow to loosen up compacted soils. "I try to fight compaction biologically, with plants," Ricardo told me.

But the biggest breakthrough, arguably, came at EMBRAPA's soybean research facility just down the road from Ricardo's farm. Brazil needed the soybean to work into its crop rotations because it is capable of forming a partnership with microorganisms to take nitrogen from the air and fix it in the soil. That limits the need for chemical fertilizer. Since the soybean evolved as a temperate crop, it is hardwired to use seasonal changes in daylight unique to that zone to cue its growth stages. Planting a temperate soybean in the tropics would produce a plant too small for mechanical harvesting. But EMBRAPA researchers managed to breed a high-yielding tropical soybean, called *Cristalina*, which swept across the cerrado.

The payoff is clear: the amount of grain that Ricardo can produce from an acre of land is close to what I get in Illinois. And the numbers for the country as a whole are impressive as well. Brazil is now the second-largest exporter of soybeans after the United States.

The growing supply of food, an expanding economy that gives people more income to buy it, and a number of farsighted nutrition assistance programs by the government have all combined to reduce hunger in Brazil. According to the International Food Policy Research Institute (IFPRI) in Washington, DC, the proportion of undernourished people in Brazil's population had dropped to 6 percent in the 2005–07 period, compared to 11 percent in 1990–92. Better yet, the prevalence of underweight children under the age of five dropped to 2.2 percent in the 2004–09 period from 6.1 percent in 1988–92.

The single biggest farmer demographic in Brazil is still subsistence growers who work less than twenty-five acres of land. In recent years, the Brazilian government has focused a lot more of its attention on the small growers it calls "family farmers," who are eligible for more generous credit subsidies than what commercial farmers can receive. It also guarantees that small farmers get to supply their produce to government nutrition programs. That is a great example of how federal nutrition programs can attack poverty on two fronts: by fighting hunger through the schools (forty-seven million students are served every day) and by creating markets for small farmers. The Brazilian government spends $2 billion annually on school feeding programs and buys at least 30 percent of the commodities it needs from these small farmers.

I met one of the small farmers who sells her goods to the government. Noildes Maria de Jesus, forty-four years old, is a single mother who lives in a simple cinder-block house with her ten children. A petite woman with her black hair pulled back, she invited me to sit in a wooden chair on her porch and offered me water as she explained that when she arrived on this land, she camped in a plastic tent. She said she chose to homestead here, deciding that it was the best way for someone with simple means to support a family. Plus, she had the labor of her kids. She farms five hectares of land, of which a half hectare is in strawberries, her big cash crop.

The government, Mrs. Noildes said, buys her strawberries for $4.50 a kilo, compared to the $2.50 a kilo she gets selling locally, which helps her to support a daughter studying at a university. I asked her teasingly whether the government's guaranteed market means that she sells her lowest-quality strawberries to the school program, saving the best for the open market. "Of course not," she scolded me. "My children eat this food, so I send my best produce to the school."

For all these successes, I don't want to paint Brazil as a country that has made no mistakes or has eliminated food insecurity. More than a fifth of Brazilians live in poverty. The poor crowd into shanties that cling to the steep hills like vertical slums, piled one above the other, not far from the fancy beaches of Rio de Janeiro. Land tenure has been a contentious issue for decades, and child labor is widespread. Thanks in part to a flood of foreign capital, inflation is high.

It's also true that Brazil's emergence in agriculture came at a cost to the larger environment. Brazil has some of the world's most progressive forest-protection laws on its books; however, loggers, ranchers, and farmers were gouging out millions of acres of the Brazilian Amazon annually by the early 2000s. This was threatening one of the world's most diverse collections of animal and plant life. Brazil lost over one hundred million acres of forest between 1990 and 2005—or roughly the area of California. The Brazilian Amazon lost one-fifth of its forest cover over the last three decades, helping to make Brazil one of the world's biggest producers of greenhouse gases. When people burn the forest to clear land, they release into the atmosphere carbon long stored in the trees.

Soybean farmers became a lightning rod for deforestation when conservation activists targeted Brazil. Europe buys a lot of soybeans from Brazil, and the publicity worried big customers such as McDonald's, which did not want to be associated with deforestation. But there has been progress: Cargill and the other big soybean exporters agreed to a moratorium on buying soybeans from farmers involved with deforestation after 2006, and Cargill even helped monitor forests to help environmentalists keep track of land being converted. The government created a forest service and gave it the mission of managing Amazon forest sustainability. State-controlled credit to farmers and ranchers can be withheld if deforestation rates don't improve. The government's space agency now prides itself on being a leader in using satellites to monitor tropical deforestation.

A group called Conservation International, or CI, is partnering with the Monsanto Company to ensure that the agricultural supply chain is in compliance with regulations, and specifically is working to prevent illegal deforestation and local extinction of species. EMBRAPA officials told me that its goal is to double Brazil's food production without taking another tree. The agency is encouraging farmers to plant more trees as part of a soil improvement strategy called agroforestry. Large farmers are required by federal law to keep 20 percent of their land in forest or woodland.

Brazil's successes have attracted the attention of global agricultural companies such as Monsanto, which now see it as an important and growing market for their products. Monsanto plans (pending regulatory approval from China, a big importer of soybeans) to soon introduce a soybean seed called Intacta RR2 PRO, which has several valuable features that should be particularly helpful in the tropics. The beans resist the herbicide Roundup and also are fortified against soybean loopers and velvet bean caterpillars, bugs particularly troublesome in that ecosystem. That can reduce insecticide use. In much of the United States, this technology is used mostly to protect corn and cotton, but it turns out to be useful for soybeans in Brazil.

Increasingly, although all products need to eventually be tested in real conditions, sophisticated agricultural research labs start and accelerate the process. Monsanto's extensive R & D facility just outside Saint Louis, Missouri, is capable of studying conditions from every point on the globe. It has over one hundred growing chambers about the size of a residential garage outfitted with lights, humidifiers, and dehumidifiers, and soil combinations designed to mimic any conditions that farmers face. Researchers can dial in longitude and latitude and the humidity and rainfall pattern from a specific period of time. Its scientists have scoured the genetic traits from crop species around the world to find the best combinations for high-yield varieties they can then enhance with other traits fine-tuned to a given environment. The process can take a decade or more from lab bench to farmers' fields. In Brazil, Monsanto scientists work closely with EMBRAPA on a number of projects. According to the company, Brazilian and Argentinean farmers now are second and third, respectively, in the adoption of advanced seeds (behind only the United States).

A MODEL FOR AFRICA?

The cerrado's emergence as a breadbasket can be an important model for Africa. In general, Brazil has more water than many parts of Africa. However, both Brazil and large swaths of Africa lie outside the fertility belts, have old and worn-out soils, and are in the tropics. Both of their populations are booming. Brazil had those natural challenges yet managed to transform itself from a net importer of basic food staples in the late 1970s into one of the world's biggest food producers and agricultural exporters. The supply of calories per capita in Brazil climbed 25 percent between 1975 and 2007.

When it comes to food security, only government can take on some tasks. Who would have helped poor farmers on this scale except for a public institution? Building a farm belt is like maintaining a military force or running an education system. It demands integrated and coordinated activities. Only the government can protect land rights, conduct large-scale research for the common good, regulate markets so that they are transparent, and create the legal support to enforce contracts. And only government can create a favorable economic climate for farmers with forward-thinking policies. In the late 1980s the Brazilian government set about dousing the hyperinflation that reached more than 1,000 percent in some years. It threw out decades of protectionism and adopted a new currency, the real, in 1994 and allowed it to depreciate against the US dollar. And it adopted open trade policies that allow farmers to import inputs when they are cheaper than domestic sources.

Clearing the way for multinational firms to invest in Brazil triggered a flood of capital into the country's farm sector, bringing the most up-to-date technologies to Brazilian farmers and new suppliers willing to provide credit. Brazilian agricultural exports became more attractive to foreign buyers, as moving the real to a floating exchange rate made Brazil a low-cost supplier of food. The government also provided cheap credit and other subsidies to its farmers.

Brazil's experiences and future development could be a big help to Africa's farmers. EMBRAPA already has its own researchers conducting outreach work in Ghana, Mozambique, and Senegal, and has launched a $7 million, five-year program that uses the internet to match Brazilian agricultural scientists with African scientists interested in whether techniques that worked in Brazil could work in Africa. Our foundation has funded several projects in which growers on the land most like the cerrado—what Africans call the "Guinea savanna"—were taught soil conservation techniques that poor farmers can afford.

Agricultural experts I know who have worked in both Africa and Brazil are optimistic that Africa's savanna can grow a lot more food than it grows now. There are large areas of land in the same latitudes as Brazil's tropical savanna, stretching from Angola east to the Indian Ocean across Zambia, Malawi, and Mozambique, that mimic the cerrado in topography, soil, and weather. Another large belt covers millions of hectares in western Africa, where it begins in the interior of Ivory Coast and crosses Ghana, Togo, Benin, and Nigeria. We need to develop these areas while also protecting the considerable existing forests and jungles within them.

It's important to acknowledge that while Brazil focused initially on helping large-scale farmers, it has given more and more support to smaller family farmers too. The governments of some African countries have been wooing large foreign farmers with tax incentives, water rights, and cheap long-term leases of government-controlled land. Some brokers are promising returns of 15 percent to 20 percent a year on African farms, which is highly unlikely. US agricultural land—where you can get parts for your tractor in a reasonable amount of time, all the fertilizer you need, and the most modern seed—has averaged a return of about 6 percent over the past thirty years.

The potential for Africa's savanna is real. Africa's leaders will blow their best chance in a generation to lift up their people if they don't concentrate on helping their own small farmers. African countries won't replicate the success of the cerrado by giving more help to foreign investors than to their own farmers. Allowing foreign large-scale mechanized agriculture to come in doesn't create enough local jobs, and shipping those crops back out of the country helps mostly the foreign farmers and the government officials who sign the deals.

To fight hunger most effectively in many places around the globe, we must share our growing knowledge of how to breathe life into stressed and depleted soil. That takes sustainable agronomic practices, a firm will, and committed government institutions. What Brazil has accomplished on the cerrado gives me hope.

Chocolate-Covered Opportunities

Joe Whinney is the CEO of an organic premium chocolate company called Theo Chocolate based in Seattle, Washington.

Joe is not a guy who scares easily.

Let me explain.

I first met Joe a few years ago on a trip to the Democratic Republic of the Congo, one of the most food-insecure, conflict-plagued countries in Africa. We were visiting a local NGO called Green House, which is trying to improve the livelihoods of local farmers by teaching them how to improve their yields of cocoa and attain access to premium cocoa markets. The DRC can be chaotic, not to mention dangerous. Armed militia and factions with shifting loyalties are constant threats. Joe, who travels to many exotic and complicated places to source cocoa, was low key and unfazed by everything. I realized right away that he was not your typical food company CEO. And the more I talked with him, the clearer that became.

Joe is from Philadelphia. He was a good student in high school, but he grew impatient and dropped out during his senior year, before graduation. Joe and a buddy pooled their money, bought a sailboat, and began an adventure in the Caribbean. But after three months, Joe went ashore in the Central American country of Belize, and he decided he wanted to do something productive with his time and energy. He went to work for an NGO that was fighting to preserve indigenous species in the face of increasing development pressures. It didn't take long before Joe realized that to accomplish that, you have to figure out how to improve the livelihoods of people living in and near fragile ecosystems, so they don't see destroying the rain forest and endangered species as the only way to survive.

One of the projects the NGO was exploring was helping the Belizeans expand the market for their high-quality cocoa. Major chocolate companies, including Hershey's, had operations in Belize and liked the quality of the local product. Joe went out to learn about farming this crop. The first day he showed up on a cocoa plantation to work with the local farmhands, they handed him two things: an old rice sack with a car seatbelt sewn onto it as a strap, and a shotgun. They gave no explanation. "I wondered, 'Do you shoot the trees to shake off the pods?'"

Joe watched his coworkers and saw that wasn't it. They told him his job would be to collect cocoa pods rolling down the hillsides of the plantation after the workers pulled them off the trees. He put down the gun and began chasing the mango-sized pods. Before long, he reached for a pod and realized there was a snake as thick as a baseball bat next to his hand. He jumped back, but he was intrigued and pointed it out to a worker nearby.

"Get the gun, boy!" his coworker yelled. The plantation was also a prime habitat of a snake species called the fer-de-lance, which is extremely poisonous, aggressive, and territorial. It hunts in pairs. (What's not to like?) Joe handed the gun to his coworker, who shot the snake. "The other guys barely looked up," he says. Before long, the occasional sound of a gun firing was just part of Joe's workday. He came to appreciate how hard the local people worked, for little money, and that the simple act of parting leaves or moving to a new tree could be deadly.

Joe talks about how many cocoa farmers around the world have never seen the finished chocolate that results from all this labor—and how the journey that cocoa takes from tree to truffle is not even remotely imaginable from looking at a raw cocoa pod. "The pods are like a cross between a little football and a pumpkin," he explains. At the end of his first day, Joe saw the workers open the pods and eat the milky white, creamy pulp inside them. "It's absolutely delicious. I could not believe that the Milky Way bar I had stolen from my brother's Halloween bag could come from this."

He was hooked. Joe felt empathy for the local people, and he could see that cocoa was a premium crop that could improve their livelihoods, but only if they could access global markets. "By the early 1990s, I was trying to source organic chocolate. I was buying beans, taking risks, and selling lots to ADM and other companies. But I realized there was nothing proprietary about what I was doing, and a large manufacturer could just step in and take the market. I started my own chocolate company in 1994, but we couldn't turn a profit trying to develop the farming side. Nobody cared about cocoa. In the 2001 market, my funding dried up. There wasn't money around to do the development work. I realized if I didn't get profitable fast, it was over. If the business doesn't perform financially, nothing else matters. The business had been too mission heavy, and I didn't focus on nuts and bolts."

He assessed what he had learned, and he figured out a better way to go. By 2004, Joe and a partner had formed Theo Chocolate in Seattle. He was determined to pursue "enlightened capitalism," but capitalism nonetheless.

BEYOND GOOD INTENTIONS, CREATING NEW CHOICES

Joe is what some call a "social entrepreneur." The term has become a buzzword in development, and it can apply to a wide variety of both nonprofit and for-profit enterprises. This sector of innovation is one I am excited about, and I expect it to produce lots of good ideas in coming years. As a foundation, we have only begun to get involved with some of these entrepreneurs and projects, and I don't know which forms will be the most successful. But what is so crucial is that the projects develop markets and jobs. They go beyond good intentions and aid, and create sustainable solutions.

There are start-ups with narrow business models, such as selling smart-phone apps to help rural farmers check grain prices, or even small, regional crop insurance companies that collect premiums and pay claims through cell phone credits. In India, there is a company using cell phone texting to alert residents in different parts of a city that water is about to be directed to their local spigots. Even some very poor people find this service worth the small cost, because it means a family member who otherwise would have to wait by the spigot for hours can go to school, or get a job.

I recently met a social entrepreneur with a broader vision forged in an unusual setting. Jake Harriman graduated from the US Naval Academy in 1998 with plans of pursuing a military career. In 2003, he was a Marine leading a platoon defending a road in Iraq in the early phases of the war. A car driving erratically headed straight for their position; fearing it was an enemy suicide mission, Jake and his team moved toward it, weapons pointed. The frantic driver stopped and got out and ran toward them, shouting, just as another vehicle sped up behind the car and Iraqi soldiers got out and began peppering the car with bullets. Jake and his men killed the attackers. The driver went back and lifted his seriously wounded young daughter out of the car. His wife and baby girl were already dead. "He was coming to us for help," Jake soon realized.

Jake learned that the Iraqi army had been trying to force the man, a farmer, to take up arms and fight. "I saw the consequences of extreme poverty on his face—he had no choices," Jake says. During his tour of duty he realized many combatants were not trained soldiers. They were simply poor farmers whose families were starving; the military would convince them to come fight (or do suicide missions) in exchange for food. Jake, who grew up on a farm, said he realized that to defeat terrorism he had to put down his weapon and work on extreme poverty. Within two years he had left the military and enrolled in Stanford University's MBA program. He then started Nuru International. (*Nuru* is the Swahili word for "light.")

Nuru's approach—ongoing in Kenya and now expanding to Ethiopia—is not based on aid. Nuru is a nonprofit and works on several aspects of community development designed to broaden the choices available to people and empower them to make their own decisions. In terms of agriculture, I'm interested in three particular elements of Nuru's model. First, it makes loans of seed and fertilizers to farmers and then teaches them the skills to maximize yields so they can pay back the loans—nothing is given away. In four years of working in Kenya, some farmers have seen 300 percent increases in crop yields.

Second, Nuru launches a for-profit company run by local entrepreneurs and a management team it helps to train. The company develops several business units, such as a transportation service to help farmers get surplus crops to market. In many regions of Africa, for example, poor farmers are exploited because they can only sell to traders who have vehicles and come to their village. Many farmers can get better prices if they take their surplus directly to a market, but they can't get it there. In this instance, Nuru helps develop a local business by purchasing a vehicle to bring fertilizer and seed to the village and transport local farmers' crops to market for a reasonable fee. Farmers get better prices and, as a result, can afford to pay the fee, so the model is sustainable. Nuru's ongoing involvement makes sure newly created companies keep reinvesting profits into the community.

Third—and this is in line with our conviction that development should be about putting yourself out of business—Jake says he's giving Nuru a seven-year exit strategy anywhere it initiates a program. This helps focus the community's attention on what it must learn to do to sustain the successes without outside assistance. "In the traditional NGO world I think we've created a glass ceiling where we can't break through and solve extreme poverty," Jake says. "The existing organizations don't believe they can do it and we've created so much dependency for aid, but they won't admit their mistakes.

"In Silicon Valley, entrepreneurs succeed because they realize when they're wrong they have to react to the marketplace and change. I want us to be transparent about our mistakes and keep changing." For example, there was a point when Jake, like us, thought drilling wells was a way to make a big impact and he started doing that. But also like us, he realized that was actually a short-term fix. "You have to do an entire value chain intervention. You can't just come in and build infrastructure, especially in areas of rural poverty. You have to find local entrepreneurs with good ideas and help them develop the ability to grow their business and access markets."

Poverty is not about how much money people earn or live on per day, says Jake, it's about living without choices that represent basic human rights. "Just because of the GPS coordinates of where someone is born, they may have no choices," he says (that sounds a lot like the Marine version of the ovarian lottery). But with comprehensive development plans that emphasize local solutions, market access, and leadership training, he says, "we think we can break the glass ceiling on extreme poverty."

Another interesting angle on social enterprise is a nonprofit organization called CITA (Centro Independiente de Trabajadores Agricolas), based in Yuma, Arizona, with offices in Mexico as well. Started by an innovator named Janine Duron, the company has a goal to improve livelihoods by supplying hardworking legally certified labor to for-profit farmers in the United States. In that sense, it competes with for-profit placement agencies. We made our first grant to CITA in 2007, just as it was getting started as a farmworkers-led organization that would serve the interests of farmworkers while simultaneously meeting US farmers' demands for access to a legal labor pool. We partnered with Catholic Relief Services to support CITA, but it is not a traditional NGO. CITA serves as a sort of labor broker, a matchmaker between farms and seasonal agricultural workers. CITA helps Mexican laborers obtain visas and legally raise their earnings by roughly 1,000 percent. (In Mexico, they can make about US$10 per day; on US farms, they earn US$10 per *hour*.) These workers are not taking American jobs. They are filling critical seasonal positions that large farmers can't otherwise fill legally. According to CITA, the 1,434 manual farm jobs they placed in 2012 paid workers about $3 more per hour than the minimum wage, while those employers received five or fewer applications from Americans. That is why farms sponsor them through the H-2A visa certification process, pay well above minimum wage, and cover other costs such as housing and transportation. (Our foundation partnered with Arizona State University to research why low-income Americans in the area are not applying for these jobs; one reason could be that a combination of welfare benefits can be comparable to what Americans can earn working in the fields.)[1]

On several occasions I visited CITA in San Luis, Mexico. On this trip, Eva Longoria accompanied me to learn more about the challenges facing migrant workers. *Photo: Howard W. Buffett*

It takes guts to try these new ideas, and I hope projects such as these will eventually replace short-term aid programs that ultimately change little in the long term. We need value chains and dynamic local economies that can carry on in a fair, sustainable way after NGOs and philanthropists have moved on. Joe and his partners and management at Theo, for example, are determined to bring the dynamics of markets and financial leverage into communities battling poverty. Theo is committed to fair trade, transparent farming and environmental practices, and good treatment of farmers. "I wanted to create a company with heart and soul, and that could create commerce in a way where everybody won," says Joe.

Helping the DRC is a special mission for me. Its people have suffered, and its extraordinary ecosystems have been under siege for decades. Roughly 70 percent of the population have suffered chronic undernourishment over the past decade, but hunger is only the beginning. It ranks last in the 2011 United Nations Human Development Index, which measures life expectancy, education, and income. More than five million people have perished since 1998 due to conflict, disease, and poverty, many of them in the eastern part of the country, where we focus a lot of our attention. By some estimates, as many as forty different identified armed groups have battled for control of different areas, which is complicated by the rich resources in the country, including oil, copper, cobalt, diamonds, and coffee.

The DRC is one of those places where the situation is so unstable and unpredictable that many organizations just won't risk going in. For a long time, we were one of the few American private foundations willing to try to work there. Fortunately, that is beginning to change. The trip where we met was organized by an organization that the actor-director Ben Affleck created (and for which our foundation provided start-up funding) called the Eastern Congo Initiative; it is working to raise awareness of the area and bring in philanthropists and other potential investors.

COCOA BUYERS ARE LOOKING FOR NEW SOURCES, BUT QUALITY IS KEY

The Congo has significant agricultural potential. And there are some interesting dynamics in the cocoa market today that favor DRC as a source, as I learned by traveling with Joe. Cocoa beans grow on cacao trees, which typically grow in the shade of taller forest foliage in hot, moist climates. Today much of the world's supply of premium cocoa comes from West Africa, where the climate has been getting steadily hotter and drier and where widespread deforestation has limited the growth potential for cocoa. Many chocolate companies are expanding their sourcing of cocoa. At the same time, premium chocolates are a fast-growing market, while traditional sources are experiencing lower yields.

Because they benefit from the shade of taller trees, cacao trees grow well in a forest; the destruction of forest for charcoal jeopardizes the DRC's ability to develop or sustain a cocoa crop. *Photo: Howard G. Buffett*

Green House identified cocoa as a crop that offered a lot of potential to raise the standard of living in the DRC for several reasons. First, the initial harvest is within three years of planting, and it does not require annual replanting. Second, it commands good prices on the global market. Finally, cocoa is not as susceptible to theft by militia that roam the region, as its true value cannot be realized until it is processed.

That's the tricky part: the postharvest handling of cocoa is essential for ensuring high quality. After being harvested by hand, the leathery pods are cut open and the seeds scooped out and piled so that the sugary pulp can ferment. This process liquefies the outside of the pulp and seeds and reduces the seeds' bitter taste. Then the material must be spread out and dried. It's at this stage that the beans typically are shipped, but mistakes in fermentation or drying can render a shipment worthless—most commonly from mold that forms if the beans are shipped before proper drying. Farmers learning to grow cocoa have to follow these procedures carefully. Initially, Joe was skeptical, but he talked with the farmers during our visit. "What impressed me about DRC was the commitment of the farmers," he says. "They were so engaged and aggressive and thirsty for opportunity." Joe bought 250 tons of cocoa from them. "It's a challenging place to work," he reflects, but "the genetics of the trees there are really good."

A cocoa farmer involved in the project we are funding told us, "They tell me I was living on $1 a day and that now I am living on $6 a day. I don't know about that. What I know is my family is no longer hungry and I can send my children to school." *Photo: Howard G. Buffett*

In the spring of 2012, the first container ship carrying DRC cocoa arrived in Seattle. Within a week, Joe's R & D team determined that the quality was good enough to use in chocolate. By late September, Theo introduced the first two chocolate bars: Pili Pili Chili, which features not just cocoa but also organic vanilla and spicy peppers from the Congo; and Vanilla Nib, a mix of cocoa, creamy vanilla, and crunchy cocoa nibs. Theo sells them through a number of US grocery chains such as Whole Foods. Joe has since increased his commitment by another ninety tons.

Theo has made sure that a portion of the proceeds from the chocolate sales go back to Green House to keep helping develop resources on the ground. The way Green House figures it, the first shipment of cocoa alone will help twenty thousand people living in the region, increasing household incomes and improving access to vital services. But more importantly, this effort to supply Theo is putting in place the training and value chain connections that have a chance to pull many people out of extreme poverty for some time, with a mechanism they control. "Unless you create a path to market, you're pushing on string," Joe says, adding that Theo could end up sourcing the bulk of its cocoa in the future from the DRC if the quality and transparency of the project remain high.

It's exciting that smart, tough entrepreneurs such as Joe and some of these other innovators appreciate how crucial markets and jobs are to sustainable livelihood development. I hope these social entrepreneurs do what all good entrepreneurs do: learn from one another's experiences and help everybody do well by doing good. For my next trip to a cocoa operation in fer-de-lance country, I will not only watch for this dangerous snake; thanks to Joe's insights, I will keep an eye out for its hunting partner too.

Fired Up in Ghana

I can't think of one good thing to say about slash-and-burn agriculture. It depletes the soil. It wears out farmers. It destroys animal habitats and pollutes the air. It releases carbon better left in the soil. But there is another problem that I haven't mentioned: out-of-control fires.

In Ghana's Ashanti country lives a brilliant, humble man who knows a lot about those fires. Kofi Boa was born in 1955, the youngest of four children. He grew up in the village of Amanchia, southwest of Kumasi, Ghana. He has one of fourteen common first names in Ghana because, like many Ghanaians, he is named for the day of the week he was born. (Kofi means "boy born on Friday.") His father died when he was six years old, but his mother continued to farm the family's cocoa plantation.

When he was about twelve, he came home from school one afternoon and could not find his mother. He asked around, and the neighbors gave him vague answers. They seemed uncomfortable talking to him. Finally, one of the men told him that his mother was still at the farm, where a fire was raging. Some of the local men had gone to help her.

Cocoa fields during the dry season are especially flammable because cacao trees drop their leaves, creating a carpet of dry kindling. What's more, this kind of fire is economically disastrous to a farmer because newly planted cacao trees take at least three to five years to produce a crop. Kofi begged to go help fight the blaze, but the adults refused. That night his mother returned home devastated. "She was crying. The entire cocoa farm was destroyed. All of it burned," Kofi recalled.

To make ends meet, his mother hired herself out as a caretaker farmer for other landowners, and slowly she made enough money to replant and restore the family's income. But Kofi never forgot the damage or the pain that the fire caused his mother. "I developed a hatred for fire on the farm. I wanted to understand how to farm without fire."

That quest ultimately brought Kofi and me together in a concrete block shed in Fufuo, Ghana, in 2007.

Ghana, a former British colony once called the Gold Coast, sits on Africa's Atlantic coastline between Ivory Coast and Togo. Although it still has considerable poverty, Ghana is a rising star and has a stable democracy; its economy has been growing because of an oil boom and it's one of the world's leading exporters of cocoa and gold. Mining its reddish soil—which the Chinese are doing aggressively these days—yields not only gold but also bauxite, manganese, natural gas, and some diamonds.

During Kofi Boa's childhood, slash and burn had become the norm around the Ashanti region (and in much of Africa), but he learned that there was an alternative. "There were then very old people in the village who told me when they started farming they would cut the maize down after harvest but leave it on the ground for a year, and then come back and plant again. That technique was called *proka*."

MEET MR. MULCH

Many farmers use slash and burn to claim new farmland from forest when soil wears out and stops producing healthy yields of crops.

Farmers chop back vegetation and then burn it to open up the land. In Ghana, many farmers also go through fields and burn what they consider "trash": postharvest stalks and dried weeds or plant stubble. They sometimes use burning to drive out poisonous snakes and mice. But that practice leaves soil vulnerable to rain and wind, diminishing its ability to hold moisture, and reducing the organic material in the soil. The gist of traditional proka style, however, was mulch: plant residues and other organic matter left on or even carried to the rows in between the planted crops. The mulch helps the soil retain moisture, which is crucial in a rain-fed agricultural system such as Ghana's. As it decomposes, the mulch also raises the biomass and organic matter in the soil. The other element of this farming style is to plant crops—ideally, legumes such as cowpeas, which fix nitrogen—between rows of maize, for example. That stabilizes the soil and keeps it from washing away.

It is not hard for me to imagine Kofi as a determined young man, going around to farmers in the area to talk about what happened to his mother's cocoa farm and trying to learn how he might prevent a fire from ever hurting his family again. He has a deep, serious voice and also a sly, dry sense of humor. As he finished the story of the fire and his research into proka, he said, "And from then on I became Mr. Mulch."

When I visited Fufuo in 2007, I had not heard about Mr. Mulch yet, but I had heard about the strides that farmers in Ghana were making in conservation agriculture. By 2000, one hundred thousand farmers in Ghana were using no-till agriculture on forty-five thousand hectares. Kofi was working for Ghana's Crops Research Institute, and he and two colleagues—one from Ghana and the other from the International Maize and Wheat Improvement Center (CIMMYT)—had coauthored and published a study on no-till technologies in Ghana. It revealed that, in normal rainfall years, no-till farmers obtained maize yields 45 percent higher than those of farmers who did not use no-till. After adopting no-till, average family labor was reduced by 31 percent; land preparation and planting, by 22 percent; and labor for weed control (with glyphosate herbicide), by 51 percent: from an average of 8.8 man-days per hectare to 4.3 man-days per hectare.

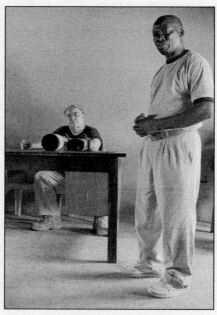

I was impressed watching Kofi discuss with farmers in Fufuo how reduced tillage systems could create better yields with less work.
Photo: Howard W. Buffett

No-till agriculture, Kofi found, provided three distinct benefits: It increased water available to the plant in dry years, because the mulch kept more moisture around the plant and roots and kept the soil temperatures cooler. It permitted the planting of a second edible crop as the cover crop. And the mulch helped keep in the field a larger number of beneficial insects that fed on destructive pests. Among other benefits, no-till brought increased food security to families from the larger yields and created more time for other income-generating farming or trading activities.

Those yield increases would get any farmer's attention. I wanted to see and hear the details for myself. I drove to Kumasi from Accra, the capital city that is on the coast, and met a group of local agricultural experts. As I often do, I was wearing one of my T-shirts that says "Nebraska" in block letters. A wiry, energetic Ghanaian made a beeline for me, his eyes focused on my shirt. It was Kofi. He smiled, held out his hand, and said, "Cornhusker."

That had never happened to me in Africa before. It turned out that Kofi had been in Lincoln, Nebraska, from 1991 to 1993, when he was studying agronomy and reduced tillage at the University of Nebraska. He was a skilled soccer player, but he became a lifelong fan of Nebraska football. I later learned that when he was getting his master's degree in the United States, he drew such an admiring crowd while practicing soccer by himself in a local park that parents recruited him to coach a local boys' team that won a championship.

Kofi's greeting put me in a great mood, but his passion for conservation agriculture put me in an even better one. I could sense his deep connection to the issues smallholder farmers faced. Perhaps most importantly, he was as fixated on helping farmers take care of and improve their soil. He farms himself, raising citrus and cocoa. "I'm not somebody doing this to get promoted," he said intently, "I'm doing it for my research and my own farming needs. And I always try to respond to the needs of Ghana." We traveled together to the town of Fufuo, where he had invited farmers to come and discuss conservation agriculture methods with me. I was impressed with their enthusiasm for the new methods and the good yields they were seeing. As I left, Kofi pumped my hand again and said, "Go Big Red!"

We've been helping to support Kofi's research ever since. Today he is doing rigorous experiments designed to convince farmers that taking care of the soil pays off in better yields for less labor. He sees his role as teacher and even evangelist. On a demonstration field in Ashanti, he regularly hosts groups of farmers, local extension of-

ficers, and students, and discusses the dramatic gains in moisture
retention he gets from cover crops and mulch around the maize, taro,
and a variety of vegetable crops he has planted on the hillsides of
this farm. "This technology is knowledge intensive," he says. "The
farmers benefit from coming here to see these test fields, but coming
on their own is hard, so I bring them here." He sends a bus to pick
up farmer groups and walks them around his demonstration fields
to show them how and which cover crops to plant and shows them
evidence of the healthy productive main crop that results.

"The three elements we talk about are: minimal disturbance to
the soil—just opening it up enough to put in the seed; a diversified
cropping system; and crop rotation," he explains. "We haven't had
rain in two months, but things are still growing."

Always a teacher, Kofi tells me he has printed up a banner with
two photos: one photo of a green, lush jungle and next to it a photo
of a patch of what looks like dry, bare earth. He'll ask the farmer
groups, "If you were to grow maize on these two fields this year,
which one do you think will give you a better yield and why?" One
of my foundation team staffers filmed a video on a recent visit to
Kofi's demonstration plots. When Kofi asked the group to vote, the
majority picked the green patch, which would have required slashing and burning the existing vegetation. Then Kofi pointed to the
brown earth. A lone farmer shyly raised his hand.

"Why are you voting for this?" Kofi asked. I'm told that the
translation of what the farmer said was: "Because we can reclaim the
brown land, and we came here today to learn how to do that. If we
don't learn, then if we cut down the trees and green to plant, it will
just become the brown."

Kofi beamed and applauded. "*Yes!* That is *so* right!"

Kofi has several test plots in the region, where he takes soil sam-
ples and measurements of ground moisture. He uses a cover crop
called Mucuna here because "if you harvest the seeds from it, you
don't have to buy more. For smallholder farmers to make a profit,

you have to reduce inputs. We want to put in more biology and bring down the chemistry. With an integrated system, you can bring down use of herbicides and fertilizer."

One of the research initiatives we're helping Kofi with is Sustainable Soil Management for Improved Food Security, a five-year research study conducted in several different climates, or what he calls agroecological regions, in Ghana: coastal savanna, forest, forest-savanna transition, and Guinea savanna. Together those represent the greater part of West African growing conditions. Kofi is evaluating the effects of tillage, cropping systems, and soil amendments (such as chemical fertilizer and compost) on the overall sustainability of crop production. It should provide a comprehensive data set on carbon dynamics and conservation systems in West Africa. The results should also improve farm management and our understanding of carbon sequestration in the various zones. Those results can be of use across the entire continent.

BEYOND BLIND FAITH

Reducing the need for farm labor in Ghana may be important in coming years. In some African countries, there is a large supply of labor, but not everywhere. Chinese mining companies have changed the local farm economics in Ghana in the last few years by paying a daily wage almost three times what farm laborers can make. Kofi, worried, says, "If we don't figure this out, Africa is going to be a mess. Youth don't want to do farming. They see it as a primitive activity. Early morning in the villages, big trucks come to collect workers for the mines." He says farmers he works with who would once be able to hire two or three people to help plant or harvest now have to work their fields alone, as the mining companies are paying triple what the farmers can afford. Naturally, everything on a farm with less labor takes two or three times as long. Eliminating steps such as hoeing the field or slashing and burning new land to reclaim it saves these farmers valuable time and money.

Kofi Boa's commitment to conservation agriculture inspires me, and the careful studies he performs on these test fields help spread the word that conservation agriculture is serious farming. It's about increasing yields today and protecting the soil for tomorrow. What's most impressive about Kofi is his devotion to gathering good data. "What has happened is that arguments have been based on blind faith," he observes. "Now we are getting the data to support what we are doing."

Similar research projects in other areas of Africa are beginning to show the same impressive results about the value of conservation agriculture. In the Maniema Province of the DRC, we supported a three-year effort to get farmers to use methods that don't involve plowing up soil but instead retain moisture and store carbon. We're developing hard data consistent with predictions by the Food and Agriculture Organization of the United Nations that conservation agriculture can offset up to 1.8 tons of carbon emissions per hectare per year. In the Kailo, Kasongo, and Kabambare territories of Maniema Province, researchers reported a substantial yield increase (up to 100 percent) for cassava, cereals, and some pulses from these conservation agriculture techniques. (Pulses are crops like peas or lentils, harvested only for their seeds.)

From the moment that Kofi became interested in finding a better way to farm than slash and burn, his motivation has been to educate himself and marshal the resources to help his people: his mother, his family, his community, his region, his country, his continent. I meet more and more smart, motivated, committed African scientists like Kofi, who have come to the United States or gone to Europe for advanced study in agronomics and other disciplines and then gone back home to help their people. The last time I visited College Station, Texas, Dr. Ed Price at the Borlaug Institute introduced me to one of his talented researchers, Dr. Macaire Dobo, a cell biologist. He is an intense, precise-speaking man who was born in Ivory Coast to a plantation owner with sixteen children. He attended the university in Ivory Coast and came to Texas A&M in 2002 to pursue a PhD. Around that time, a civil war between the north and south factions erupted in his country.

Dr. Dobo never strayed from his goal to return to Africa and help produce new rice strains that would be hardier and higher yielding, to attack poverty and food insecurity. In 2006 he returned to Ivory Coast and joined the University of Abidjan as an assistant professor of molecular genetics, and he also worked at the West African Rice Development Association (WARDA) facility, where he was trying to develop higher-protein rice strains. Unfortunately, by 2010, conflict over land and ethnic politics flared up again, and his lab was burned down. The universities were closed, converted to military bases, and remain closed today. More than two hundred thousand refugees fled their homes, and another ten thousand people were killed. Dr. Dobo feared for his family's safety, so he brought them to Texas, and Ed hired him at the Borlaug Institute.

It's important that Dr. Dobo can continue to use his talents to battle hunger. He is now working on high-protein rice strains for Iraq with special features that make them more marketable there, such as an appealing aroma. High-yielding ambar rice is highly acceptable on the international market for foreign-exchange earnings, and the hope is that it can bring poor farmers more money and prevent internal tribal conflicts. Ivory Coast's loss is Iraq's gain. However, how tragic for that struggling African country that a man with such talents cannot work in his homeland as long as the instability and violence continue.

Ed Price often makes an important point about this. Westerners have had a tendency to "send in" scientists and saviors to Africa, but they don't always integrate the talents and knowledge of scientists with the minds and hearts of a Macaire Dobo. Africans such as Kofi and Dr. Dobo are motivated by the idea of permanent change, not just a successful "project."

In 2013, I went back to see Kofi in Ghana. I was so impressed with what he's doing that we have decided to support an idea that Kofi has been thinking about for years: we are going to help him develop Africa's first Center for No-Till Agriculture, which will be located near Kumasi. The center will not only coordinate and promote research into the techniques that provide the best results for smallholder farmers but also serve as a resource for cross-sector partnerships and agribusiness development. The foundation has developed successful collaborations with John Deere and DuPont Pioneer as well as local Ghana-based organizations to demonstrate a new suite of conservation-based products from these companies. Combined with knowledge sharing of agronomic practices, we hope this will lead to a vibrant market for small-scale conservation-based cropping systems and appropriate equipment for smallholder farmers. Farmers who visit the center to learn about conservation agriculture will also learn about financing opportunities, if they choose to purchase conservation-based equipment. Our goal is to support agribusiness through a demand-based approach to philanthropy, in which charitable dollars catalyze private sector markets. We're hoping that the center's outreach activities and Kofi's dedicated leadership will make the center well known throughout Ghana, and then West Africa, and eventually across the continent of Africa.

Kofi also wants to inspire the next generation. His son Kwadwo Amponsah graduated from the Kwame Nkrumah University of Science and Technology in Kumasi with a degree in economics. He has been working with his dad on our research projects in Ghana. Kofi wrote recently in an email: "I am seeking to get him to do advance studies in the socioeconomics of no-tillage farming to make the two-party team [Kofi and Kwadwo] more solid to continue championing the course of no-tillage farming in Ghana and ultimately in Africa as a whole." In talking about his father, Kwadwo told one of our foundation's team members in Ghana, "The thing about him is that he works hard. When it comes to work, there is no joking around. He keeps track of time, and he stays on track. The way my dad farms is attractive to me—but the way others do it scares young people off."

Kofi Boa is a hardworking hero of conservation agriculture. And his heart is always in the right place. Go Big Red.

Story 36
Buy Local!

Some opening lines can wreck your whole day. In farming, it's "You know that tractor part that was supposed to be ready by today . . . ?" or "You know how the rain was supposed to hold off until Friday . . . ?" At the foundation, the phrase usually arrives in an email or letter and begins: "A no-cost extension request is warranted . . ."

A couple of years ago, I received an email from an NGO with a project we were supporting in South Sudan. This was a well-drilling effort, and the original plan we funded seemed straight-forward. The email said that the project was behind schedule, and here is just a partial list of the reasons why the project leader was asking for a change in the original project terms (a "no-cost" extension means the recipient has not spent the money he already has, so he's asking for more time to complete the project, not more money):

He had trouble keeping staff focused during a political campaign.
He had trouble keeping staff focused during the preparation of postelection celebrations.

He underestimated labor costs, which made it harder for him to hire staff.

He underestimated how much local material costs would rise.

Local government offices had a larger turnover in personnel, and so permit processes and other approvals were slower than anticipated.

There was postconflict psychological depression among the staff.

Nearby regions had developing conflicts, and that had everyone on edge.

Unseasonal rainfall had created flooding, which created impassable roads.

The flooding also made some airstrips unusable.

The equipment turned out not to have enough horsepower to get the job done.

The equipment broke, and it had taken six months to get parts.

With a list like that, I was surprised there was no mention of a dog eating the paperwork.

I gnash off layers of tooth enamel when I get "updates" like this one. Will development organizations ever learn to anticipate challenges and plan for them in a realistic way? One of the most common flaws of these failed efforts is complexity. The more volatile and fragile a situation, and the less developed the roads and other infrastructure are, then the simpler a plan needs to be in order to work. NGOs sometimes respond that these are difficult environments, and you have to expect such setbacks. Well, that is my point. When I say we need a simpler plan, I don't mean an "easy" plan. I mean a plan that is not so prone to come apart. I mean a plan that anticipates problems and has built-in backups and options when elements break, as they inevitably will.

I wrote back: "The current model most are working from is inadequate at best and a failure at worse. This is not an accusation or a criticism directed at [you], it is an observation based on looking at multiple projects that consistently miss their targets. If these were businesses, everyone would be broke by now!"

On the other hand, every once in a while a surprise shows up that makes me smile and might even help me hang on to my molars for a few more years.

A BETTER LIFE FOR HONDURANS

In October 2012 I received a letter from the Republic of Honduras's president, Porfirio Lobo Sosa. He invited me to visit with him and see the local implementation of a global pilot program of WFP called Purchase for Progress, or P4P, which our foundation helped launch in 2007. We have supported P4P in four Central American countries—Guatemala, El Salvador, Nicaragua, and Honduras—and I have visited them several times to see how the programs are doing.

This report was the most dramatic I'd ever received from a head of state: "More than half of the grain required by the School Feeding Program . . . is currently supplied by farmers involved in the P4P project," the president wrote. "The program is now considered one of the most successful programs of our government, covering 85 percent of school-aged children in 20,000 schools across the nation. . . . Our government is aware of the need to promote agricultural development as part of the country's economic growth and sustainable food security in order to give a better life to Hondurans."

In a country like Honduras, where one-third of the population live on less than $1 per day, success stories are not so common that any of us can afford to take them for granted. The president's endorsement of the importance of agriculture in a country with huge numbers of subsistence farmers is also significant. But the larger story behind this letter is not just about a promising program. I think it reinforces the importance of a style of philanthropic investment that we call "catalytic funding," which we think is a better model for more efficient and sustainable progress.

Honduras, bordered by Guatemala, El Salvador, and Nicaragua, has an extensive coastline on the eastern edge of Central America. That makes it vulnerable to the chaotic storms that spin around the Caribbean. The country's export revenues come mostly from agricultural products—fruit, coffee, and sugarcane—but it suffered devastating damage from Mitch, the 1998 hurricane that wiped out at least 70 percent of Honduras's transportation systems and crops.[1] Hurricanes and prolonged heavy rains not only wreck agriculture but also can prevent access to food and other basic necessities. As if that's not difficult enough, prolonged droughts in recent years have affected the food and nutritional security of the most vulnerable populations in the southern and western regions of Honduras. These regions are environmentally degraded and include a high concentration of small-scale subsistence farmers. The droughts have caused a sharp decrease in the production of basic grains—crops much of the population relies on for survival. Chronic malnutrition can reach more than 48.5 percent in rural areas.

ENTER P4P

WFP implements P4P through a network of partnerships. In Honduras the main partner is the government. P4P is part of a food assistance program, but it is not about dropping off bags of food or seed and hoping that good gets done. What P4P does is help smallholder farmers do something we take for granted in American agriculture: stabilize their production process and access markets. As we saw with value chain development in Afghanistan, markets are not automatic. Markets do not appear magically when farmers have a surplus. In Honduras, as around the world, a smallholder farmer existing on the brink of food security all year long is never sure whether he or she will have enough surplus to try to sell. If there is a surplus, there is not always a way to get it to a market at a time when it still has value.

WFP addresses food insecurity brought on by conflicts, droughts, floods, tightening food markets, and the global economic slowdown.

To provide relief, it buys more than $1 billion worth of commodities every year, and it increasingly buys the commodities from farmers in the regions where the aid is needed.[2] That's a lot of purchasing power. Purchase for Progress is an innovative vehicle that leverages the WFP's networks to create a stable and reliable market for small-holder farmers' output. Instead of taking the money the developed world donates toward famine relief and other aid programs and then going back and buying crops and staples from the developed world and shipping it to these struggling regions, P4P cuts out two steps and uses the funds to purchase aid *locally* from farmers who are themselves struggling. That is not necessarily "easier," but it is simpler and, I believe, a stronger model. It not only satisfies an immediate need, such as food for hungry schoolkids, but also the presence of a strong, stable buyer for local crops creates an incentive for smallholder farmers to learn to farm better and more efficiently.

David Stevenson is a former WFP executive who did important early work in the 1990s connecting smallholder farmers in Africa with WFP's demand for food commodities. "The biggest market failure we have in the developing world for small-scale farmers is getting a buyer," he points out. "Often you either have no buyer, or you have only one buyer who has his own costs to cover and wants low prices. Farmers need to be connected to markets."

Earlier, I talked about the problem with monetization. Some-times the aid available does not match the aid needed in a country. For example, the United States has corn available for shipping, yet the most pressing need in a region may be not corn but perhaps a different grain or other kinds of assistance—maybe even funding to pay rent and keep the NGO office open, or trucks, or even fuel. Beginning in the 1980s, NGOs that received in-kind aid from the United States were allowed to sell surplus commodity aid locally and use the money for other needs.

As we discussed, dumping surplus grain on a local market depresses the prices local farmers can receive. An NGO selling on the open market may be undermining the same people it is training to improve their grain yields. Also, why ship all that grain as aid when it is not going to end up helping hungry people? Given the high cost of shipping, why not just send the money, which would allow the NGO to buy what it needs locally, therefore supporting the smallholder farmers you are there to help?

In 2013 the World Food Programme will supply food relief to more than 90 million people in 75 countries, much of it through local purchase programs. *Photo: Howard G. Buffett*

Europeans realized that monetization was a bad idea. (Are you listening, Washington?) Around the same time that monetization began, European aid programs started sending funds to countries where local farmers were producing surpluses for sale and authorizing the NGOs there to spend the funds locally for food to give hungry people.

By the mid-1990s, there were enough direct aid funds coming to WFP that the program dispatched David Stevenson, then a United

Nations World Food Programme emergency officer, to Uganda to use local procurement of food aid to help with the Rwandan crisis triggered by the genocide. His job was to buy food from local farmers to help the displaced Rwandans, as well as refugees from South Sudan coming into Uganda. He grew frustrated, however, because of contract defaults. The local food traders in stressed conditions sometimes would agree to supply crops to the program, but then they would not deliver those crops. It might be because of weather or quality problems, but sometimes the problem was a basic issue: that the farmers did not understand or respect contracts. If market fluctuations offered them a better price—or something happened, and they needed the money sooner rather than when the WFP program would pay—they would "side-sell" the crop early; this meant there was a high risk that WFP would be left without food supplies to distribute to those in need. "I could see it was an admirable idea," David says, but it was difficult to count on because of the way WFP was cobbling together the commitments. He set about trying to figure out how to make it work better.

David moved around working as a local procurement officer in African countries such as Uganda, Tanzania, Ethiopia, and the Ivory Coast. In 1998 he moved from Addis Ababa to Abidjan to set up WFP's regional procurement operation for West Africa to help with Sierra Leone and Liberia humanitarian operations. He kept working on more reliable ways to procure the food locally, and gradually the amount of aid WFP distributed shifted more and more to local purchase. One of the key elements was encouraging local governments to link food procurement for school feeding to small-scale farmers, so there was more stability and infrastructure. In 2004 David took over responsibility for WFP operations in Zambia and began to further develop this approach. Experiences like those led by David, as well as many other WFP staff worldwide, laid the foundation for what later became one of WFP's most innovative initiatives.

The watershed moment came three years later when Josette Sheeran, who previously was undersecretary for economic, business, and agricultural affairs in the US State Department, came to run WFP. I worked closely with Josette at WFP, where I am an ambassador against hunger. I found her to be a visionary leader. By 2007, WFP had increased its local purchase to several hundred million dollars, and Josette realized that the program could do more good with the same amount of money and create more sustainable markets for farmers in the process.

Several different connections came together. Coincidentally, I had met David in Zambia earlier in 2007. He was country director at the time, and he was a good sport holding on to a rope around my waist while I took photos leaning out of the Cessna we used to visit different development projects in the country. Zambia was struggling after drought and flood cycles and also issues with pest infestations and animal invasions of fields. David wanted to try to develop livelihoods around the perimeter of animal habitats to attack the poaching problem with a legal, productive alternative. WFP partnered on a program designed to ease conflict, in which poachers would hand in guns and snares, and then get paid in food and be trained in food production.

Four of the most notorious poachers of elephants and rhinos in Zambia handed in their guns and snares, accepting food for work and committing to learn conservation farming. *Photo: Howard G. Buffett*

I could see that David was both creative and practical. He kept track of the lessons he learned on the ground. He knew that WFP wanted to expand its local purchase program, but he worried that it might not find sustainable ways to do so. The Bill & Melinda Gates Foundation was mulling over a proposal to link local purchase to school feeding programs in many countries to create an anchor market, but David felt WFP should think even more broadly and consider any and all food needs to give the program the greatest possible buying power.

It made sense to me, and our foundation wrote the first check to support P4P under the leadership of David. We eventually gave more than $12 million to establish a P4P office in Rome and launch an integrated program in seven countries. David became P4P coordinator and head of WFP's policy and strategy branch.

After a meeting in Omaha with Bill Gates, Jeff Raikes, now the CEO of the Gates Foundation, Josette Sheeran, and me, the Gates Foundation committed $62 million to support P4P. About the same time, the government of Belgium also joined in. Our foundation helped P4P launch in the African Countries of Sierra Leone, Liberia, and Sudan, as well as the Central American nations of El Salvador, Honduras, Guatemala, and Nicaragua; while the Gates and Belgian support allowed P4P to be implemented in a total of twenty-one countries.

MAKING PRODUCERS MORE STABLE

There was another wrinkle to how P4P developed that came from an experience I had in Mexico later that same year, 2007. Jerry Steiner, who is executive vice president of sustainability and corporate affairs at Monsanto, invited me to visit the Educampo Project in the Mexican states of Jalisco and Chiapas. Run by a foundation called Fundar, with help from Monsanto and other private companies, Educampo had taken 1,500 farmers, organized them into 131 farmer groups, and then conducted intensive training in both better farming techniques and what it called the "social aspects": specifically, the business elements of farming, such as negotiation techniques, credit, and even purchasing crop insurance. The results were amazing: a 300 percent increase in productivity among the farmers involved in the Chiapas group the first year, a significant increase in their incomes, and the expectation that the farmers would help repay Fundar so that the program could expand. The success they were having even in poor areas impressed me. The farmers worked hard, and for the first time, some were hiring a half dozen workers, so the increased productivity helped the whole community. "Before this project, we did not exist as part of the economy," one Chiapas farmer told me.

The original P4P design was mainly about purchasing production from farmers, but it didn't address their farming techniques or how stable their production was likely to be going forward. We went to Josette and David to discuss what I considered a bottleneck in the original design: if P4P was going to work, we needed to help farmers develop skills and processes to meet the production criteria. As I observed in Mexico, training is a valuable investment.

Planning for sustainability is the essence of catalytic funding. If you distribute the seeds and fertilizers, what happens when you leave? They run out. It's the sand castle and tide problem. However, if you make the market connections and teach the farmers to use credit, and to respect and carry out contracts, you have given them tools to buy their own inputs, manage their businesses effectively, and be active in the market in the future.

And so today in Honduras, you have farmers such as Lucrecia Santos Galindo, who is one of sixteen female smallholder farmers from the farmers' group Light and Life Production Associative. According to a P4P report, once a week Lucrecia and neighbor farmers attend school in the field, where they learn new agricultural techniques, proper handling of supplies, and improved practices in the demonstration plots. "This project has changed our lives," Lucrecia told the

P4P team. "Before, we produced only eight to ten bags per hectare; now we produce thirty-five to forty bags per hectare. Thanks to all the support we have received in training, supplies, and equipment, we can now produce seeds with high quality. Now *I* set the prices! I know the quality of grain that I produce and know that they cannot cheat me."[3] In her region in northern Honduras, more than 2,500 small producers benefit from P4P.*

Today Josette Sheeran is president and CEO of the Asia Society, while David Stevenson is now director general of a branch of the Canadian International Development Agency. And yet P4P keeps growing. The new head of the WFP, Ertharin Cousin, recently told the UN Committee on World Food Security, "P4P improves the nutrition of rural families and reduces the cost of food assistance programs."[4] We are hopeful that it will be renewed in 2014, when its pilot phase is over, and we are constantly talking with WFP about new variations on this central, strong program design. P4P has helped a half million farmers in twenty-one countries and is bringing healthy, needed food to food-insecure people in distress. In Tanzania, the government signed a deal with WFP allowing the program to purchase up to two hundred thousand tons of maize from the National Food Reserve Agency, which buys from the nation's own smallholder farmers. This program will help Tanzanian smallholder farmers secure a more dependable and fairer market for their crop, and WFP can use the food for assistance programs for people in crisis throughout the region, including those in Kenya, Somalia, and South Sudan.

Little is simple in the world of development. An old friend of mine from an NGO likes to remind me, "Actually, Howie, it *is* rocket science." Some days I think it may be even harder than rocket science

---

* Many analyses of the post–Hurricane Mitch damage in Central America showed that in locations where conservation agriculture techniques had used cover crops and no-till practices, there was far less damage, less soil erosion, and more topsoil. So the techniques that P4P is teaching stand to better protect these vulnerable farmers' livelihoods from future storms as well.

because some plans are doomed by factors that will never appear in an equation, from unruly elephants to staff members distracted by "postelection celebrations." But P4P is a solid idea that is changing the face of aid in all the right ways, shaped by committed people. Governments are vital to making P4P work and several, including Honduras, have embraced it. It is becoming part of the fabric of meaningful investment in both agriculture and hungry children in places such as Honduras. It was not easy to launch, it is not easy to execute, but it is a robust, game-changing idea that doesn't break just because of a flood or election celebrations or a manager getting reassigned. It's a basic approach that smart people can adjust to a given culture, circumstance, resource base, and need.

Story 37
Hungry for Data

"If you eat food every day, you should care about the people who don't."

It's a simple statement, but well put by my friend and fellow philanthropist Eva Longoria, the actress. Eva and I were introduced by a mutual friend who knew we were both interested in improving the livelihoods of food-insecure people in the United States. Eva has visited us in Decatur and taken her turn harvesting corn. ("This is more glamorous than the set of *Desperate Housewives*" she said in the combine.) However, we've talked about how easy it can be for Americans not to see the hunger that is all around us. "Out of sight, out of mind," Eva puts it. Right now we're working together on an exciting pilot project to try to illuminate and do something about food insecurity in Eva's home state.

Eva grew up in Corpus Christi, Texas. The youngest of four girls, she was well acquainted with having to stretch to make ends meet. To help put herself through college, she worked several jobs, from burger flipper at a fast-food chain to aerobics instructor. But she says she never thought much about hunger. The Longorias never worried about where their next meal would come from. Her mother was a special education teacher, and her father worked on the local army base, but it turns out that he grew a lot of the family's food himself. "We were never allowed to eat fast food," Eva explains. "We grew watermelons, squash, strawberries—all kinds of fresh food. I ended up hating squash because we ate so much of it, but we would pick carrots out of the ground, rinse them and dry them off on our jeans, and eat them."

Approximately ninety-one thousand people are food insecure in the counties surrounding Corpus Christi in southeast Texas, and the Food Bank of Corpus Christi serves food to nineteen thousand people in any given week. Overall, Texas has one of the lowest average costs per meal of any state in the United States ($2.37). Nonetheless, it has 4.6 million food-insecure people, including 1.8 million children. That is 18.5 percent of the population, or almost one in five Texans. Like me, Eva says she did not appreciate the nature and extent of hunger in the United States until she had some unusual experiences that revealed how hidden hunger can be.

Several years ago, some friends and colleagues asked Eva to help produce a documentary about the lives of migrant agricultural worker families. Called *The Harvest/La Cosecha: The Story of the Children Who Feed America*, the 2010 film was shot in Texas, Michigan, and Florida, and it follows several migrant families during their travels picking hundreds of pounds of food per day yet often struggling to put food on their own tables. Eva explains: "We were shooting with a family of migrant workers, and we went with a mother to a supermarket, and she looked at the sign that said one tomato was $1.29. She had been paid $1 for picking an entire bucket of tomatoes the day before. She just could not understand how she could be paid so little for a product that was going to be sold for so much that she could not afford to buy it." The same family that picked and boxed fresh, nutritious fruits and vegetables all day long had to rely on a less expensive, much less nutritious, high-fat, high-carbohydrate diet. "Seeing that is a heartbreaking exposure to where food really comes from," Eva adds. "Not from a pretty place in the store called the produce section, but from the work of people who sometimes are going to bed without a meal."

THE PICTURE CLEARS

Until recently, many national and local government officials—and even food banks themselves—have had a murky picture of hunger in their districts and communities. The only reason *I* know those statistics about Corpus Christi is because of a relatively new interactive online tool that our foundation helped fund, managed by the Feeding America organization. Introduced in 2011, it is called Map the Meal Gap, and it is one of those big, new, and simple ideas that I think will help a wide variety of organizations attack US food insecurity in creative and effective ways.

Right now, if you live in the United States, you can go to your computer, and in a matter of minutes, you can call up these same food-security statistics I rattled off above for Texas, or for any county in the entire country.* To help local leaders make sure that elected officials have a clear picture, the statistics also are viewable by congressional district. You can learn exactly how many people are food insecure in your community, the extent of child food insecurity, and the average cost of a meal in your state. You can learn what percentage of food-insecure children are income eligible for nutrition programs. (That means their families' incomes put them at or below 185 percent of the poverty level.)

Why is this information a big deal? We all know there are poor people, homeless people, and distressed families living in shelters. But we tend to underestimate how many Americans miss meals a number of days each month. Many of us don't realize, for

---

* Visit www.40Chances.com/MMG to access Feeding America's Map the Meal Gap tool.

example, that some food-insecure people actually own their own homes. There are elderly people who do not show outward signs of poverty or distress but who must make a choice between medicine and food each month. There are children changing schools two or three times a year because they are moving from a car parked in a driveway at one relative's house to a couch at another relative's house after a parent's layoff or the foreclosure of their home. A hot lunch at school may be their only complete, nutritious meal of the day.

The insights from this database can be very dramatic. Take Maryland. In 2010, that state had the nation's highest median income—more than $70,000, compared to a national average of $49,000. Yet despite the state's overall prosperity, Map the Meal Gap revealed that the same year, more than 700,000 Maryland residents were food insecure and together they missed more than 125 *million* meals.[1] Sometimes elected officials aren't aware of the extent of food insecurity among their constituents—and sometimes they are not inclined to *want* to become aware of it. However, a tool like Map the Meal Gap is the antidote for bureaucratic head-in-the-sand behavior. I like the transparency of this project, and the fact that anyone can use the online tool, from an elementary school student writing a report to economists in the Congressional Budget Office.

I have been looking more closely at poverty and food insecurity among US farmworkers lately, particularly in light of calls for immigration reform. In 2010 our foundation purchased land in Arizona to use for research purposes, and that state is grappling with serious fallout from the political rhetoric surrounding immigration. In many cases, farmers are finding it more and more difficult to hire sufficient labor to harvest their crops. That is true not only in Arizona but also in other states. Americans often do not want these jobs, yet we turn away hardworking farm laborers trying to support their families in a way that strengthens US agriculture and contributes to the overall food security and food safety of our country.

I don't have the answers for resolving the immigration debate, particularly in our volatile political climate, but there is another difficult irony today in US agricultural communities dependent on migrant labor. In California, which leads the nation in agricultural production, two counties that fall into the top five for highest agricultural sales are also among the top 10 percent of counties with the highest food-insecurity rates: Merced and Fresno.[2] Farming in California's Central Valley, where Merced and Fresno are located, is dramatically different from the high-volume corn, soybean, and wheat farming I do in Illinois. In my state, only a few workers with modern equipment are needed to farm hundreds of acres, but farming California's many high-value specialty crops is much more labor intensive. Vegetables, nuts, and fruits must often be hand harvested, which means the same amount of farmland as what I have in Illinois would require hundreds of seasonal workers. As Eva's film pointed out, these workers are essential to the US farm economy, yet their lives are difficult, and their children suffer. They move from harvest to harvest and may be in and out of schools frequently. Not surprisingly, many never finish high school. And even though these workers pick and handle hundreds of pounds of fresh fruits and vegetables each day, they cannot afford to buy that same food, and studies have shown that the overwhelming majority of farmworkers eat diets high in fat and low in fruits and vegetables.[3]

A NEW TOUCH POINT IN TALKING ABOUT HUNGER

Map the Meal Gap is the kind of information tool that helps everyone who cares about situations such as hunger get a more accurate and useful picture of what hunger looks like in these communities. Its power lies in its simplicity. But some very smart statistical and computational brains are behind making the data so accessible and simple.

As I mentioned, this tool was created for Feeding America, the nation's leading domestic hunger-relief charity. In 2009 several food banks in the Feeding America network had tried to work together to construct a portrait of hunger in their communities. On one hand, these folks had access to the best, boots-on-the-ground information—they were working every day in the communities where the need was greatest. Yet they struggled with trying to match data sets that often were incomplete, were outdated, or did not easily correlate between regions. Some were using poverty as a proxy for food insecurity, but that is not always an accurate measuring stick. For one thing, the price of an average meal in some parts of the country can be twice what it is in other areas, creating a much more dire situation for those living in more expensive regions. More than half of all food-insecure people live in households with incomes above the poverty level, notes Elaine Waxman, vice president of research and nutrition at Feeding America, and that can mean they do not qualify for federal nutrition programs. They rely instead on charitable emergency food programs to meet their needs. Also, not everyone *below* the poverty level is food insecure. Some otherwise low-income individuals have more access to other social networks to obtain food, such as connections to farms or family.

Feeding America put together an advisory group and contacted economist Craig Gundersen, who is considered one of the foremost experts on food security in the United States. Gundersen, a professor in the Department of Agricultural and Consumer Economics at the University of Illinois, has a research agenda that concentrates on the causes and consequences of food insecurity in the United States and on the evaluation of food assistance programs. He had spent considerable time working with the available statistics and creating equations that brought in relevant variables. "Food banks have been asking for more localized information," says Dr. Gundersen. He adds that there were many surprises for groups working in hunger relief, including areas where food insecurity was as much as three times higher than local organizations had figured, particularly in the volatile period after the recession hit in 2008.

"The immediate payoff was its ability to fuel advocacy work," says Elaine Waxman. "But it has become a touch point for anyone speaking to the topic of hunger and nutrition. Food banks became creative in terms of plotting the locations for their activities, making sure their backpack programs [programs where children bring home food in their backpacks after school or during the summer], for example, were located in the areas of highest need. Map the Meal Gap helps you spot where the holes are." And the data begin to suggest other uses in terms of identifying populations for different kinds of studies, such as a pilot program Feeding America is working on examining the links between food insecurity and diabetes.

At the broadest level, Map the Meal Gap has reengineered the way Feeding America approaches outcomes, explains Maura Daly, its chief communication and development officer. "We've measured service in the past as the number of people fed, but it turns out that is not a very accurate way of doing it. Now we can measure in terms of the meals delivered to a community, where we know the extent of food insecurity down to the county level. It's becoming a backbone for local hunger relief organizations to measure their own success."

Thanks to MMG, we know that there are several counties in Texas where 50 percent of the children are at risk of hunger. Eva Longoria feels a special desire to support these families. "I think the keys to these households are the women," she says. "They control the choices, but one in four Latina women in the US is below the poverty line." In conjunction with the Eva Longoria Foundation and the nonprofit Accion USA, we are helping to fund a micro-credit program to lend capital to low-income Latina women. We will use Map the Meal Gap data to target communities facing the most food insecurity. Accion has helped all kinds of Texas entrepreneurs secure microloans for businesses ranging from pie shops, to personal care services, to florist shops. The women who qualify for our fund will apply for loans between $500 and $25,000, and they will receive training in finance and help in how to grow a business. We're going to work closely with them, and analyze the program every six months to make sure it's on track. And we're going to analyze how the participants' level of food security changes after they become involved.

As a farmer, I don't spend a lot of time on the kind of abstract equations and correlations that are Dr. Gundersen's life's work. But I have a deep appreciation for the value of good information, be it weather predictions or more accurate demographic data on the true nature and extent of hunger in a community. The idea that questions once relegated to ballpark guesses can now be answered in a few keystrokes on a website is not just innovative, it is inspiring new ideas and, we hope, better approaches.

Our food's journey from the field to the table can be complicated. Here Eva Longoria learned about large-scale grain production by operating a combine to harvest corn on our Illinois farm. Using Map the Meal Gap data, we are partnering with Eva's foundation to fight hunger in the US. *Photo: Howard W. Buffett*

The Power of a
Piece of Paper

José Martín lives in a small community in the municipality of Es-quipulas, province of Matagalpa, Nicaragua. José, thirty-six, is the father of three young children. He has worked as a farmer his whole life. He started on his parents' farm, where they taught him to work the land to get ahead, but he dreamed of having his own property instead of spending money renting land to grow his crops.

Many subsistence farming families in the area share this dream, but for a long time, it was almost impossible for them to achieve it. To obtain legal title to land in Nicaragua, the government requires a landowner to hire an attorney and provide evidence that the land belongs to the farmer, either through the sale documents or by affidavits from neighbors that the family has worked the land for many years. The normal fees to follow this process and pay attorneys can top the equivalent of $2,000.

In 2004, when José made a good profit from growing beans, he was able to buy one *manzana* (1.7 acres) of land from a neighbor. He obtained a document for the land, a sales-purchase agreement written by a lawyer, but it was not entered in the public registry. He discovered that this lack of paperwork meant even though he might no longer be paying rent, the current owner had the right to reclaim the land. José says, "I knew that the document that I had for my land was not worth much, and I was very afraid of this . . . but it was worse to have nothing. For a long time, I didn't try to find out what to do; first of all, because I didn't know where to go, and the other thing was the cost. They [at the municipality] told me that it was very expensive."

These are the dilemmas that farmers trying to obtain title to the land they work face around the world. So many, like José, are hardworking, determined people who nonetheless find the bureaucracy and the expense of navigating complicated and sometimes corrupt systems to be overwhelming. The good news is that some organizations are finding ways to help these smallholders navigate the process and feel the pride and security of owning their land.

We have been working with Catholic Relief Services in Central America on an initiative called Agriculture for Nutrition. A4N focuses on supporting smallholder farmers to develop business skills, a market focus, and financial savvy so they can enter and thrive in a larger economy. The program teaches sustainable agricultural techniques, for example, but it also educates farmers about saving and lending and investing in infrastructure assets.

A4N is implemented locally by the Diocesan Caritas of Matagalpa. In 2009, A4N began expanding its work in José Martín's area and held training sessions to improve farmers' general knowledge about farming techniques. Based on their recommendations, José expanded his crops to include different vegetables he could sell. But when it came to investing in the soil with fruit trees to protect it or with other long-term improvements, he was hesitant. He knew that at any moment he could lose the property. "Imagine, I did not even put a fence around it," he says. To invest in the soil with cover crops or irrigation would just increase the chance that the owner would want the land back.

But in May 2010, A4N conducted a detailed assessment. After it determined that more than 1,500 of the 2,500 participants in A4N in Nicaragua lacked legal title to their farmland, it moved to help. The project initiated a large land legalization process for José Martín and over 1,376 other participating farmers. The organization worked with local municipalities to reduce the fees, and it helped the farmers complete the requirements. By September 2011, Señor Martín had become the official owner of his farm.

Increasingly, Nicaraguan farmers will be able to invest in their land as owners, bringing greater stability to their families and future generations. *Photo: Howard G. Buffett*

The property is now registered. Although it is only a small area, José Martín says it is sufficient. Now he can improve the land with trees, better water systems, and cover crops, and take maximum advantage of support from A4N and other projects. José told CRS that being part of A4N has benefited many aspects of his life. "I have even learned to improve my relations with my family and to understand and value what my duties and rights are. A4N has helped us in many farming-related ways, but it is the titling of our property that has made a great difference. . . . At the beginning, I never expected it because it was something that no one had been able to resolve for us, not even the central or municipal governments."

CRS sent me a report in which one of its staffers detailed José's story, but I have seen for myself the light in the eyes of farmers holding the titles to their land. In the fall of 2011 I visited the Nicaraguan village of Guasuyuca. I went to help inaugurate a newly built maize and bean storage processing center—an extremely valuable asset for this community of farmers. Shortly after we arrived, I saw a new wooden outhouse building nearby and stepped inside to use the facilities. A local man who didn't realize I was inside started hammering nails into a piece of trim on the side of the not-quite-finished latrine. I yelled, "Hey, you could have just knocked!" When I came out, we all had a good laugh.

Throughout my visit, I could feel a lot of energy and optimism in this community, but by far the most fun was meeting with small groups of farmers, all dressed in their Sunday finest. One group came holding their land titles, and they were so proud to show them to me. A tall, thin farmer showed me his papers and talked about how he had a lot of children and that the land title meant so much to his family. His eyes watered, and he became so emotional that finally the local CRS staff comforted him, and the interpreter stopped translating. The farmer was convinced that God had intervened and delivered a miracle. A CRS staffer later explained to me that originally about 30 percent of the farmers thought they had legal title, but the A4N team discovered that less than 10 percent actually did. These people had been frightened at the beginning of the process, so the A4N's accomplishment in resolving the titles was a huge relief. Now their investments in the land and in learning to improve it would benefit them and their families permanently.

One of my most gratifying moments was when a small group of farmers in Nicaragua showed me their land title documents. *Photo: Howard G. Buffett*

In another village, CRS let me hand land title documents to farmers. This was an unbelievably powerful experience. I could see the excitement and pride on their faces. I don't think I imagined it when all the men and women I gave documents to that day walked away a little taller.

LAND RIGHTS CAN IMPROVE OUTPUT, INCOME, EVEN GRADUATION RATES

In many other regions in the world, the mood is not so happy. According to the NGO Landesa, which has been working on land reform since 1981, 75 percent of the world's poor live in rural areas where land is a fundamental asset and a primary source of income, security, opportunity, and status. Yet more than half these families lack either access to land or a secure stake in the land they have often farmed for generations.

Former law school professor Roy Prosterman started Landesa, originally called the Rural Development Institute (RDI), in 1981. Today the organization has worked in fifty countries. Landesa has compiled data showing that land rights are a significant advantage for subsistence farmers. In regions around the world that Landesa has surveyed, annual family income increases by 150 percent when farmers secure land rights, and agricultural production typically increases by 60 percent. Investments in property improvements double, as do high school graduation rates.[1]

Land tenure for farmers around the world is a critical issue, yet the details and peculiarities of politics, local laws, tribal customs, and farm management practices mean that it has to be addressed one country at a time. Dr. Gaye Burpee, who is the senior advisor for agriculture and climate change in Latin America and the Caribbean for Catholic Relief Services, explains: "Central America has different laws for obtaining land titles in each country. Because of past conflicts over landownership, trying to do in Guatemala exactly what CRS did in Nicaragua, for example, would have put families at risk and may have resulted in violence."

Still, memories of this A4N project in Nicaragua inspire me to keep working on land tenure issues and looking for creative new approaches geared to local realities. What an honor and privilege it was to hand a legal title document to a hardworking farmer who now is certain that he is farming land that he owns and can pass down to his children.

Story 39
Farmer of the Future

By Howard W. Buffett

Big steel-sided field sheds are common on farms in the US heartland. Most, like the two we have on the property I farm in Nebraska, are just massive garages. They're drafty, with high ceilings and walls lined with tools, chains, and boxes of parts and machine oil. Usually a tractor and other pieces of farm equipment that need servicing or shelter are parked in the middle of a concrete or gravel floor. The "décor," if it can be called that, includes old seed bags and maybe a calendar from a farm supply store. Unless it's windy, it can seem colder inside a farm shed in winter than outside.

Clay Mitchell's shed in northeastern Iowa, on the other hand, is more like a wizard's lair—and a toasty one at that. There are tall racks of tools and parts, wrenches, tractor parts, and other gear you'd expect, but also network switches, cables, and sensors. There is a huge Irish wolfhound named Smoogie who is Clay's field general for deer management during growing season but who lounged on a soft bed when I visited the shed in January 2013. There is a fertilizer applicator that has a number of custom elements Clay and his father have designed for farm equipment, such as section control to fine-tune the amount and location of the fertilizer application, and an independent steering mechanism so both the tractor and the applicator are controlled by GPS for maximum efficiency.

But there is also a spotless, automated bathroom, which is so nice that I don't imagine even my four sisters would complain about using these facilities. There were still some Christmas decorations on the counter, and I watched family portraits and farm photos flash across a digital photo frame on a nearby wall. My sense is that the Mitchells want everyone to feel welcome here. During my visit, I spoke with a young woman from a neighboring farm who was working with Clay's dad, Wade, on a roof cover for a small tractor. Clay explained that Wade is a mentor to many young farmers in the area. "I'm going to Iowa State University next year," she told me, with plans to pursue a career in agriculture.

Up near the ceiling, a four-foot-high light indicator from an old John Deere foundry flickered. The industrial-strength heater kicked on, and had the place almost fifty degrees warmer than the icy twenty-six degrees outside. Clay and Wade have rigged up hundreds of sensors around the farm that they can program this "marquee" to monitor with blinking light patterns, such as when the heater is running or a fertilizer tank is running low and somebody needs to drive a tender out to fill it up. The light marquee may be vintage, but there is a good reason that *Time* magazine once called the Mitchell Farm "the farm of the future."

IMPATIENT FOR CHANGE

Clay Mitchell, forty, is considered one of the most progressive, innovative crop farmers in the United States. Over a decade ago, he was the first farmer in the Midwest to use GPS-steered farm equipment. The equipment innovations are significant, but what is most important to my father and me is that the Mitchells are committed to preserving soil, making chemical use as efficient as possible, and also—and this point is critical—doing it in a way that delivers profits to farmers. Clay is a tireless advocate for no-till farming and long-term approaches, and, in the spirit of forty chances, he believes in mentoring and in evangelizing the lessons he's learned so that other farmers benefit. Even though change comes far too slowly for his taste, he gives me reason to hope that US agriculture is moving in the right direction.

Five generations of Mitchells have farmed this region about an hour northwest of Cedar Rapids, near the small Iowa town of Buckingham. Clay's great-great-grandfather moved his family here from Ireland. They launched a family farming operation to support themselves. Today Clay farms with his great-uncle, his dad, and his cousin. Clay himself is quiet but intense. He keeps a desk in the machine shed, and during my visit, he leaned against the corner of it with his laptop open to show me a PowerPoint presentation of some findings from incredible experiments he had conducted.

In 2009 he hand-tagged individual bar codes on 1,200 corn plants in four locations on his farm. Then, throughout the growing season, he took multiple, frequent measurements of many variables, including stalk thickness, number of leaves, water penetration in surrounding ground, fertilizer utilization, photosynthesis, and more.

One objective was to measure effects of what is called "controlled traffic" on a field, which refers to confining the paths that farm equipment travels over and over, and using wide wheels on the equipment to disperse the weight and create less soil compaction. Soil compaction is a major issue in farming, for several reasons. Compacted, dense soil creates a crust, and young plants have trouble breaking through it. In addition, it inhibits plant roots from growing and taking up nutrients, and prevents water from penetrating the soil. That can inhibit growth, create runoff, and reduce yield. Clay's data showed that water infiltration in controlled-traffic fields can be upwards of twenty times the rate in fields where farmers are driving heavy equipment all over on narrower tires.

Those numbers grabbed my attention: efficient water use is something that is only going to get more important in farming in the future. For example, on our foundation's farm in Arizona, there is already serious concern over water volume rationing, and water is only going to become more precious—and more expensive.

Clay and I discussed how his data on compaction do not necessarily provide a straightforward answer to water efficiency: infiltration rates vary by soil types, for example. It's also influenced by factors such as whether rainfall has been fairly steady over time: steady rainfall tends to soften soils and improve infiltration, whereas long dry periods can make some soils harden like concrete. However, soil compaction is an important phenomenon to study in more depth and in more places—not only to make water use as efficient as possible but also to prevent runoff, which erodes soils and transports fertilizers and pesticides to river systems and other environments where they don't belong.

The data fascinated me, especially the time and labor required to take the ongoing measurements. But our time together was starting to get tight, and Clay had a whole section of his presentation about the efficiency of pesticide spraying. One machine that he and his father invented works with different nozzles to vary the size of the droplets emitted to cover the plant leaves so that they don't drift in the air and deliver "sublethal" doses that encourage pesticide resistance. As I checked the time, Clay seemed chagrined. "Okay, I'll try to go through this quickly," he said. Then he frowned and looked up, grimacing a little. "No, actually, I can't. I can't do this quickly."

I smiled. Clay is so data driven and analytical that he can't conceive of cutting corners.

We got to know Clay several years ago. He gave my dad a call to talk about conservation farming. Clay and his wife drove to Decatur, and my father took them to lunch. Then my dad invited him to visit our foundation's farm in South Africa. Clay and I both attended the World Economic Forum in Davos, Switzerland, in 2012. That event featured impressive speakers, heads of state, and titans of business, but the hour or so when I sat down and talked with Clay was my favorite part of the trip. He is on a mission to get farmers around the world to farm in a more sustainable way, and he is trying to inspire government leaders to craft policies to support that goal. But as a fifth-generation farmer steeped in Midwestern farming culture, he is acutely aware of the inhibitors of making that change happen.

As my father touched on earlier, farming in the United States has a rich history and a particular ethos. Traditionally, fathers have passed down their techniques and wisdom to the next generation. While there has been consolidation in recent decades, it's still true on many farms that families have worked the same parcels of land for generations. Farmers are subject to the laws of supply and demand for their prices, but subsidy designs, inadequate or missing data, or other much less scientific factors can also influence their behavior and financial success.

There have been incredible spikes in farmland prices in parts of the Midwest in recent years. The day I visited Clay, a nearby parcel had sold for $17,000 per acre. In Iowa, land carries what's called a CSR rating—that stands for "corn suitability rating." It is an assessment, in many places done decades earlier, about the potential of that land to produce corn. The trouble is, it's a static measurement. "It's like selling a classic car based on the condition it was in when it rolled out of the Ford assembly plant on day one," Clay said. The measurement does not assess how the land has been treated since the day it was given its rating. And yet it's not uncommon for a farmer selling land not to give more information than that rating in terms of describing its quality. As Clay explained, recent land values are not necessarily high because a given parcel is so valuable from a productivity standpoint. Rises in commodity prices have meant that farmers have more cash on hand than they've had in the past, and, as Clay pointed out, "If all you've ever wanted is that parcel of land that goes right up to yours so you could square off your field, and there is a guy on the other side who feels the same way, when it finally comes up for sale, you are going to pay a lot for it. It may be the only chance in your life you'll ever have to get it."

IT'S HARD TO HIDE ON A TRACTOR

Tradition and peer pressure also influence farmers. A unique element of farming in our part of the country is that, unlike the diversified "salad bowl" farming of fruits, nuts, and vegetables in California or the southern US, Midwestern corn, wheat, and soybean farmers all tend to do the same thing at the same time, whether it is disking, planting, fertilizing, or harvesting. When you're out in your corn-field, you see what the farmer in the next cornfield is doing. You may be waiting for the right weather to spray, but if you see a neighbor start, you get anxious and may scramble to hurry up and do the same. If he upgrades his irrigation pivot, you start wondering if you should go shopping too. I'm told that farmers were not always this competitive, but with so many renting land and needing to demonstrate performance to their landlords through high yields, I know for a fact that they are today.

It's hard, maybe impossible, to farm in secret. When a farmer tries something new, word spreads. He's asked about it at the coffee shop, at the farm supply store, and in line at the bank. It's a lot of pressure. Raised eyebrows from a neighbor make some farmers nervous. It can be a disincentive to try new things, and, when you do, according to Clay, there can be a tendency to stick too long with an approach that doesn't work very well, just because you're now known for doing it. Innovation isn't easy. Pride may make a farmer throw good labor and money after bad.

But one of the biggest issues Clay sees as undermining smarter farming practices is that we don't have accurate mechanisms or data to represent the true cost of treating land badly. Earlier in the day, as we drove around the area, he pointed to a farmer's field with lots of rolling hills on it. "That guy is losing so much soil. He's got ditches below the downhill slopes, and the county comes and hauls the soil away," he said, referring to all the soil that runs off the hills, building up and clogging the ditches by the road. The farmer uses traditional chisel plowing at the end of his harvest season, ripping up the corn-stalk residue from the old crop and turning over the top foot or so of soil and then just letting it sit fallow all winter. This practice is the standard for the majority of grain farmers in the United States, and one of the problems with it is that it "looks" neat. "I call that a Dorian Gray farm," said Clay. "There is massive erosion, and he's lost hundreds of years of soil, but you till it up, and it *looks* good." A worked field gives the appearance of meticulous care. "No-till farm-ing takes more deliberation and precision," Clay admitted. "Tilling is an easy way for a farmer to cover up a lot of his mistakes. If he has weeds, he can cover them up. If his fields get compacted, he can till to loosen the upper portion of the soil. If he gets gullies after a rain-storm, he fills them in with dirt. He is degrading the land, but he doesn't see the cost of that."

Conservation farming, on the other hand, demands that a farmer leave the residue from the previous crop on the ground, where it adds to the organic matter of the soil as it decomposes. And it can involve the planting of cover crops. Cover crops can help fix nitrogen and hold the soil in place in rain and wind, but they tend to be low-lying plants that give a field a messy, weedy appearance. "The irony of plowing is that you use it to cover up your problems, and doing that makes the problems worse," Clay noted. It's almost like an alcoholic waking up with a hangover and taking a shot to feel better. It gives some im-mediate relief but only adds to the addiction. Clay has a photograph of a farm on a hill where the placement of a telephone pole years ago limited how closely the farmer could plow and plant. What's shock-ing is that the chunk of land around the pole is now four or five feet higher than the hillside around it. Over the expanse of his whole field, that represents thousands of tons of topsoil that have washed down the hill, probably into gullies and some portion ultimately to a river system, never to return. Clay says that since it takes five hundred or more years for natural sources to produce an inch of topsoil, "It's a disaster to lose even an eighth of an inch a year of topsoil," he explained, "but when it's happening, you don't notice it."

There is no easy way to measure the economic impact of soil erosion. You pay an invoice for seed and fuel, but the bill from Mother Nature will be paid by future generations. *Photo: Howard G. Buffett*

Clay's personal and family history has shaped his strong feelings and his experimental and creative approaches. Wade stressed the importance of education with his boys starting young. Clay says his dad taught his brother, Guy, enough physics and math by age four (not a typo) that he qualified for his ham radio license. Clay earned a degree in biomedical engineering from Harvard University. He found an outlet for his energy as a collegiate ski racer, but his heart never left the farm. Between his junior and senior years, he bought two hundred acres in Iowa.

Clay's background is not typical, but his love of farming and his passion for helping farmers improve their technology and methods are infectious. He admits that he gets frustrated with how slowly farmers are changing their behavior, and he's concerned about consolidation in agriculture, which tends to favor crop yields over soil stewardship. However, the Mitchells consistently outproduce their neighbors by 20 percent to 30 percent, numbers that should persuade even the most stubborn old-school farmers to consider changing their ways.

On the bright side, the Mitchells get a lot of visitors to this shed, lately more than Clay says he can even handle. That's a good sign. Representatives from major companies such as John Deere and Trimble Navigation come here to look at new ideas Wade and Clay come up with or to drop off a piece of equipment that the Mitchells want to incorporate into a new design. They avoid formal arrangements, however. "We have an open door, and they have an open door to us," Clay explained. "If we worried about intellectual property and all that, it would take months to do anything. We just explain what we want to do, and they trust us [not to go off and try to commercialize it on our own]. We can get a new part or piece of equipment here in a week"—compared to six months just to negotiate an intellectual property agreement.

We talked about ways to try to promote better farming. These days Clay splits his time between Iowa and the San Francisco Bay Area, where he and a college ski teammate have started an investment company called Fall Line Capital right in the heart of Silicon Valley. (A fall line is the most efficient path down a hill.) It seems curious: a farmland investment firm in California's high-tech heart. But Clay is looking for new ways to force changes in farming practices that utilize market levers. The fund invests in farmland that Clay believes has potential to be more productive—not on the basis of emotional factors or outdated measurements but on the basis of its actual quality and potential to respond to good soil management and conservation farming techniques. I find this to be an interesting and creative approach. Being located in Silicon Valley also gives Clay and his partner an eye on emerging technologies they can apply to this effort, such as soil-sampling technologies to analyze soil quality right in the field in real time, which a Mountain View, California, company is developing.

FARM OWNERSHIP IS CHANGING

Sometimes small, simple, low-tech changes can make a big difference too. Clay said it is hard to find land-lease contracts with language requiring renters to use conservation techniques. The terms are not standard. This area of contract law has not developed yet. We discussed whether our foundation might help support the preparation of sample contracts that could be a resource for farmland owners interested in preserving the value of their soil. He mentioned an interesting reality: a large percentage of farmland owners in Iowa today are women, often farmers' widows who end up leasing the family land to contract farmers instead of farming it themselves. According to data from *Successful Farming* magazine, 70 percent of farmland will change hands in the next two decades, and 75 percent of that land will be transferred to women.[1] In cases where new farm owners have not had much involvement in the operation of the farm, they may not be well versed in either farming contracts or the principles of conservation farming. One solution could be conducting an outreach program that provides resources such as standard contracts that focus on land management and preservation. That sounds simple enough, and could prove to be an incredibly useful tool.

Another aspect of incentivizing farmers to be good stewards of the soil involves the government conservation programs available today. The government pays Clay $40 for each acre of his farm planted with cover crops such as rye and radishes, which he figures costs him $30 an acre. We spent nearly an hour discussing government subsidies, as well as conservation efforts such as the Conservation Stewardship Program.

The Conservation Stewardship Program (CSP) encourages young farmers like me to farm without tillage, preserving our greatest asset: soil. *Photo: Howard G. Buffett*

Like us, Clay wants to see improvements in the way the government incentivizes conservation-minded behavior, focused first and foremost on better soil management practices. "The truth is, it just doesn't make sense to have price support subsidies anymore," said Clay. "Our real problem as a nation is that we are no longer on the leading edge of farming practices anymore. It's amazing that Brazil and Argentina are ahead of us in soil management techniques like no-till." Clay notes that there are huge no-till operations in places like Kazakhstan, where literally millions of wheat acres are being farmed using no-till—versus only perhaps 30 percent of US farms, and perhaps only 5 percent of them are exclusively no-till.

Farming is challenging under any circumstances. Clay laughs at the memory of working alongside his dad when he was a boy, and their machine shed did not have heat. In those days, his dad would farm with his brother and sons and work on equipment during the day, and then put in a full-time shift in a foundry at night. According to Clay, it taught him the value of both hard work and analysis. "Most farmers are used to getting a recipe from John Deere or Monsanto," he reflected. "We want to say, 'Be introspective on your farm.' We don't have a 'system' here. It's not like following a twelve-step plan, and it will all work. There is no magic potion." Each farm has different soil profiles and different conditions, and, therefore, each farmer needs to research options tuned to those conditions and adjust. "We use a different approach to experimentation. We're trying to drill down to what makes a difference in yield."

Clay Mitchell believes, as we do, that when it comes to feeding people, soil is the world's most vital asset. If you treat soil properly, erosion won't claim it. And effective conservation techniques with a commitment to good stewardship can make our soil, as Clay put it, "an oil well that never runs dry."

A New Approach to Governance

"I don't want to put any pressure on you," I said to former British prime minister Tony Blair, "but I had Shakira out here, and she did this perfectly the first time."

We were sitting in the cab of a harvesting combine on one of our foundation farms near Decatur. It was a windy, cool early fall day in 2012, and we'd just made one pass down six rows of roughly seven-foot-high corn. That was the easy part. This implement is fully GPS enabled and has auto steering. We pointed the combine header, which looks like a rack of torpedoes, toward the rows we wanted to harvest. Then we switched on the auto steer, and we collected around 150 bushels without having to touch the steering wheel. But at the end of the pass, we had to turn, and the maneuver demanded a quick switch to manual controls as we reset the line of the combine to harvest the next set of rows. Tony did a great job, although when he realized he'd run over a small section of corn, he grimaced and said, "Sorry, Howard, I've just cost you money there."

I often invite people I like and work with to visit our farms in Illinois. I like to make farming real for those who haven't experienced it, especially when we are working together on issues related to food and agriculture. Inviting down-to-earth, sincere people to a farm is a fun way to get to know them better. Tony Blair is not only a brilliant, accomplished leader but also a good sport who doesn't take himself too seriously. He arrived at the farm in jeans and boots, and, on our way to the cornfield, I asked if he'd ever driven farm equipment. A member of his staff ribbed him: "Please—he hasn't even driven a car in twelve years!" Tony laughed as hard as the rest of us. And when we finished, he was excited to send a photo of the combine to his thirteen-year-old son, Leo.

Tony Blair spends time in my combine, which I use as a rolling office.
Photo: Howard W. Buffett

More important, I find that everyone I host for a ride in a combine cab comes away from the experience more thoughtful about modern farming and food. There are a half dozen farming steps that a combine literally "combines": from the cab, you see cornstalks fall and feed into the headers. Then the chains pull the cuttings into what's called the threshing drum in the belly of the machine. There the kernels separate from the cob, and the chaff is blown out the back of the combine. I enjoy seeing the amazed look on my visitors' faces as they glance directly back and see corn kernels or soybeans pile up in the clear window of the tank. In a matter of seconds, plant stalks taller than our heads have been reduced to a food item they instantly recognize. My guests start to realize that much of what they've eaten in their lifetime began as the plants we're driving through, and, more than likely, that their food has touched the same kind of equipment. Food doesn't come from the store. It comes from the soil on a farm. Until you see it, you may know that, but you don't "get it."

It seemed only right to offer the former British prime minister this experience, because I'd had the pleasure at breakfast at our farmhouse that morning of discussing his area of expertise: high-level governance, which for a long time felt as foreign to me as harvesting corn is to him.

In 2008 Tony Blair launched his Africa Governance Initiative (AGI) to create a different framework for working with African governments. He is trying to teach the basic principles of running a peace-seeking, effective, responsive government to the leaders of some of the poorest, most conflict-ridden and disorganized countries on the planet. As he explains, for so long, the rest of the world has focused on the flawed dictators and crises of Africa. We are discouraged by governments that seem corrupt or unresponsive to their own people. But he is convinced that a new generation of leaders offers an opportunity to change this narrative and look at this situation in a new way. I'm finding that his optimism is giving me hope as well.

After he launched AGI, I had been hearing about the former prime minister's efforts in Africa but had not paid close attention. In early 2012, while on an airplane I picked up a copy of a magazine with a cover story on him. I read that, so far, he's been invited to work in Rwanda, Sierra Leone, Liberia, Guinea, and South

Sudan, and he can point to some good progress. In Sierra Leone, for example, his team helped the government implement a health care initiative that has cut the number of children in hospitals dying from malaria by 80 percent.

I began learning more about Tony Blair's approach at a point when I was frustrated by the lack of progress on many of our projects in Africa aimed at reducing food insecurity. Another statistic was bothering me too: in 2003, African heads of state had gathered in Maputo, Mozambique, and signed the Maputo Declaration, which pledged to increase public investment in agriculture to a minimum of 10 percent of their national budgets and to raise sector growth by at least 6 percent by 2008. On a continent with hundreds of millions of subsistence farmers, and where more than half the population in most of the fifty-four countries depends on agriculture for survival, my opinion is that even a 10 percent investment in agriculture by any country is woefully inadequate. It should be at least 30 percent, and it should include investment in infrastructure such as roads, storage facilities, credit systems, and other tools designed to help farmers access markets. At the time (and I believe it is still true as I write this in mid-2013), only Burkina Faso, Ethiopia, Ghana, Guinea, Malawi, Mali, Niger, and Senegal met or exceeded the 10 percent target.[1]

I thought, "How can anyone from outside any of these countries overcome this basic gap in commitment? How can our foundation help create a new, progressive agricultural climate in countries where the leaders refuse to invest in their own people? If they won't support their own agricultural systems, what can we achieve? Would it be better in the long run if I make adherence to Maputo the minimum criterion for us to get involved, and try to increase pressure on governments to invest in this sector? Or should I pull back altogether and increase my attention to other food-insecure regions such as Latin America, where, in my experience, more governments are better attuned to agriculture?" These are not easy questions to answer.

THE CONVERSATION IS CHANGING, SO SHOULD WE

But as I read the article on the former prime minister, I was struck by the themes he addressed. Africa, he said, has been in crisis for decades, but we have to stop responding to crises by just handing out aid. He said a new generation of emerging leadership was different: better educated and more focused on trying to get these countries to be active players in the global economy. His tone and his optimism were clear, but he also had a new way of thinking about development. I started paying more attention to his speeches and efforts, and I thought the gist of his thinking came through particularly well in a 2012 speech he gave to the CEO Africa Summit in London. In this speech, called "A New Approach to a New Africa," the prime minister explained why he thought there was an opportunity right now for progress:

> Twenty years ago, a conversation with African leaders would often be dominated by the legacy of the past, often a colonial legacy. Today there is impatience with such a dialogue about history. There is instead an urgent desire to focus on the future.
>
> Governance has traditionally been the poor relation of the development community, usually consigned to broad brush civil service reform programs, training days and the like. Actually in its proper sense it is utterly fundamental. And in the modern world, it is the one thing that, unlike capital or technology, simply can't be imported. It means prioritizing; focusing; putting in place the people and the systems to deliver. There is a mass of footloose capital looking for an outlet for investment today. Whether they come to country A or country B depends, of course, on things like resources, such as oil or minerals; but it also crucially depends on having in place a proper system for attracting that investment, treating it predictably, having a legal system that functions fairly and it depends on a minimum level of infrastructure.

The old way, where the rich world gives and the poor world passively receives, looks increasingly out of date. African countries must be in the driving seat of their own development, setting the priorities and making the decisions. Where aid is needed, it should get behind these priorities and use and strengthen the government's own systems. I believe, with the right kinds of support and the right policies, Africa can be free of dependence on aid within a generation.[2]

In the face of conflict-related crises and starving children, discussion about governance had always seemed abstract to me. The immediate need to feed people or help them restart agricultural systems seemed more critical. But one of my forty-chances lessons is that after a decade of supporting different aid projects and agricultural initiatives, it is often governance-related issues inside a country that undermine otherwise important and valuable efforts, rendering them temporary at best, or, at worst, useless.

We recently sent one of our foundation program officers to evaluate some of our funded projects in several poor and conflict-ridden countries, including Sierra Leone, Liberia, DRC, and South Sudan. His report was noteworthy for the number of extreme experiences he had on a single trip. In the northeastern region of DRC, he learned that a rebel-controlled group had started demanding that all NGOs and developmental organizations pay taxes to them, violating the laws of the official DRC government and forcing most NGOs in the area, including staffers of the N2Africa project he was visiting, to leave the region at least temporarily. "For emergency and relief purposes, some NGOs fly their staff via cargo planes into this region for a few days, deliver all the emergency items, and then fly them out as soon as the delivery is complete," he reported.

In South Sudan, meanwhile, his vehicle was stopped on the road to the capital city of Juba. He had to wait an hour while a United Nations team demined the road. In Liberia, he took a photograph of a giant mud pit pretending to be a road. He'd been sloshing and bouncing along on it for more than six hours to review a test field on a seed project. In the photo is a Land Cruiser SUV stranded up to the running board in red mud.

You can always try to plan or work around any one of these specific situations, and yet ultimately inadequate infrastructure and these governments' inability to keep order and set priorities for development undermine virtually all development. I sometimes think Americans hear phrases such as "Africa has poor roads," and it's like hearing "New York City's Times Square is crowded on New Year's Eve." They nod in agreement, even though they have no idea what it's like to operate and move around a country with villages that cannot be accessed in any practical sense except on foot or perhaps by animal cart or motorbike. But for countries such as Sierra Leone or South Sudan, the roads are such significant impediments to getting *anything* done, yet often nobody in government owns the problem. There is no organized assessment of the roads' current state or what a better system would look like. Government ministers may ask would-be investors in the country to build roads as opportunities arise, but often those roads are one-offs that get built to a mining area or a destination of interest to the investors. They aren't designed according to a long-term plan. Our program officer's report was another reminder to us that all the high-technology and smart seed development and committed individuals such as Joe DeVries or Ed Price cannot get traction, literally or figuratively, in situations where the roads are so muddy or otherwise impassable that commerce simply stops—unpredictably.

These are huge barriers to progress, and there are times when even the best-intentioned individuals say with a sigh, "Here we go again. TIA." But Tony Blair is pointing out that many of Africa's new generation of leaders want to do the right thing for their people, and we should figure out how to help them, beginning with very basic organizational help and assessing what skills are needed. AGI often uses a quote from 2011 Nobel Prize winner President Ellen Johnson Sirleaf of Liberia, from her 2009 book *This Child Will Be Great: Memoir of a Remarkable Life by Africa's First Woman President.* President Johnson Sirleaf talks about how a population "bypassed by education for so long, who have been deskilled by years of war and inactivity," just does not hold the skill base or capacity to get an array of seemingly basic things done. ". . . There you stand, trying to rebuild a nation in an environment of raised expectations and short patience, because everyone wants to see change take place right away. After all, they voted for you because they had confidence in your ability to deliver—immediately. Only you cannot. Not because of the lack of financial resources but simply because the capacity to implement whatever change you have in mind does not exist."

ORDER AND PROCESS

The term *capacity* is key, as we talked about in the story about our water initiative. As President Johnson Sirleaf points out, there may not be a single person in a small, developing country with the necessary skills and training to address a critical situation. There often is no resource or manual of what corporate managers call "best practices." There is no established, accepted method for setting priorities and creating systems to manage projects from beginning to end. Many governments have never used the most basic governance tools such as meeting schedules and public calendars. Staff positions have been doled out by patronage and tribal connections rather than filled by experienced or trained personnel. Some ministries just depend on individuals coming to the government office and waiting their turn on a given day to be seen and discuss an issue. The loudest and most persistent actors get the attention.

Tony Blair and his team have convinced me that reliable, repeatable governance processes are crucial. They don't appear miraculously when a new administration is elected. The advantage of the

AGI model is that it can operate at two levels: Tony Blair will go only where governments invite him to go. But once that step takes place, he can stand shoulder to shoulder with a country's top leaders. They respect his experience and stature and listen to his thoughts on the importance of good governance and the priorities that create a stable foundation. And then AGI dispatches skilled teams to work with counterparts at the key ministries. These are the front lines where it is crucial to institutionalize systems and procedures so that basic, critical priorities such as infrastructure improvements don't always end up subordinate to whatever crisis is simmering on any given day. AGI's work is focused not specifically on agriculture but on helping governments set priorities and then manage toward those goals. Improving livelihoods and shoring up infrastructure—everything from roads to electricity to water management—are key to reducing food insecurity, so I discovered a lot of overlap in the governance issues Tony Blair is focused on and those that would reinforce and support what we are trying to accomplish as well. Specifically, we have decided to help fund AGI's efforts in Liberia and Sierra Leone. Both have been ravaged by conflict and we are familiar with their issues because we have funded initiatives in both countries for years. We understand why, without progress on the governance front in those countries, there can't be sustainable progress in improving food security.

Every country must summon the particular will and discipline to invest in its own people, own its own challenges, and benefit from its own success. Tony Blair's attitude and approach represent a new way of thinking and attacking some of the underlying fundamentals that are pushing these conversations in a positive direction. He's doing what our foundation cannot do itself, but what we believe must happen for our work to be successful.

Epilogue:
A Pessimistic Optimist
Returns to Prague

In the summer of 2012, I traveled to Prague because writing this book reawakened so many memories of our Czech exchange student Vera Vitvarová and that pivotal post–Prague Spring summer of so many years ago. HWB went with me, as he had heard me talk about this time in my life as leaving such a lasting impression.

Today Vera has four children and is a social worker who assists young individuals with disabilities. Her father, Milos, died recently at the age of ninety, while her mother, eighty-six, was doing pretty well. About seven years ago, Vera moved out of the flat where I had stayed, because she had adopted a son with some physical disabilities, and it was too difficult for him to navigate to the top floor.

It was fun to reminisce about our experiences together: standing in line at the grocery store and having to boil water for everyone's once-a-week bath. Vera reminded me that I had complained bitterly when we could buy only a couple of Coca-Colas at a time from a hotel (literally the only place in Prague where Coke was sold) because they were expensive. She laughed over the fact that I had wanted to buy two dozen! I met her children, including one of her sons, who is a big, strapping guy. I smiled at Vera and made a gesture flexing my muscles about him. "Strong!" I said. "Like his mama!" she growled back at me.

Remember that feeling you got when you were going out on a date for the first time? That was about how I felt when I got off the airplane in Prague in 2012. It had been forty-three years since I had seen Vera. I walked through Immigration and I immediately recognized her. As we hugged, it was as though I had never left. *Photo: Howard W. Buffett*

I knew about Prague's resurgence over the years, but I had never been back. HWB had visited a couple of years ago and talked about what a beautiful and interesting city it was. For me, it was wonderful to see that a place so grim and at times frightening as Prague was during those tense years in the late 1960s could, in fact, recover and be so vibrant and beautiful today. The bullet holes in the walls of buildings have been patched over. The same streets where people lined up for hours to buy stale bread and potatoes are now full of ice-cream parlors and sweet shops, internet cafés, and mobile phone stores. Vera and I laughed about the time we went to the countryside during my first visit, and I saw some Russian soldiers I wanted to photograph. That was strictly forbidden, so I had her pose as if I were taking her picture and then moved the lens at the last minute. Today tourists are everywhere, smiling, laughing, and snapping pictures at will. For fun, I asked HWB to take a photo of me with a female Czech police officer. He could not appreciate how impossible such a shot would have been in 1969.

Life can get better. Challenges can be overcome. Determination and hard work can make a difference. A city whose people could not count on where their next meal was coming from is now thriving. I returned home with a renewed spirit. I will always be a pessimistic optimist, but the effort to lift people out of the dehumanizing and painful state of food insecurity will always be worth it. And sometimes it will even work.

Acknowledgments

We wish to acknowledge the following individuals who made this book possible:

Our family, Warren and Astrid Buffett, Susan A. Buffett, Peter and Jennifer Buffett, Pam Buffett, Lili Buffett, and "the girls," Erin, Heather, Chelsea, and Megan.

A special thank-you to a group of individuals making the most of their forty chances, many of whom helped bring our stories to life: Ben Affleck, Padre David Beaumont, former Prime Minister Tony Blair, Jake Blank, Kofi Boa, Debbie Bosanek, Paul Brinkley, Gaye Burpee, Dan Cooper, Colonel Kurt Crytzer, Maura Daly, Shannon Sedgwick Davis, Joe DeVries, Mansour Falls, General Wamala Katumba, General Stanley McChrystal, General David Petraeus, General David Rodriguez, General John Uberti, Allen Greenberg, Kate Gross, Paul and Ali Hewson, President Paul Kagame, Ann Kelly, Don and Mickie Keough, Francis Kleinschmit, Rob Lalka, Annette Lanjouw, Tim LaSalle, Eva Longoria, Amani M'Bale, Graham McCulloch, Shakira Mebarak, Maria Emma Mejia, Laura Melo, Emmanuel de Merode, Zlatan Milisic, Clay Mitchell, Jim

Morris, President Yoweri Museveni, Trevor Neilson, Doug Oller, Laren Poole, Ed Price, Jose Quiroga, Andy Ratcliffe, Jorge de los Santos, Sheriff Tom Schneider, Ritu Sharma, Josette Sheeran, Carlos Slim, Anna Songhurst, Jerry Steiner, Roy Steiner, David Stevenson, Amanda Stronza, Vera Vitvarová and her family, and Joe Whinney.

Thank you to those who have supported our foundation's efforts: Archbishop Desmond Tutu, Dennis Avery, Susan Bell, Matt Berner, Herminio Blanco, Sabra Boyd, Nicki De Bruyn, Tracy Coleman, Trisha Cook, Erica Dahl-Bredine, Jim Doherty, Sarah Durant, Jendayi Frazer, Catriona Garde, Francis Gatare, Bill and Melinda Gates, Helene Gayle, Paula Goedert, William Hart, Tarron Hecox, Molly Heise, Wolfram Herfurth, Jim Houlihan, Judy Inman, Charlie Jordan, Patrick Karuretwa, Muhtar Kent, Scott Kilman, Jon Koons, Kepifri Lakoh, Alex and Lani Lamberts, David Lane, Marla Leaf, Marco Lopez, Tom Mangelsen, Emily Martin, Angela Mason, Patti Matson, Lucy Matthew, Louise Mushikiwabo, Ron and Jane Olson, Laura Parker, Nic Prinsloo, Ambassador Kenneth Quinn, Richard Ragan, Domenica Scalpelli, Sheryl Schneider, Robert (Hondo) Schutt, Jim Shafter, Raj Shah, Daniel Sheehan, Dennis Sheehan, Tom Sloan, Willem VanMilink, Mike Walter, Rosa Whitaker, Molly and Mike Wilson, and Ambassador Andrew Young.

We also thank these individuals who have provided support and counsel over the years: Mike Albert, Jorge Andrade, Dwayne Andreas, Marty Andreas, Marianne Banziger, Dwayne Beck, Spencer Beebe, Brian Beyers, George Kwaku Boateng, Jeff Boatman, Julie Borlaug, Kevin Breheny, Deputy Sheriff Tony Brown, Lane Bunkers, Michelle Carter, John Cavanaugh, Sue Cavanna, Michael Christodolou, Eric Clark, Kathleen Cole, Hank Crumpton, Ed Culp, Sheriff Mark Dannels, Gabriela Diaz, Natalie DiNicola, John H. Downs Jr., Jamie Drummond, Marc D'Silva, Ann van Dyk, Loren Ehlers, William B. Eimicke, Ezekiel Gatkuoth, David Gilmour, Ricardo Gomes de Aravjo, Bill Green, Charlie Havranek, Paul Hicks, Jim and Nadine Hogan, William Holmberg, Marlyn Hull,

Bashir Jama, Mary Obal Jewel, Kathy Kelley, Joey King, Peter Kinnear, Jim Kinsella, Dave Koons, Margaret Lim, Peter Lochery, Jonathan Lynch, Liz McLaughlin, Sheriff Mike Miller, Gus Mills, Jeannie O'Donnell, Kay Orr, Fred Potter, Ed Prussa, Christine Rafiekian, Jeff Raikes, Deb Ray, Bill Roberts, Eugene Rutagarama, Alberto Santos, Dan Schafer, Sue and Walter Scott, Neale Shaner, Senator Paul Simon, Jamie Skinner, Mark Smith, Todd Sneller, Mark Suzman, Scott Syslo, Scott Terry, David Thomson, Schuyler Thorup, Camilla Toulmin, Lucas Veale, US Marshal Adam Walter, Don Wenz, Mike Wenz, Otto Wenz, Wayne Wenz, Jerry White, Layne Yahnke, Mike and Gail Yanney, Bryan Young, and Bob Zhang.

I also want to thank our agent Jillian Manus, who recognized the value in a book that could help us share with others the lessons we have learned over many years. Her introduction to Simon & Schuster gave us a great team that was committed to supporting our efforts. We would not have been able to publish this book without the hard work of our editor, Ben Loehnen; our publisher, Jonathan Karp; or the tireless efforts of Richard Rhorer, Lance Fitzgerald, Meg Cassidy, Lisa Erwin, Mara Lurie, Marie Kent, Emily Remes, Brit Hvide, Irene Kheradi, Gina DiMascia, Brittany Dulac, Jill Putorti, and Michael Accordino. And we could not have asked for a better partner and collaborator than Joan O'C. Hamilton. She listened to and synthesized our thoughts and experiences in a way that made the process productive, and the insights meaningful. She paid meticulous attention to every detail and, more importantly, made it fun. We thank Joan for making this book a reality.

Notes

Introduction: One Shot at a Warlord

1. The US Department of State estimates that at the height of LRA activities, two million people were displaced, and UNICEF estimates that sixty-six thousand children were abducted, http://www.state.gov/r/pa/prs/ps/2012/03/186734.htm.
2. http://www.fao.org/newsroom/en/news/2005/102562.
3. http://www.wfp.org/hunger/stats.

Story 1: The Day I Heard the Clock Tick

1. http://faostat3.fao.org/home/index.html.
2. http://feedingamerica.org/hunger-in-america/hunger-studies/map-the-meal-gap.aspx.
3. http://www.fao.org/infographics/pdf/FAO-infographic-SOFI-2012-en.pdf.
4. http://www.fao.org/nr/sustainability/food-loss-and-waste/en.

Story 2: Prague, 1968: The Soviet Army Eats First— "We Just Get What Is Left"

1. Background on the Soviet invasion at http://history.state.gov/milestones/1961-1968/soviet-invasion-czechoslavkia.

Story 3: From Bulldozing Dirt to Building Soil

1. *US Agriculture: Feeding the World and Investing in Our Future,* Howard G. Buffett Foundation, 2010.

2. http://www.ncga.com/upload/files/documents/pdf/WOC%202013.pdf.
3. For a fuller picture of the Ethiopian famine, see http://www.time.com/time/world /article/0,8599,1915544,00.html.

Story 4: Devon's Gift

1. For more background on these schools, see http://www.hrw.org/news/2010/04/15 /senegal-boys-many-quranic-schools-suffer-severe-abuse.

Story 5: Because "Al Called"

1. http://www.un.org/geninfo/bp/enviro.html.
2. For more background on the Convention on Biological Diversity, see http://www .cbd.int/history.
3. http://www.wineportfolio.com/sectionLearn-Great-French-Wine-Blight.html.
4. http://www2.nau.edu/~bio372-c/class/sex/cornbl.htm.
5. Statistics from H. G. Buffett, *Research in Domestic and International Agribusiness Management,* vol. 12 (Greenwich, CT: JAI Press, 1996).
6. http://rainforests.mongabay.com/20elsalvador.htm.

Story 6: The Ovarian Lottery

1. To view the interview, see http://www.charlierose.com/guest/view/1368.
2. Carol Loomis talked at length with Warren Buffett about his giving plan: http:// money.cnn.com/2006/06/25/magazines/fortune/charity1.fortune.

Story 7: Reality Has a Nutty Taste, Especially When Fried

1. http://www.fao.org/ag/AGP/AGPC/doc/Counprof/malawi/Malawi.htm.

Story 8: Where Hunger Hides

1. More information on ADM at http://www.adm.com/en-US/news/Facts/Pages /20Facts.aspx.
2. http://feedingamerica.org/hunger-in-america/hunger-studies/map-the-meal-gap .aspx.
3. Population data from Google Public Data.

Story 9: Loved but Lost

1. I am grateful to physicians from the United Nations World Food Programme for their assistance in preparing this material. For more background, see http://www .who.int/nutrition/topics/malnutrition/en/index.html.
2. http://www.unicef.org/media/files/Community_Based__Management_cf_Severe _Acute_Malnutrition.pdf.

Story 10: Empty Calories

1. For more information on micronutrient deficiencies and undernutrition in Guatemala, see http://www.who.int/nutrition/topics/en/ and http://reliefweb.int/report/guatemala/breaking-malnutritions-cycle-guatemala.
2. http://www.micronutrient.org/english/View.asp?x=620.
3. http://www.cdc.gov/obesity/adult/causes/index.html.
4. In his 2007 book *Dirt: The Erosion of Civilizations*, David Montgomery spells out the gradual decline of productivity caused by extensive tilling and grazing on slopes, which disrupt food production and can force relocation of local populations.

Story 11: Little Cromite

1. For background, http://www.bbc.co.uk/news/world-africa-14094194.
2. http://www.irinnews.org/Report/94037/SIERRA-LEONE-Amputees-still-waiting-for-reparations-almost-10-years-on.
3. http://data.worldbank.org/country/sierra-leone.

Story 12: Sex and Hunger in Timbuktu

1. For background on trafficking in the US, http://thecnnfreedomproject.blogs.cnn.com/2011/06/17/trafficking-and-the-u-s.
2. http://2001-2009.state.gov/g/wi/rls/rep/crfgm/10105.htm.

Story 16: Shakira

1. See the history of school feeding in the US at http://www.fns.usda.gov/cnd/Lunch/AboutLunch/ProgramHistory_2.htm and in *US Agriculture: Feeding the World and Investing in Our Future,* Howard G. Buffett Foundation, 2012.

Story 17: A Franciscan Padre in the Sierra Madre

1. http://www.drugwarfacts.org/cms/?q=node/1988.

Story 18: Gorillas Versus Guerrillas

1. For more on Virunga's gorillas and crises, see http://ngm.nationalgeographic.com/2008/07/virunga/jenkins-text.

Part 3. Hard-Learned Lessons

1. Dambisa Moyo, "Why Foreign Aid Is Hurting Africa," *The Wall Street Journal,* March 21, 2009, http://online.wsj.com/article/SB123758895999200083.html.

Story 19: Can This Village Be Saved?

1. Estimates of land mines in Angola vary by a wide margin. The NGO Halo Trust,

an NGO, has been clearing mines in Angola for seventeen years: http://www
.halotrust.org/where-we-work/angola.

Story 20: A Complicated Legacy

1. http://www.unicef.org/publications/files/Tracking_Progress_on_Child_and
   _Maternal_Nutrition_EN_110309.pdf.
2. For more background on fertilizer use in India, see this video report prepared
   in 2010 by the *Wall Street Journal*: http://live.wsj.com/video/over-fertilized-soil
   -threatens-india-farmlands/81484D0D-5086-4AEE-AD84-E22C62AA89DD.
   html#!81484D0D-5086-4AEE-AD84-E22C62AA89DD.
3. http://www.cgdev.org/doc/events/9.6.06/9.6.06/BorlaugGreenRevolution.pdf.

Story 21: For Yields to Go Up, We Have to Look Down

1. Jeremy Grantham's thoughts can be found in his firm's July 2011 *GMO Quar-
   terly Newsletter:* "Resource Limitations 2"; also in http://www.nytimes.com
   /2011/08/14/magazine/can-jeremy-grantham-profit-from-ecological-mayhem
   .html?pagewanted=all&_r=0.
2. http://www.fao.org/newsroom/en/news/2008/1000874/index.html.
3. *Losing Ground: Iowa's Soil Erosion Menace and Efforts to Combat It* (Des Moines, IA:
   Soil Conservation Service, 1986). Access report at http://www.whybiotech.com
   /resources/tps/ConservationTillageandPlantBiotechnology.pdf.
4. From Juergen Blaser, Alastair Sarre, Duncan Poore, and Steven Johnson, *Status of
   Tropical Forest Management 2011* (Yokohama, Japan: International Tropical Timber
   Organization, June 2011).

Story 21½: Owners Make Better Farmers

1. http://www.fao.org/docrep/015/i2497e/i2497e00.pdf.

Story 23: What Does Doing Better Look Like?

1. http://www.nytimes.com/2006/12/26/world/asia/26tsunami.html.
2. E. Kessler, *The International Community's Funding of the Tsunami Emergency and Relief: Local Response Study Overview* (Bangkok: Asian Disaster Preparedness Center,
   2005).
3. From *After the Tsunami: Human Rights of Vulnerable Populations* (Berkeley, CA:
   Human Rights Center, University of California, Berkeley, October 2005).

Story 24: "Who Came Up with This Crazy Idea?"

1. http://www.gao.gov/assets/330/320017.html.
2. As of mid-2013, several aid organizations, including CARE and the international
   NGO OXFAM, have become more vocal in calling for aid reform in Washington,
   but several other charities have joined agribusinesses and shippers in opposing

changes to current monetization policy. For background see http://www.nytimes
.com/2013/04/05/us/politics/white-house-seeks-to-change-international-food
-aid.html?smid=tw-share&_r=2&.

3. http://www.gao.gov/assets/330/320013.pdf and http://archive.gao.gov/t2pbat2
/152624.pdf.

Story 25: A Six-Beer Insight

1. http://www.haguejusticeportal.net/index.php?id=9502.
2. General information about Sudan and South Sudan from http://www.cia.gov
/library/publications/the-world-factbook/geos/su.html.

Story 26: Less Than Sparkling

1. http://www.fao.org/nr/water/docs/WRM_FP5_waterfood.pdf.

Story 27: Elephants and Experts

1. http://www.cnn.com/2012/02/20/world/africa/cameroon-elephants-killed/index
.html; http://www.nytimes.com/2012/09/04/world/africa/africas-elephants
-are-being-slaughtered-in-poaching-frenzy.html?pagewanted=all&_r=0.
2. http://www.academicjournals.org/IJBC/PDF/pdf%202010/Sept/Monney%20
et%20al.pdf.

Story 28: Can Smarter Carrots Save Soil?

1. Total based on data collected by the US Department of Agriculture.
2. http://www.ers.usda.gov/topics/farm-economy/farm-commodity-policy
/government-payments-the-farm-sector.aspx#.UXI5QL9Vf_4.
3. According to the US Department of Agriculture Economic Research Service,
about a quarter of the nation's population lived on farms in the 1930s, when not
quite half of the population lived in rural areas, which is a broader category. See
Carolyn Dimitri, Anne Effland, and Neilson Conklin, *The 20th Century Transfor-
mation of U.S. Agriculture and Farm Policy*, no. 3 (Washington, DC: United States
Department of Agriculture Economic Research Service, June 2005), http://www
.ers.usda.gov/media/259572/eib3_1_.pdf.
4. *Historical Statistics of the United States: Colonial Times to 1970* (Washington, DC:
US Bureau of the Census, 1975), part 2.
5. According to the US Environmental Protection Agency, less than 1 percent of
the US population now claim farming as an occupation, and about 2 percent of
the US population live on farms. See http://www.epa.gov/agriculture/ag101
/demographics.html.
6. Robert Hoppe and David E. Banker, "Structure and Finances of U.S. Farms: Family
Farm Report, 2010 Edition," USDA Economic Research Service, Economic Information Bulletin (EIB-66), July 2010, http://www.ers.usda.gov/publications
/eib-economic-information-bulletin/eib66.aspx#.UXsox4IrcXw.

7. http://www.nrcs.usda.gov/wps/portal/nrcs/detail/national/technical/nra/nri/?cid=stelprdb1041887.

Story 29: Chains That Unlock Potential

1. Andrew Lawler, "Remains of Bamiyan Buddhas Yield Additional Details About Statues' Origins," *Washington Post*, March 5, 2001, http://www.washingtonpost.com/wp-dyn/content/article/2011/03/05/AR2011030504131.html.

2. http://www.unodc.org/documents/data-and-analysis/tocta/TOCTA_Report_2010_low_res.pdf.

Story 32: Does Aid Plant Seeds of Violence?

1. This trip was where we got to know Dr. Ed Price of the Norman Borlaug Institute for International Agriculture at Texas A&M University. This meeting in Jalalabad was where we finally traveled when the fog lifted in Kabul.

2. http://www.state.gov/secretary/rm/2012/1½00353.htm.

3. *World Development Report 2011: Conflict, Security, and Development* (Washington, DC: The International Bank for Reconstruction and Development/The World Bank, 2011), http://siteresources.worldbank.org/INTWDRS/Resources/WDR2011_Full_Text.pdf.

4. http://www.grain.org/article/entries/128-the-soils-of-war;http://www.nytimes.com/2010/10/09/business/global/09raisins.html?pagewanted=all.

Story 33: Opening What Once Was Cerrado

1. Analysis by the Institute on the Environment—a collaboration between the University of Minnesota's Global Landscapes Initiative (IonE) and McGill University's Land Use and the Global Environment Lab—using EarthStat data.

2. By comparison, in 2012 the US Department of Agriculture had $2.53 billion in discretionary funds for agricultural research, education, and extension programs. See http://www.fas.org/sgp/crs/misc/R40819.pdf.

Story 34: Chocolate-Covered Opportunities

1. http://ilpil.asu.edu/research/qualityproductivity-projects/buffett-foundation-project/.

Story 36: Buy Local!

1. National Climatic Data Center, http://www.hurricanescience.org/society/impacts/environmentalimpacts/terrestrialimpacts.

2. As the world's largest humanitarian agency, WFP is a major buyer of staple food. In 2011 WFP bought US$1.1 billion worth of food—more than 70 percent of this in developing countries. See http://www.wfp.org/purchase-progress.

3. http://www.wfp.org/stories/ahora-la-que-pone-los-precios-soy-yo.
4. http://www.wfp.org/eds-centre/speeches/remarks-ertharin-cousin-executive-director-un-world-food-programme-committee-wor.

Story 37: Hungry for Data

1. United States Census Bureau, American Community Survey 5-Year Estimates, 2006–2010, http://www.census.gov/acs/www/; Craig Gundersen, Elaine Waxman, Emily Engelhard, Theresa Del Vecchio, Amy Satoh, et al., "Map the Meal Gap: Child Food Insecurity 2012" (Chicago: Feeding America, 2012), http://feedingamerica.org/hunger-in-america/hunger-studies/map-the-meal-gap/~/media/Files/a-map-2010/2010-MMG-Child-Executive-Summary-FINAL.ashx.
2. Based on the market value of agricultural products sold from the 2007 USDA Census of Agriculture; Gundersen et al., "Map the Meal Gap 2012."
3. Gail Wadsworth and Lisa Kresge, "Hunger in the Fields," Civil Eats, September 26, 2011, http://civileats.com/2011/09/26/hunger-in-the-fields.

Story 38: The Power of a Piece of Paper

1. http://www.landesa.org/infographic-land-rights-matter.

Story 39: Farmer of the Future

1. http://www.agriculture.com/family/women-in-agriculture/farm-families/this-l-is-her-l_339-ar26202.

Story 40: A New Approach to Governance

1. http://www.nepad.org/foodsecurity/agriculture/about.
2. http://www.tonyblairoffice.org/speeches/entry/a-new-approach-to-a-new-africa.

Index

Page numbers in *italics* refer to illustrations.